Doing Global History

Doing Global History

An Introduction in Six Concepts

ROLAND WENZLHUEMER

BLOOMSBURY ACADEMIC
LONDON • NEW YORK • OXFORD • NEW DELHI • SYDNEY

BLOOMSBURY ACADEMIC
Bloomsbury Publishing Plc
50 Bedford Square, London, WC1B 3DP, UK
1385 Broadway, New York, NY 10018, USA

BLOOMSBURY, BLOOMSBURY ACADEMIC and the Diana logo are trademarks of
Bloomsbury Publishing Plc

First published in 2017 in Germany as *Globalgeschichte schreiben* by Narr Francke
Attempo

First published in Great Britain 2020

Copyright © Roland Wenzlhuemer, 2020

Translated from German by Ben Kamis

Roland Wenzlhuemer has asserted his right under the Copyright, Designs and
Patents Act, 1988, to be identified as Author of this work.

For legal purposes the Acknowledgements on p. xi constitute an extension of this
copyright page.

Cover image: Hollow plaster globes produced in the London factory of George Philip and
Son (1955). (© Harry Kerr / Getty Images)

A catalogue record for this book is available from the British Library.

A catalog record for this book is available from the Library of Congress.

ISBN: HB: 978-1-3501-0601-7
PB: 978-1-3501-0600-0
ePDF: 978-1-3501-0602-4
eBook: 978-1-3501-0603-1

Typeset by Deanta Global Publishing Services, Chennai, India
Printed and bound in Great Britain

The foundation of my work is my family.
I dedicate this book to them.

Contents

Figures

Acknowledgements

This book combines the thoughts and groundwork from many different discussions and scholarly contexts. It has grown over the course of many years, sometimes faster and sometimes slower. A number of clever, creative and patient people let themselves be drawn into the project, which both delights me and fills me with gratitude. I subjected Martin Dusinberre to many of my early ideas, and he rescued me from several. Andreas Hilger, Christoph Streb and Benedikt Stuchtey read the manuscript carefully and provided me with valuable insights. The members of our superb team at the Chair of Modern History at Heidelberg University and later LMU Munich spared neither themselves nor me. Ben Kamis translated the manuscript from German to English and from academese into understandable language. These people and others deserve my deepest thanks.

1

Global history

The grasp of global history

Global history tends to be overestimated – especially in terms of its potential. The expectations made of it have escalated in step with the rapidly growing attention it has been attracting in the broader discipline of historical research. As German historian Sebastian Conrad, among others, observed in his recent and very accomplished introduction to global history, the original inspiration for a global approach to history emerged from the conviction of many historians that the analytical tools familiar to us can no longer provide an adequate interpretation of history in the age of globalization. Conrad has noted two defects that global history was not prepared to accept: the fixation on the nation state as the primary (and sometimes only) frame of reference and the concomitant 'methodological nationalism',[1] as well as deep-seated Eurocentrism, which has paralysed history's perspective and given it a predetermined standard. For Conrad, global history was and is principally an attempt to address these two 'birth defects' of modern historical research.[2]

That is a noble goal, but it is no small challenge for a field that is still in its adolescence. And as global history comes to be more firmly established in the broader field of history, new tasks and challenges are constantly emerging. For example, in his prolegomenon to the inaugural issue of the *Journal of Global History*, Patrick O'Brien prophesied that global historians would choose to liberate themselves from 'disciplinary boundaries, established chronologies and textual traditions for the construction of European, American, Indian, Japanese, Chinese or other national histories'.[3] Martin Dusinberre, in a recent but memorable intervention, stated that global history would have to admit a multiplicity of different voices.[4] Not to mention the claims that all this must also be accompanied by the progressive internationalization of research practices.[5]

These thoroughly justifiable desiderata, which all speak to serious imbalances in historical research, imply in their sum heavy theoretical and methodological burdens for global history to carry. The defects that global history is to overcome are precisely the fundamental problems of theory and method that plague history as a field of study, ranging from the dangers of parochialism and the (im)possibility of objectivity to finding the proper scale for frames of reference and disciplinary boundaries. Taken to its logical conclusion, the research programme sketched previously is effectively a call for a basic reconceptualization of history that would necessarily entail new organizational forms and scholarly practices. Given the magnitude of these calls, global history alone cannot answer them by decentring,[6] transcending the nation as a frame of reference or rendering disciplinary boundaries obsolete. The entire field of history must follow its example.

It should be no surprise that such an expectation – which is in fact a whole collection of aspirations – can quickly become overwhelming, which begs the question how one could possibly meet this expectation and with what tools. How exactly can global history address the problems that its own proponents have identified and simultaneously initiate a fundamental recalibration of historical research as a whole? In other words, what is global history after anyway? What questions drive it? And more importantly, how can the knowledge it produces be used to help overcome, say, Eurocentrism or methodological nationalism? There has already been much debate about the driving questions and objectives of global history, but it has unfortunately failed to take the next step and reconnect with the broader aims of the field. Dominic Sachsenmaier has suggested that defining global history presents a 'necessary impossibility'.[7] This impossibility reveals the cleft between the goals devised by historical theory and the questions that drive historical research. Many have pondered and written about what global history *is*, and this common question has led to vastly different answers.[8] However, the related questions of what global history can achieve in the broader field of historical research, what means are at its disposal to make interventions, how its perspective and tools can help to make good on its considerable promise have been treated much less explicitly.

Indeed, this has inspired the central question of this book: what can global history achieve and how? Teaching and research in global history cannot help but be overwhelmed by the demands sketched earlier because they provide no clear line of approach or fundamental research questions. That is one reason why research in global history ought to be considered as a mode of problematization and critical reflection that can, at best, lead to partial improvements, not as a comprehensive remedy in itself. Andrea Komlosy's introductory textbook on global history provides an apt example. In terms of Eurocentrism, Komlosy takes revealing Eurocentric thought patterns and imagery to be the task of the field: 'Global history endeavours to understand locally conditioned worldviews in their respective contexts.'[9] From this point of view, the proper task of global history is to uncover, not necessarily to overcome. The goal should be to reveal persistent imbalances in historical thinking beyond simple generalizations, to refocus historical research when established modes of interpretation are inadequate, by means of clear and operationalizable research questions. In the scope of expectations one can make of global history this one is fairly reasonable.[10] Changing and broadening perspectives can accentuate the problems sketched earlier and lead to critical reflection on parochial views and fixations on implicit standards. That is within the grasp of global-history-as-perspective. But it cannot overcome these basic features of historical thought – not even by proliferating its sites and standards. I will come back to this point at the end of this introductory chapter.

Global history as perspective

The question remains as to what global history can achieve. What curiosity drives it? What should it try to show? But also, of what tools should global history make use, and how are the questions it poses to history to be operationalized? This book will attempt to address these and other questions. Of course, it is not the first book to do so. For years historians have been pondering how to characterize global history's research programme. There is also lively discussion about the approaches and methods of global history. However, these two elements – that is, what curiosity drives research in global history and the methods it requires – are seldom directly calibrated to each other. Rather, they are often oddly treated in isolation from each other. Research questions in global history tend to lack operationalizability, leaving a gap between theoretical claims and implementation in the empirics. With this book I seek to provide some building blocks to bridge precisely this gap without succumbing to the illusion that these few pages, concepts and case studies will suffice.

Rather, I would like to show how a few already existing concepts in global history can not only accentuate how global frames of reference and activity can shape the thoughts and deeds of historical actors, but also to embed these in a broader historical context. To do so, the book must apply various concepts that will need further elaboration. In general, though, they all relate to the notion of connection – in terms of global history, a global or transregional connection – which is the conceptual fulcrum of the ideas presented here. It is what holds this book together, what makes the individual case studies (all of which unfolded in entirely different historical settings) communicate with each other.

Connection, of course, is hardly a new or unfamiliar term in global history.[11] On the contrary, it is one of the most commonly used terms in the field, which has contributed to it becoming a sort of terminological panacea. In order to make the term more than just an arbitrary label, it must be analytically sharpened. What are global connections, and how can they be grasped theoretically and methodologically? What distinguishes global connections from other kinds of connections? What makes such connections historically relevant? Finally, what do they contribute to global history's research programme? Different conceptions of how to conduct research in global history suggest different answers to these questions. Engaging with these answers will help to frame the notion of connection used here.

Recently, more and more global historians are beginning to re-evaluate the theoretical and methodological underpinnings of the field and seek to build sustainable conceptual foundations for its further development. Despite their common engagement with the concept of global history, their contributions cover vastly different grounds as already a glance on the relevant publications of the last few years reveals. Sebastian Conrad asks what global history is by examining where it comes from and what it is supposed to achieve.[12] In a volume originating from the opening conference of the Oxford Centre for Global History, the editors seek to provide examples of how the goals of global history can be pursued and which methodologies could serve in this regard.[13] Martin Dusinberre muses about whether it can or should be a goal of global historical writing to give a voice to those overheard in the past and by other strands of historiography.[14] Sven Beckert's and Dominic Sachsenmaier's recent volume *Global History, Globally* traces the commonalities and differences in global historical practice around the globe.[15] Jeremy Adelman, on the other hand, doubted the suitability of global history to engage with the questions of a re-nationalizing world and provoked a lively discussion in the field.[16] A recent response to Adelman's critique by Richard Drayton and David Motadel can be found in the *Journal of Global History*.[17] These are only a few examples that testify to a renewed interest in the conceptual foundations of global history. As diverse as they are in their tasks and outlooks, one common feature of all these considerations – sometimes raised explicitly, sometimes touched upon implicitly – is the question whether global history has a concrete object of study or whether it is rather a complementary perspective on the human past.

Sebastian Conrad prominently claims that in his understanding, global history has a specific research object. The extent to which global history can be applied as a perspective depends, as Conrad says, on the structural conditions of global integration; that is, it depends on whether global connections have durably established themselves structurally.[18] According to Conrad, nuanced treatments of global connections only become possible when global history as perspective and as research object are combined. Conrad holds this to be the most promising path for research in global history to take and claims that the most nuanced studies in recent years have followed this approach.[19] I argue that applying global history as a perspective on the human past – a perspective that specifically looks at the significance of global connections in a particular research context – renders it a much sharper analytical tool.

Global history as a history of connections

Of course, identifying and describing global connections does not explain anything in itself. Like all historical phenomena, they must be carefully contextualized, and their historical significance must be analysed and weighed with consideration. The question is how best to make sense of global connections' impact and how to grasp their particular qualities. The principal goal of global history ought to be to show how global connections emerge from human activity, and how they in turn affect people's thoughts, feelings and choices, which can occur within or without structurally stable conditions. Therefore, such conditions are better thought of as part of a multifaceted context in which the interactions between human actors and global connections should be situated. The intellectual energy and attendant analytical focus in global history should be directed at the interface between human activity and global connections. Accordingly, some of the field's most important questions are: What makes global and transregional connections historically relevant phenomena in the first place? What separates them from local and regional connections that serve the formative elements of all human communities? To what extent do global connections operate differently? What are their special qualities that justify talking about global history as a distinct perspective in the first place?

   These questions might seem self-evident, but they are far from it. Indeed, when taken seriously, they are particularly difficult to interpret and to answer, but tackling them also promises at least two benefits for research in global history. First, the question as to the analytical particularities of global connections automatically leads to other factors that influence people's thoughts, feelings and actions, resulting in broader contextualizations and deeper assessments of the investigated phenomena. Processes of global integration and structuration as well as the efficacy of global structures, whose thorough treatment receives an entire chapter in this book, appear as one factor among many. Second, focusing on the quality of the connections themselves produces a conceptual abstraction that touches the core of what global history seeks to understand about the world and isolates it from any particular context in order to recontextualize it in specific cases. This abstraction should guide research in global history. It secures the field's conceptual independence and allows it to make a contribution to the discipline of history that goes beyond a mere world historical synthesis or a recapitulation of other fields' research questions, like those of, say, postcolonial or area studies.

Concentrating thus on global connections in no way constricts the perspective of global history, nor does it undermine the status of integration processes as objects. On the contrary, it allows the well-trained gaze of global history to pan very different areas without losing touch with the basic explanandum. How and why do people in very different locations and contexts create global and transregional connections? And how do these connections, in turn, affect people? These seemingly simple questions suggest no lesser project than to fathom the depth of global connections. The plumb might indeed hit a shallow bottom, meaning that transfer and exchange may be of little consequence in many cases, but such a result must be possible in any reasonable assessment. The point is to situate global connections in a constellation of many factors, even if this means that their role will sometimes be negligible.

To return to the objectives of global history mentioned at the beginning, a focus on global connections led and sharpened by a conceptual abstraction should demonstrate, even more clearly than has been the case in other fields, that restricting analyses to national histories is insufficient, that there is no place for Eurocentrism in history and that many voices have been silenced or drowned out. However, these problems are not exclusive to global history; they are challenges that must be tackled by any historical research. Consequently, history as a whole should take heed of these views.

Global history and globalization

This book is not a typical introduction to global history. It does not seek to cover the subfield of global history systematically, as many renowned authors have recently attempted. This book does not review the history of how global history has been written.[20] It does not treat particular methods of global history,[21] nor does it present a list of possible research topics in global history.[22] Still less does it concern itself with the institutionalization of global history and the profile associated with it in academia.[23] It does not even map the potential and pitfalls of various approaches to global history.[24] Rather, the book is conceived as an introduction to research practice, and it seeks to accomplish this by clarifying the concepts in the field and by combining theory and empirics to the greatest degree possible.

Theory, here, implies constructing abstract concepts whose terms will allow deep penetration of global historical phenomena, not mere superficial descriptions. With an eye to developing valid generalizations in global history, this book aims to formulate key questions that will enable a number of already existing terms in the social sciences and humanities to be used fruitfully in global history. The process of adapting these terms to the new context should simultaneously achieve the requisite operationalization of the research questions. They close the gap between theory and empirics, which, as experience has shown, is a recurrent problem. The empirical application of the revamped concepts then follows concrete, clearly defined case studies.

The case studies, which make up the central portion of this book, also prominently feature the term 'globalization'. Although it is not among the six concepts selected for this introduction, it is connected to them and in many ways lends them their dynamism. Moreover, treating the concept of globalization first helps to show how helpful it can be to shift such terms from description back to analysis, from the particular to the general. This term, globalization, is ubiquitous in studies on global history. Many scholarly debates implicitly hold global history to be principally a history of the processes of globalization.[25] Some students of global history go beyond this implicit emphasis and argue that research in global history should deal explicitly with the history of globalization.[26] However, this does not mean that the term's analytical value has remained undisputed. Recently, economic historian Gareth Austin reinvigorated an intervention by Frederick Cooper, who had questioned the analytical usefulness of the concept of globalization for African history.[27] Today, Austin wrote, 'Cooper's scepticism … is shared by a high proportion of global historians, whether particularly focused on Africa or not.'[28] While such a claim is notoriously difficult to test, many historians' broad, largely descriptive usage of the term seems to support it.

There is nothing even close to a consensus understanding of the term in the field of global history. While this is not the place to list and evaluate the countless, sometimes contradictory, interpretations, the prominent debate between Dennis Flynn and Arturo Giráldez,[29] on the one hand, and Kevin O'Rourke and Jeffrey Williamson, on the other,[30] will provide a good idea of the diversity of opinions. The former hold globalization to denote the increase of persistent interaction among all settled continents. The latter use it to refer to global market integration. Even though both sides approach the history of globalization from a perspective strongly informed by economic history, they come to fundamentally different conclusions about what the term means. Looking further to political science, sociology or anthropology, the array of available definitions becomes somewhat bewildering.[31] To illustrate the breadth of the spectrum, Lynn Hunt recalls contributions by Jan Scholte, Robert Keohane and Joseph Nye in her chapter on globalization and time.[32] While Scholte sees in globalization nothing more than the rise of supraterritoriality,[33]

Keohane and Nye look to the globalizing effect of technologies that collapse distances of all kinds.[34]

Of course, that globalization lacks a clear and settled definition and a common conceptualization is no secret. In fact, Bruce Mazlish and Akira Iriye reassure us that this lack is no cause for concern.[35] Barry Gills and William Thompson begin their attempt to clarify the relationship between global history and globalization with the consolation that they remain fundamentally 'ecumenical and tolerant' towards other approaches and conceptualizations.[36] Such conceptual openness is certainly to the credit of the social sciences and humanities, and it will not be impugned here. I merely want to set the record straight about how the use of the term globalization in global history leads to two apparent analytical disadvantages. First, the wide range of definitions in history makes it difficult to discuss processes of globalization in different eras and from different perspectives. One prominent example of this is the perennial debate about how to pinpoint the historical inception of globalization. This question not only forms the core of the aforementioned debate between Flynn and Giráldez and between O'Rourke and Williamson but also frequently hinders global historians focusing on different eras, who may answer it in very different ways, from cooperating productively with each other. In the final analysis, when globalization began depends on what it actually is, and a variety of definitions could provide for a more inclusive dialogue on questions of global history, so it is argued. A second problem with the current terminological looseness is that most definitions are only meant to apply to particular instances in relation to quite clearly delimited topics and research questions. Although this tactic can yield considerable descriptive power, it makes them difficult to operationalize beyond the limits of their intended uses. As a result, situating globalization processes in global history is difficult – at least, if one wants to say more than that, they play an important role. Here, too, a clearer, but also more abstract, understanding of the term can be of great benefit.

But what would that look like? Jürgen Osterhammel and Niels Petersson claim to discern a common semantic core in the various concepts. They write, 'In the majority of the proposed definitions of "globalization", the factors that play a major role are the expansion, concentration, and acceleration of worldwide relations.'[37] With his definition, which is now over twenty-five years old, Anthony Giddens takes a basically similar tack but with a different emphasis. For Giddens, globalization is 'the intensification of worldwide social relations which link distant localities in such a way that local happenings are shaped by events occurring many miles away and vice versa'.[38] To abstract from Osterhammel and Petersson's and Giddens's common elements, one could say that globalization is basically nothing more than the process of detaching social interaction from spatial proximity. Such processes have abstract beginnings and endings. The beginning would be when all social interaction only occurs in the actors' immediate vicinity, and the process would be complete when the relation between social interaction and spatial proximity no longer exists. Of course, both are fictional situations that do not obtain in actual human society. Still, they can help us better to grasp this process of dissipation, for which the globe itself is the only limit.

To make the definition a little less abstract while preserving its broad applicability, one could say that globalization is a process in which patterns of social interaction display more and more long-distance connections and, thereby, indirectly cross borders of all kinds. Such a conceptualization makes no assumptions about the intensity or the effectiveness of the connections. Rather, it focuses only on their increase, which can, of course, be very slow and gradual. Thus, globalization here refers only to changes in the patterns of interaction and connections.

The practice of global history

This abstraction offers at least two advantages. First, it greatly facilitates discussion across eras and perspectives. Although the emphasis on process is one benefit, including an abstract beginning and end of the process goes further in that, while these can be stronger or weaker, they share a common qualitative basis. The abstraction helps to clarify that globalization as a process is not to be confused with, say, a period of globalization. The latter refers to an age or era in which globalization processes touch society as a whole. As to which societies met this criterion at what times, historians are welcome to disagree. Further, it is often forgotten that, beyond just the societally pertinent connections, globalization processes were profoundly relevant for the thoughts and actions of many people.

Such a minimalistic conceptualization also helps to illuminate the relationship between global history and globalization, in effect recalling the original curiosity that drives research in global history. Taking globalization as a process – one at the centre of research in global history – implies an interest in processuality, in dynamics, in change over time. This description certainly fits global history, but it also applies to other forms of historical research. Such changes in the form of increases (or, conversely, decreases) of transregional connections are of considerable interest to global history. But again, it is basically a function of the original curiosity that inspires global history, that is, to investigate the emergence and impact of global connections. Connections can also shape people and their actions, when they do not become more concentrated or change in some other way. In practice, it is true that most case studies will be situated in the context of globalization processes. It is in contexts like these that global connections most greatly affect people, their thoughts and their actions (as is always the case when people are confronted with something new). But that is not to say that the historical impact of global connections is limited to such contexts.

In concentrating on globalization processes and, with them, on the dynamics of global connections, it is easy to lose sight of their conceptual components. Clarifying the relationship between global history and globalization, then, eventually reverts back to the curiosity that originally inspired inquiry in this field and to the conceptual lenses that we can use in search of it. Hence, this book proposes six terms that might guide research in this respect. Next to the concept of connections itself, the following chapters discuss the concepts of space, time, actors, structures and transit in relation to global connections and, thus, in the context of global history. While this selection does not claim to thoroughly exhaust the potential range of research in global history, the six terms do, in their sum, offer a broad conceptual fundament solid enough to support global historical analysis. All of them are grounded in the belief that global history examines the emergence and significance of global connections. This is their common point of reference. With the help of vivid case studies, I try to highlight how changing patterns of global connections impact on notions of space and time, how actors create and simultaneously live in a web of connections, how structures shape and support connections, and finally how connections always include a phase of transit, of being-in-between.

Similarly, the subsequent chapters should not be read as introducing unprecedented neologisms or revolutionary interpretations. On the contrary, with the exception of transit, these terms are current and commonly used in the social sciences and humanities. What this book tries to achieve is to render them more precise and fruitful for research in global history. Even though some reinterpretations of these terms are suggested, perhaps most obviously in the cases of connection and transit, the suggestions are by no means radical re-readings of established concepts. Rather, the objective is to conceptualize and systematize without losing analytical applicability, as is demonstrated for each term with a dedicated case study. Although the selected concepts derive from different contexts and are not necessarily at the same level of abstraction, what they share – at least as they are used in this book – is that they sit squarely on the fence between theory and empirics. This means that my proposed interpretations of these terms aim to be abstract and generalizable enough that they not be restricted to particular case studies, displaying clear potential to enrich global history as well as history in general. Simultaneously, though, the terms should not lose their operationalizability, and they should retain their epistemological utility in their respective case studies. Such interpretations provide us with analytical concepts in the true meaning of the term. That is, they are ideas and concepts that can help us to dissect research objects into their component parts while simultaneously allowing inferences about the broader research context and its notable mechanisms through studying those parts. Each of the terms presented here shares this ambition and objective.

The concept of global connections, already discussed in this introductory chapter, corresponds to a basic unit of observation in global history. The principal purpose of the field, which is to trace the emergence and impact of global connections, demands a more nuanced understanding of this term than even the literature on global history typically displays. Accordingly, connections must not be recollected backwards from their endings; rather, they have to be taken seriously as historical phenomena in their own right, which is a point that will recur in talking about transit. This is especially the case since global connections often become significant only after interacting with other kinds of connection. These are the key arguments relating to connections that will be demonstrated in the discussion of the so-called 'Great Moon Hoax' of 1835. In the summer of that year, the *Sun*, a New York newspaper, published a series of articles containing detailed reports of how the respected British astronomer Sir John Herschel discovered human-like life on the moon with the help of a gigantic telescope. In fact, Richard Adams Locke, the *Sun*'s editor-in-chief, wrote the texts to increase circulation. Despite a number of doubts, the deceptively real-seeming reports duped many readers and spread around the world, garnering an enthusiastic reception among countless masses. In this section, I try to show how the Moon Hoax worked, among other reasons, because of Locke's accomplished use of global connections and non-connections, which, due to their particular interplay, yielded an unprecedented situation and opportunities.

In terms of case studies, the two subsequent chapters track the history of telegraphy, which is especially well suited to illustrate the analytical qualities of space and time as concepts. In the section on space, I use a plural, relational concept of space to show how global connections are activated. Seen in relational terms, space consists of connections. When global or transregional connections come into play, spaces shift and bend, changing their relationships to other spaces. The qualitative substance of global connections and processes of globalization for the actors involved manifests itself in such shifts – so goes the core argument. The change becomes particularly tangible in, for example, the spatial tension that was common to many of the cable stations where the telegraphers went about their work in the early twentieth century. Many relay stations were in seemingly idyllic locations that were, however, very geographically isolated, like small islands in the Indian and Pacific Oceans. The personnel stationed there experienced the simultaneity of completely different spaces on a day-to-day basis through the discrepancy between their tight communicative and weak geographical ties to the world. I try to show what an unusual range of opportunities and events, what kinds of ways of apprehending the world, became possible by tracing German attacks on British cable stations on Fanning Island at the beginning of the First World War.

Without a connection to the concept of space, the concept of time is almost inconceivable. As is the case with the dynamic notion of space, time is a socio-cultural phenomenon that emerges from temporal relations between various actors, objects, ideas and events. Global connections and processes of exchange affect temporal relations, thereby becoming tangible for individual actors and entire societies, which I try to show through the shifting relation between time and space that arose in a few instances of telegraph fraud in the mid-nineteenth century. There are many cases in which fraudsters managed by one means or another to acquire important information first or to feed others false information with the aid of telegraphy, which yielded them brief windows of opportunity to profit from their exclusive knowledge. Further, global connections have also altered individual and collective perceptions of time. As one of many instances of such change, there is the case of a British telegrapher in India whose thoughts and actions reveal a perception of time that was profoundly affected by the feeling of being constantly accessible – a feeling that disturbed him deeply.

After discussing time and space, the next two chapters are devoted to two terms that guide much work in the humanities and social sciences – actor and structure – and their interrelationship, as they apply to studying global history. In discussing the concept of actors, I want to show how human actors navigate structures, while emphasizing how their activity creates global connections, thereby making them fulcrums between different spaces. To illustrate this, I examine the infamous and unprecedented mutiny on the *Bounty* in 1789, where the most diverse range of opportunities and interpretations came together on a little ship in the middle of the Pacific, making the mutiny possible in the first place. The perceptions and actions of the people involved were informed by utterly different areas and objects, which coalesced in the actors themselves. The socio-economic conditions of British plantations in the Caribbean played just as significant a role as the European image of the South Seas and the *Bounty* as a living space.

In the chapter on structures, I try to explain how actors create patterns of global connections through their activity and how these simultaneously stabilize and feedback into that activity. As an example, I consider how Mont Cenis was conquered and made amenable to transportation routes. The mountain, which had always frustrated the movement of goods and people between Savoy and Piedmont, went from a merely regional inconvenience to a global obstacle in the mid-nineteenth century. With the rise of steamships, the expansion of the European rail network and the construction of the Suez Canal, Mont Cenis suddenly became the last major impediment to traffic between Great Britain and India, which resulted in considerable structural pressure to overcome this final obstruction. The pressure eventually led not only to digging a tunnel through the mountain but also to daringly building a rail line over it.

The final analytical chapter is devoted to the concept of transit. Here I try to combine some ideas from the preceding chapters, especially the discussion of connections. The idea of transit assumes that connections consist of more than just the connected elements, which is something global history has largely ignored. Global connections exist in their own space and their own time. They are active mediators, not neutral intermediaries, between two or more connected nodes. The idea of transit tries to capture their effectiveness terminologically beyond simply how they recombine the connected points. To demonstrate the point, I survey the flight and eventual capture of Hawley Harvey Crippen in 1910. Crippen was suspected of his wife's murder in London, but he managed to abscond from the pending arrest with his mistress. The two boarded the *Montrose*, a steamer that was to convey them from Antwerp to Montreal. However, instead of the safe passage they had hoped for, the suspects were trapped in a 'cage of class', confined in a crossing that became a spectacle for a titillated global public. This case study exemplifies the interplay of very diverse kinds of connection and clearly reveals the inherent spatial and temporal dimensions of connections in transit.

As should have become clear by now, this is not a coherent, inevitable selection of cases. The six following chapters speak to each other via the conceptual approaches they introduce and discuss, not so much via the case studies whose principal aim is to provide best-practice examples regarding the analytical application of the concepts. The selection and combination of the cases ultimately reflects my own research interests, my approach to the field and the serendipity of my finds in recent years. That is the only reason why these examples are all from the so-called 'long nineteenth century', whose temporal extent I have tried to cover to the greatest degree possible. That is the only reason why all the examples display a connection – sometimes stronger, sometimes weaker – to the global British Empire. That is the only reason that they derive from European or European colonial contexts. That is the only reason why topics like telegraphy and steamships play disproportionately large roles. Thus, the selection reflects the limitations of my repertoire, but it is by no means a consequence of the analytical approach. On the contrary, each of the concepts presented here could be applied to countless other subjects of inquiry from other eras and other cultures. Indeed, that is precisely one of the key points about the concept of global history I am advocating here.

Still, before we move on to a discussion of the core concepts and their application in the case studies, the particular composition of the cases begs a final note on the issue of Eurocentrism. Even if the setting of individual studies reflects my own training and research experience in the field of European and European colonial history, the question remains whether such a focus on European (and often elite) actors of globalization can be appropriate in a book that claims to be an introduction to global history research practice. Is this not precisely the sort of Eurocentrism that global history and its neighbouring fields constantly point us to? Not necessarily, but of course with such a focus, the temptations and opportunities to go astray are everywhere. To explain: Eurocentrism, or indeed any other variant of centrism, does not refer to the practice of studying European (or any other given) history or testing hypotheses in this particular setting. Instead, it refers to the danger of consciously or unconsciously essentializing the European (or any other) experience and treating it as a universally applicable standard against which others are measured or categorized. The problem, of course, is that the more we focus on European issues, actors or background settings, the likelier it is that at some point we will – willingly or otherwise – find ourselves essentializing certain aspects of our studies. Global historical research is not immune to these temptations, and certainly I am not. Global history itself cannot overcome the ubiquitous temptations of centrism. However, as pointed out earlier in this chapter, its focus on global connections can help us to reveal imbalances and essentializations. Global history helps to see and understand Eurocentrism. It has helped me to find it in my own studies and tackle it best as I could. Still, I am convinced that I have overlooked things, that there are still manifestations of Eurocentrism in the following case studies that I am not aware of. Global history will help you, the reader, to recognize and counterbalance these remaining instances.

Notes

1 Ulrich Beck, among others, has adopted and problematized this term. It refers to the widespread tendency in the social sciences and the humanities to take the nation state as the primary unit of analysis and/or to derive the key analytical categories from the organizations of the nation state. See Ulrich Beck, *Macht und Gegenmacht im globalen Zeitalter. Neue weltpolitische Ökonomie* (Edition Zweite Moderne). Frankfurt am Main, 2002, 81ff.

2 Sebastian Conrad properly addresses defects in modern social sciences and humanities more generally. For reasons of clarity, I focus here on history as a discipline. Sebastian Conrad, *What Is Global History?* Princeton/Oxford, 2016, 3–4.

3   Patrick O'Brien, 'Historiographical Traditions and Modern Imperatives for the Restoration of Global History', in: *Journal of Global History* 1/1 (2006): 3–39, 4.

4   Martin Dusinberre, 'Japan, Global History, and the Great Silence', in: *History Workshop Journal* 83/1 (2017): 130–50.

5   Andreas Eckert, 'Globalgeschichte und Zeitgeschichte', in: *APuZ* 62/1–3 (2012): 28–32.

6   Natalie Zemon Davis, 'Decentering History: Local Stories and Cultural Crossings in a Global World', in: *History and Theory* 50/2 (2011): 188–202.

7   Dominic Sachsenmaier, *Global Perspectives on Global History: Theories and Approaches in a Connected World*. Cambridge, 2011, 70.

8   For example, compare the utterly different lines of argument in the two books bearing the title *What Is Global History?* by Crossley and Conrad; Pamela Kyle Crossley, *What Is Global History?* Cambridge, 2008; Conrad, *What Is Global History?*.

9   Translation from German original: 'Globalhistoriker bemühen sich, regional bedingte Weltsichten in ihrem jeweiligen Kontext zu verstehen.' Andrea Komlosy, *Globalgeschichte. Methoden und Theorien*. (UTB Geschichte, Bd. 3564.) Wien/Köln/Weimar, 2011, 14. Unless otherwise indicated, translations have been done by Ben Kamis on the author's request.

10 See, for example, Komlosy, *Globalgeschichte*, 8 and Sebastian Conrad, *Globalgeschichte. Eine Einführung*. (Beck'sche Reihe, Bd. 6079.) München, 2013, 12 und Ders., *What Is Global History*, 11–14. Although Conrad claims in explicit terms, especially in *What Is Global History*, that global history represents a particular perspective and that it has a particular research object.

11 Patrick O'Brien holds focusing on connections to be one of two dominant styles in global history, the other being characterized by comparison. The subtitle of Christopher Bayly's landmark book on the birth of the modern world evidences a similar conception of global history. Andrea Komlosy also points to connections and comparisons, the symmetry and appropriateness of which will be discussed briefly at the beginning of the next chapter. O'Brien, 'Historiographical Traditions'; Christopher Bayly, *The Birth of the Modern World, 1780–1914: Global Connections and Comparisons*. Oxford, 2004; Komlosy, *Globalgeschichte*, 9.

12 Conrad, *What Is Global History?*.

13 James Belich et al., *The Prospect of Global History*. Oxford, 2016.

14 Dusinberre, 'Japan, Global History, and the Great Silence'.

15 Sven Beckert and Dominic Sachsenmaier (eds), *Global History, Globally: Research and Practice around the World*. London/New York, 2018.

16 Jeremy Adelman, 'What Is Global History Now?', in: *Aeon*, 2 March 2017, https://aeon.co/essays/is-global-history-still-possible-or-has-it-had-its-moment (accessed 1 June 2018).

17 Richard Drayton and David Motadel, 'Discussion: The Futures of Global History', in: *Journal of Global History* 13/1 (2018): 1–21.

18 Conrad, *What Is Global History?*, 11–12 and 67–72.

19 Ibid., 10.

20 See, for example, Sachsenmaier, *Global Perspectives* (especially chapter 1); O'Brien, 'Historiographical Traditions'; Patrick Manning, *Navigating World History: Historians Create a Global Past*. New York, 2003 (especially Part I); Conrad, *Einführung* (especially 29–52); Conrad, *What Is Global History?* (especially 17–36); Sebastian Conrad and Andreas Eckert, 'Globalgeschichte, Globalisierung, multiple Modernen. Zur Geschichtsschreibung der modernen Welt', in: Dies. and Ulrike Freitag (Hrsg.), *Globalgeschichte. Theorien, Ansätze, Themen*. Frankfurt am Main, 2007, 7–49.

21 See, for example, Komlosy, *Globalgeschichte*.

22 See, for example, the second half of Conrad, Eckert and Freitag (Hrsg.), *Globalgeschichte. Theorien, Ansätze, Themen*; Conrad, *Einführung* (especially 193–247); Cátia Antunes and Karwan Fatah-Black (Hrsg.), *Explorations in History and Globalization*. London, 2016; Wolfgang Schwentker, 'Globalisierung und Geschichtswissenschaft. Themen, Methoden und Kritik der Globalgeschichte', in: ders., Margarete Grandner and Dietmar Rothermund (Hrsg.), *Globalisierung und Globalgeschichte*. (Globalgeschichte und Entwicklungspolitik, Bd. 1.) Wien, 2005, 36–59, 39.

23 See, for example, Sachsenmaier, *Global Perspectives* (especially chapters 2–4).

24 This corresponds roughly to the explicit goal of the case studies collected in Boris Barth, Stefanie Gänger and Niels P. Petersson (Hrsg.), *Globalgeschichten. Bestandsaufnahme und Perspektiven*. (Reihe 'Globalgeschichte', Bd. 17.) Frankfurt am Main, 2014.

25 See, for example, Boris Barth, Stefanie Gänger and Niels P. Petersson, 'Einleitung: Globalisierung und Globalgeschichte', in: dies., *Globalgeschichten*, S. 7–18; Grandner, Rothermund and Schwentker, *Globalisierung und Globalgeschichte*, especially Dietmar Rothermund, *Globalgeschichte und Geschichte der Globalisierung*, 12–35 and Schwentker, 'Globalisierung und Geschichtswissenschaft'; Antunes and Fatah-Black (Hrsg.), *Explorations*; Christopher A. Bayly, '"Archaic" and "Modern" Globalization in the Eurasian and African Arena, *c.* 1750–1850', in: Anthony G. Hopkins (Hrsg.), *Globalization in World History*. New York, 2002, 47–73; Anthony G. Hopkins, 'Introduction: Globalization – An Agenda for Historians', in: ders. (Hrsg.), *Globalization in World History*. New York, 2002, 1–10.

26 This applies especially to Bruce Mazlish in his various formulations of a 'New Global History'. See, for example, Bruce Mazlish, *The New Global History*. New York/Abingdon, 2006; Bruce Mazlish and Akira Iriye, 'Introduction', in: dies. (Hrsg.), *The Global History Reader*. New York/Abingdon, 2005, 1–15.

27 Frederick Cooper, *Colonialism in Question Theory, Knowledge, History*. Berkeley/Los Angeles, 2005; Ders., 'What Is the Concept of Globalization Good For? An African Historian's Perspective'. *African Affairs* 100/399 (2001): 189–213.

28 Gareth Austin, 'Global History in (Western) Europe: Explorations and Debates', in: Beckert and Sachsenmaier (eds), *Global History, Globally*, 21–44, 23.

29 Dennis O. Flynn and Arturo Giráldez, 'Born with a "Silver Spoon": The Origin of World Trade in 1571', in: *Journal of World History* 6/2 (1995): 201–21; Dies., 'Born Again: Globalization's Sixteenth Century Origins (Asian/Global Versus European Dynamics)', in: *Pacific Economic Review* 13/3 (2008): 359–87.

30 Kevin H. O'Rourke and Jeffrey G. Williamson, 'When Did Globalisation Begin?' in: *European Review of Economic History* 6/1 (2002): 23–50; Dies., 'Once More: When Did Globalisation Begin?', in: *European Review of Economic History* 8/1 (2004): 109–17.

31 Jürgen Osterhammel and Niels Petersson provide a very good initial survey of the various approaches in their small but brilliant text on the history of globalization. Jürgen Osterhammel and Niels P. Petersson, *Globalization: A Short History*. Princeton/Oxford, 2005, 5–11.

32 Lynn Hunt, 'Globalisation and Time', in: Chris Lorenz and Berber Bevernage (Hrsg.), *Breaking up Time: Negotiating the Borders between Present, Past and Future*. (Schriftenreihe der FRIAS School of History, Bd. 7.) Göttingen, 2013, 199–215, 201.

33 Jan Aart Scholte, *Globalization: A Critical Introduction*. 2. Aufl. New York, 2005.

34 Robert O. Keohane and Joseph S. Nye, 'Globalization: What's New? What's Not? (And So What?)', in: *Foreign Policy* 118/1 (2000): 104–19.

35 Mazlish and Iriye, 'Introduction', 2.

36 Barry K. Gills and William R. Thompson, 'Globalizations, Global Histories and Historical Globalities', in: dies. (Hrsg.), *Globalization and Global History*. New York/Abingdon, 2006, 1–15, 4.

37 Osterhammel and Petersson, *Globalization*, 5.

38 Anthony Giddens, *The Consequences of Modernity*. Stanford, 1990, 64.

Further reading

Adelman, Jeremy, 'What is Global History Now?' in: *Aeon*, 2 March 2017, https://aeon.co/essays/is-global-history-still-possible-or-has-it-had-its-moment (accessed 1 June 2018).

Beckert, Sven and Sachsenmaier, Dominic (eds), *Global History, Globally: Research and Practice around the World*. London/New York, 2018.

Belich, James, Darwin, John, Frenz, Margret and Wickham, Chris, *The Prospect of Global History*. Oxford, 2016.

Conrad, Sebastian, *What Is Global History?* Princeton/Oxford, 2016.

Crossley, Pamela Kyle, *What Is Global History?* Cambridge, 2008.

Drayton, Richard and Motadel, David, 'Discussion: The Futures of Global History', in: *Journal of Global History* 13/1 (2018): 1–21.

O'Brien, Patrick, 'Historiographical Traditions and Modern Imperatives for the Restoration of Global History', *Journal of Global History* 1/1 (2006): 3–39.

Osterhammel, Jürgen and Petersson, Niels P., *Globalization: A Short History*. Princeton/Oxford, 2005.

Sachsenmaier, Dominic, *Global Perspectives on Global History: Theories and Approaches in a Connected World*. Cambridge, 2011.

2

Connections:
The Great Moon Hoax

Connections in global history

Christopher Bayly gave his path-breaking work on the birth of the modern world a suggestive subtitle: *Global Connections and Comparisons.*[1] Taking its cue directly or indirectly from this phrase, the general historiographical approach of global history has often been described as focusing on 'trans-border processes, exchange relations as well as comparisons in the context of global relations',[2] as Sebastian Conrad summarized it in his German-language introduction to global history. Patrick O'Brien used the same definition in his prolegomenon to the first issue of the *Journal of Global History*, which appeared in 2006.[3] The first and most basic point to note, here, is that the terms 'connection' and 'comparison' are of two very different kinds with respect to their import for historical research. Comparison is a method, a tool of inquiry. It can be employed in very different forms of historical research. Conceptually, it has no special relationship with global history.[4] Connections, though, are basic units of analysis in global history. They are the building blocks of all forms of contact, exchange and network, and questions relating to the development of such connections as well as their meaning for historical actors are, accordingly, of great interest. Their historical efficiency is established, and their significance to the economic, social or cultural relations of a particular region or time is investigated. This approach is guided by the conviction that we cannot understand or explain the thoughts and actions of historical actors – in effect, history itself – without understanding extra-regional connections, their local manifestations and the interplay between them and intrinsic factors.

Thus, transregional connections are the basic units of observation in global history. They are the key elements of influential concepts, like transfer,[5] connected or entangled history,[6] and contact zones.[7] Hardly any study in global history can make do without the concept of connections, and this book is no exception, given that they guide the analysis of the various examples. Actors create them (as in the mutiny on the *Bounty*), structures forge them and, thus, they react back on the actors (see Mont Cenis). They create new spaces and temporal frameworks (see telegraphy). Therefore, global connections are undeniably significant in answering the questions of global history.

However, the very centrality of connections hints at a fundamental problem of global history: all forms of human thought and activity are embedded in complex patterns of connections and exchange patterns. All forms of social organization are based on this fact. Interpersonal connections and interactions are the basis of all forms of socialization. In consequence, all humanities and social sciences are always and automatically concerned with the relevance of such connections, and history is no exception. The upshot for global history is that its approach does not complement existing modes with a focus on *connections* but with its attention to *transregional, global* connections. The key question is, therefore, what distinguishes such global exchange processes and the attendant border crossings from other kinds of connections in theoretical terms. Why and how must interactions over long distances and across borders be viewed and investigated differently? How do their effects on the thoughts and actions of the respective actors differ conceptually from the basic connection patterns that prevail in any community? While these questions might seem trivial and their answers self-evident, reflecting on them forces us to analytically sharpen our conventional concept of connections and to examine the effects of factors like spatial distance, national borders and cultural differences, to name but a few.

Global connections have hardly been explicitly conceptualized in global history and, as a result, there has been little deliberate engagement with the problem sketched earlier. Even though the term 'connection' is ubiquitous in the relevant research, it is almost always used descriptively, which makes it difficult to tackle these important questions. This conceptual gap is most probably a result of how we tend to view connections, especially in relation to two points. First, we tend to think about connections from their ending points. We think about the people, places and things that are connected or are being connected with each other, and that is where we look for the effects of contact and exchange, which we then examine as factors of human thought and action. This implies that global history tacitly focuses on those connected, not on the connections themselves. Connections are usually thought of merely as quasi-neutral intermediaries – a point I will discuss in more detail in the sixth case study relating to the concept of transit.

Second, we tend to think of connections in binary terms, as either on or off, as existent or non-existent. Studies in global history have in many cases sought evidence of a connection between objects whose connectedness had gone unnoticed, but this kind of approach does not do justice to the complexity of historical circumstances. Connections always appear in the plural, and they affect each other. Relations between particular actors and their communities are always based on assemblages of different kinds of bonds. Assemblages of global connections have to traverse great distances, including a wide variety of borders and obstacles, which affects some kinds of connection in the assemblage more than others. Some are more effective over short distances. Some cross borders, while others do not. In contrast to local connections, the interplay among the individual connections changes, which, in turn, affects their qualities. The composition of these assemblages not only varies from one situation to another but also distinguishes global processes of exchange from local ones. One could say that global and local connections differ in terms of the interplay of the various connections and non-connections in such an assemblage, depending, of course, on the historical context in question.

If global history seeks to productively and reliably trace transregional connections through history and to assess their significance precisely, it will need, at the very least, a nuanced, adaptable understanding of connections on both of these levels. First, connections have to be taken seriously as historical phenomena in their own right that exist in their own space and time. They have to be considered mediators and not mere intermediaries, to borrow a couple of terms from actor-network theory, if we are to develop an integrated picture of connections and connected objects. How this could look in practice will be illustrated with a concrete case study in the section on transit. Second, global history must attend to the diversity and intricacy of global connections. The following example is an attempt to empirically elucidate this intricacy and its significance to the thoughts and actions of historical actors. It should show, among other things, that global connections did not just continuously stabilize through the nineteenth and twentieth centuries but also could be unstable, perceived, imagined, vague and interrupted without losing importance for people's thoughts and feelings. The 'Great Moon Hoax' of 1835 and its historical echoes demonstrate the point.

In April 1836, the editor of the *Athenaeum* – a London magazine on literature, science and art – felt obliged to enlighten his educated readers as to the truth of recently disseminated moon observations:

> The absurd accounts lately referred to in our daily papers, about some extraordinary discoveries made by Sir John Herschel, are now said to have been originally put forth in America. How this may be, we know not, but a correspondent has obligingly forwarded to us copies of the *Granada*

Free Press newspaper, in which we find a 'full, true, and particular' report, professedly copied 'from a Supplement to the Edinburgh Journal of Science', [...] [t]he papers are admirably written, and we would willingly have given our readers a taste of their quality, but it would have required more space than we could conscientiously spare for a mere joke.[8]

For the learned readership of the *Athenaeum*, then, it was at best a well-written joke, the incredible story that had been spreading from North America, over the Caribbean,[9] and then to Europe and beyond for months. For our purposes, it is an especially appropriate case study for several reasons. First, the so-called 'Great Moon Hoax' was itself in many ways a global phenomenon. The story spread from New York over vast regions of the world, and it was widely repeated and discussed. Moreover, the keen interest in observing the moon and in astronomy also indicates a certain globalized self-perception among the people of the time, the early nineteenth century. The sighting of extraterrestrials crystallized this perception in the world community. Second, and more importantly, the 1835 moon hoax highlighted diverse layers in the history of connections. The hoax was only successful due to deft handling of global connections and non-connections that interacted in an assemblage, the anatomy of which I will now outline.

The moon ...

On Friday, 21 August 1835, the *Sun*, a New York daily newspaper, printed an assortment of twenty-seven news snippets on its own behalf.[10] Hidden in this list, directly after the note that the *Sun*'s editorial offices had recently moved, the following message appeared:

Celestial Discoveries. The Edinburgh Courant says-'We have just learnt from an eminent publisher in this city that Sir John Herschel, at the Cape of Good Hope, has made some astronomical discoveries of the most wonderful description, by means of an immense telescope of an entirely new principle.'[11]

Following a common practice of the time, the New York paper quoted a Scottish newspaper directly – or at least professed to do so. The reference was to the *Edinburgh Courant*, which was told by a publisher that the famous British astronomer John Herschel (Figure 1) had made revolutionary astronomical discoveries with the aid of a giant telescope. There were no details as to the exact circumstances, nor was there any hint that further statements on this

FIGURE 1 *Sir John Herschel, photographed by Julia Margaret Cameron, April 1867. Courtesy of the Metropolitan Museum of Art 2013.1116.*

subject were to be expected. These few lines comprised the entirety of what the *Sun* had to say about the matter on that Friday.

It is fair to presume that the readership initially paid little attention to these lines in the Friday edition – assuming that they were widely noticed at all. The *Sun* was the first penny paper in the United States, and it was principally sold by paperboys on the street. Its readers were typically more interested in notable events in and around New York than in the latest scientific discoveries. Therefore, the heading of 'Celestial Discoveries' was perhaps only partially meant as a Friday teaser to generate suspense and to arouse the readers' curiosity, but it was quite definitely a deliberate act of deception intended to lend subsequent articles greater retrospective credibility. With that unassuming little message on 21 August 1835, the *Sun* launched the Great Moon Hoax, which not only captured the interest of the New York public but also spread deep into the American west and extended even to Europe.

Four days later on Tuesday, 25 August, the *Sun* printed the first of six long articles on the subject.[12] The text itself was printed directly on the first page and, due to its considerable length, covered most of it. The editors did not deign to include an explanation until page two:

> We this morning commence the publication of a series of extracts from the new Supplement to the Edinburgh Journal of Science, which have been very politely furnished us by a medical gentleman immediately from Scotland, in consequence of a paragraph which appeared on Friday last from the *Edinburgh Courant*. The portion which we publish to day is introductory to celestial discoveries of higher and more universal interest than any, in any science yet known to the human race.[13]

The statement referred to the brief message from 21 August and, in addition to the *Edinburgh Courant*, now brought the *Edinburgh Journal of Science* into play, whose supplement was the source of the articles. The title of the main article from the front page also clearly referred to the provenance of the text that followed: 'Great astronomical discoveries, lately made by Sir John Herschel, L. L. D. F. R. S. &c. At the Cape of Good Hope [From Supplement to the Edinburgh Journal of Science.]'[14] Then came the actual copy, which, in accordance with common practice, reprinted the original content of the *Edinburgh Journal of Science* verbatim rather than paraphrasing:

> In this unusual addition to our Journal, we have the happiness of making known to the British publick, and thence to the whole civilized world, recent discoveries in Astronomy which will build an imperishable monument to the age in which we live.[15]

However, the many succeeding lines of this first report related yet very little about the revolutionary discoveries themselves. Rather, the text laid the groundwork for the coming episodes. It started tracing a narrative arc and, more importantly, formed a stable foundation for the credibility of the subsequent elaborations. A major factor in this respect was the giant, technologically innovative telescope that John Herschel was to have developed and that made the promised discoveries possible in the first place. Early on, the text foreshadowed suggestively that, once he had erected and calibrated his telescope, Herschel observed a few hours of ceremonious silence before beginning his observations in order to prepare himself mentally for the awesome discoveries.[16] The author of the article repeatedly invoked this silent pause in rhetorical flourishes – 'And well might he pause!' – to emphasize the overwhelming magnitude of Herschel's supposed discoveries without giving away the game. Not until the next paragraph did the first real clue about the sensation finally appear:

> The younger Herschel, at his observatory in the Southern Hemisphere, has already made the most extraordinary discoveries in every planet of our solar system; has discovered planets in other solar systems; has obtained a distinct view of objects in the moon, fully equal to that which the naked eye commands of terrestrial objects at the distance of hundred yards; has affirmatively settled the question whether this satellite be inhabited, and by what order of things; has firmly established a new theory of cometary phenomena; and has solved or corrected nearly every leading problem of mathematical astronomy.[17]

Hidden among many points of more academic astronomical interest, there was a hint of the actual sensation, Herschel had definitively answered the question of whether there was life on the moon, a question of great importance in the burgeoning contemporary debate about extraterrestrial life.[18] The readers could only speculate about the form of the answer for the moment, since the remainder of the text was almost exclusively concerned with the technical requirements of Herschel's research results and their transmission. First, a certain Dr Andrew Grant was introduced who, as it would later emerge, was a fictional character, an astronomer who was to have studied with William Herschel, the father, and be the right-hand man of John Herschel, the son. The report was supposedly based on Grant's first-hand information, which he was passing on with Herschel's explicit permission. The entire remainder of the article was devoted exclusively to the invention and development of Herschel's innovative telescope, which was described in excessively minute technical detail. The article's actual author evidently knew enough about optics and astronomy to concur with the contemporary state of science and technology, which he needed to plausibly describe the development of a telescope with a seven-tonne lens and 42,000x magnification. The text ended by observing that, even while constructing the telescope, Herschel had been so convinced of its potential 'that he expressed confidence in his ultimate ability to study even the entomology of the moon, in case she contained insects upon her surface', and it closed with a promise 'To be continued'.[19]

This promise was kept the very next day, on 26 August. After long passages detailing the backstory of Herschel's sojourn at the Cape of Good Hope and the process of installing the telescope there, there finally came a description of the lunar discoveries. Until 10 January, Herschel had mostly investigated the night sky of the southern hemisphere before eventually directing his telescope at the moon, where the first thing he made out was a field of dark red flowers that reminded Dr Grant of the common domestic poppy. 'And this was the first organic production of nature, in a foreign world, ever revealed to the eyes of men.'[20] In the following paragraph, the astronomers stumbled on forests whose trees were reminiscent of yews and firs. They discovered a lake and huge quartz formations, which Grant initially thought were artificial (and, thus, proof of intelligent life on the moon), until Herschel corrected him. Only after further intensive observation did Herschel finally encounter animal life:

> In the shade of the woods on the south-eastern side, we beheld continuous herds of brown quadrupeds, having all the external characteristics of the bison, but more diminutive than any species of the bos genus in our natural history.[21]

Further, the astronomers had sighted bluish unicorns and pelican-like birds diving for fish. Finally, they toasted their fantastic discovery with the very best 'East India Particular' – a Madeira vintage. The article closed with the claim that many other animals had been observed on 13 and 14 January, which were soon to be described 'in the graphic language of our accomplished correspondent'. Thus, it was a classic cliffhanger ending with the standard tease of another exciting episode.[22]

The promised episode appeared the next day, and it was markedly shorter than the previous instalments. In it Herschel discovered further species of animals, of which a special lunar breed of beaver, the two-legged beaver, was especially noteworthy. It looked almost exactly like its earthly counterparts, with the exception that it had no tail and walked on two legs. And the beaver displayed other very human behaviours:

> It carries its young in its arms like a human being, and moves with an easy gliding motion. Its huts are constructed better and higher than those of many tribes of human savages, and from the appearance of smoke in nearly all of them, there is no doubt of its being acquainted with the use of fire.[23]

The article went on to describe some of Herschel's further geological, botanical and zoological discoveries, none of which, though, could rival the novelty value of the beaver. The piece closed by saying that Herschel expected peculiar things from his coming observations, which is exactly where the *Sun* took up the thread in the fourth instalment of the story, which appeared on the next day, Friday, 28 August. It was even a little shorter than the previous day's report, making it quick and easy to read. After the relatively pedestrian descriptions of the previous day – the beaver notwithstanding – the moment for the climax had come. Herschel had come across winged humanoid creatures (a contemporary artist's renderings of which appear in Figures 2 and 3). As the fictional narrator Dr Grant described:

> We were thrilled with astonishment to perceive four successive flocks of large winged creatures, wholly unlike any kind of birds, descend with a slow even motion from the cliffs on the western side, and alight upon the plain. They were first noted by Dr. Herschel, who exclaimed, 'Now, gentlemen, my theories against your proofs, which you have often found a pretty even bet, we have here something worth looking at.[']24

The narrative yarn in this episode was deftly spun. Without much ado and only a few technical details, the reader was gratified with the great sensation: humanoid life on the moon! A few well-chosen sentences were added to pique the readers' imaginations. Dr Grant described the man-bats in some detail before falling silent:

> Our further observation of the habits of these creatures, who were of both sexes, led to results so very remarkable, that I prefer they should first be laid before the public in Dr. Herschel's own work, where I have reason to know they are fully and faithfully stated, however incredulously they may be received. [...] We scientifically denominated them as Vespertilio-homo, or man-bat; and they are doubtless innocent and happy creatures, notwithstanding that some of their amusements would but ill comport with our terrestrial notions of decorum.25

Rather than elaborating on the man-bats, Dr Grant demurred and deferred to Herschel, leaving their readers' imaginations the greatest possible freedom to embellish. The intimations about the man-bats' casual sexual habits were plenty obvious. Indeed, the subject matter must have been astonishing if even Grant refused to expound. Moreover, by postponing more detailed descriptions and deferring to Herschel, the authors of this fabrication insulated themselves against doubt and criticism. The following paragraph included notice that Herschel's own account would be published along with the verified reports of eyewitnesses, including reputable civil and military figures of the Cape Colony, among them 'several Episcopal, Wesleyan, and other ministers'.26

What could possibly follow the discovery of humanoid life on the moon? Also rather short, the fifth episode of 29 August opened without much pomp. It described the surface of the moon – volcanic activity had been found, after all. Herschel had developed another outlandish theory, according to which the volcanoes' immediate vicinity would surely be inhabited, since the 'flaming mountain'27 would provide locals with light through the long nights. Despite continued searching, Herschel and his colleagues failed to find further life

ALTRE SCOVERTE FATTE NELLA LUNA DAL SIG.' HERSCHEL

FIGURE 2 *Illustrations from the Italian translation of the* Moon Hoax. Leopoldo Galluzzo, *Altre scoverte fatte nella luna dal Sigr. Herschel, Napoli 1836.*

forms, but they did notice an architecturally fascinating temple facility, which caused them no small degree of puzzlement. The moon-men were apparently religious. Beyond that, however, they faced many unanswered questions. To rekindle enough suspense to last over the weekend, Grant was given to close:

> I by no means despair of ultimately solving not only these but a thousand other questions which present themselves respecting the objects of this planet; for not the millionth part of her surface has yet been explored, and we have been more desirous of collecting the greatest possible number of new facts, than of indulging in speculative theories, however seductive for the imagination.[28]

The final episode of the saga appeared on Monday, 31 August. It was an attempt to fulfil the expectations that had grown, and it again required the

FIGURE 3 *Illustrations from the Italian translation of the* Moon Hoax. Leopoldo Galluzzo, *Altre scoverte fatte nella luna dal Sigr. Herschel, Napoli 1836.*

use of a few narrative tricks. Right at the beginning, Dr Grant described how Herschel had soon found still more man-bats near the temple 'of larger stature than the former specimens, less dark in color, and in every respect an improved variety of the race'.[29] It was, therefore, obvious that the inhabitants of the moon differed biologically and culturally. Grant's subsequent descriptions touched on their social behaviour and societal composition. At this point the report took another dramatic turn. Exhausted after all the exciting discoveries, they had forgotten to direct the telescope's lens away from the daylight sun, and the concentrated rays ignited the building in the morning, causing considerable damage. After a week of repairs, the moon was no longer visible, so Herschel turned his equipment on Saturn. The piece covered his observations and detailed the accomplishments of William Herschel, who had, after all, discovered two of Saturn's seven moons in 1759. Only when the *Edinburgh Journal of Science* threatened to delve into the arcana of Saturn research, after already quite detailed descriptions, did the *Sun* opt to intervene:

Having ascertained the mean density of the rings, as compared with the density of the planet, Sir John Herschel has been enabled to effect the following beautiful demonstration. [Which we omit, as too mathematical for popular comprehension. – Ed. Sun.][30]

The Scottish science journal, which the *Sun* had apparently been citing verbatim throughout, then resumed its discourse on the rings and belts of Saturn – but here again the editors of the penny paper stepped in:

[But the portion of the work which is devoted to this subject, and to the other planets, as also that which describes the astronomer's discoveries among the stars, is comparatively uninteresting to general readers, however highly it might interest others of scientific taste and mathematical acquirements. – Ed. Sun.][31]

Thus, the sixth and final instalment of the series closed by saying that Herschel would be able to resume his observations on the new moon in March. Finally, there was Dr Grant's report of still other man-bats and a repeated deferral to Herschel's own publication:

We found the very superior species of the Vespertilio-homo. In stature they did not exceed those last described, but they were of infinitely greater personal beauty, and appeared in our eyes scarcely less lovely than the general representations of angels by the more imaginative schools of painters. [...] I shall, therefore, let the first detailed account of them appear in Dr. Herschel's authenticated natural history of this planet.[32]

The *Sun*'s editors added that, aside from the forty pages of 'illustrative and mathematical notes'[33] that they would spare their paper's readers, this was the end of the supplement from the *Edinburgh Journal of Science*.

... and the *Sun*

The brief summary in the previous section of the six-part report reveals not only the content of the 'Great Moon Hoax' but also how it was narratively engineered with painstaking attention to detail. The *Sun* did not bombard its readers with extravagant revelations about life on the moon; rather, it strung them along with only vague hints for days at a time. The authors of the allegedly quoted Scottish journal indulged in exhaustive technical descriptions, which invoked – terminologically as well as substantively – the state of the contemporary scientific arts. While these details were beyond most of their readers' comprehension, precisely their over-sophistication lent them credibility. Besides, the report mentioned a number of well-known scientific authorities. In addition to the protagonist John Herschel, the report mentioned his famous father William on several occasions. The name of David Brewster, a Scottish physicist, also appeared several times, which indirectly tied the reports to the *Edinburgh Journal of Science*, as Brewster had been its editor until 1832. Further, though the six reports were clearly building dramatic tension towards a climax, the flow of the narrative was repeatedly interrupted with duller discussions about the moon's topography or the technical challenges of observing it.[34] This style, as with the cliffhangers, served both to build suspense among the readers as well as to lend the reports greater credibility. And the innuendos about unspoken (or perhaps even unspeakable?) details, which only Herschel, if anyone, could relate personally were also a great titillation.

While the content of the report may have been incredible, its packaging was not. The text skilfully referred to the global (mostly transatlantic, in this particular example) connections of the time and used them to enhance its credibility. Engineering this text so convincingly would have required considerable time and trouble, vast knowledge of astronomy and physics as well as indubitable literary talent. The author was in all probability Richard Adams Locke, a journalist and the *Sun*'s editor-in-chief at the time. Even though Locke only indirectly admitted his authorship after the hoax had been exposed, nearly all clues seem to confirm it retrospectively. Many contemporaries also fingered him as the real source of the report shortly after its publication – especially James Gordon Bennett, publisher of the *New York Herald*, whose paper immediately identified Locke as the author.[35]

Richard Adams Locke was well known in New York's lettered circles, and he was respected for his acuity. In the sixth volume of *The Literati of New York City*, Edgar Allan Poe wrote of him:

> He is about five feet seven inches in height, symmetrically formed; there is an air of distinction about his whole person – the air noble of genius. His face is strongly pitted by the small-pox, and, perhaps from the same cause, there is a marked obliquity in the eyes; a certain calm, clear luminousness, however, about these latter, amply compensates for the defect, and the forehead is truly beautiful in its intellectuality. I am acquainted with no person possessing so fine a forehead as Mr. Locke. He is married, and about forty-five years of age, although no one would suppose him to be more than thirty-eight. He is a lineal descendant from the immortal author of the 'Essay on the Human Understanding'.[36]

Richard Adams Locke was born in 1800 in Somerset, England (even though he later listed New York as his place of birth), and the Locke family was relatively well off, propertied and busy. Among other influential ancestors, the philosopher John Locke (1632–1704) had been a member of the family. However, the line of descent between him and Richard Adams Locke was not direct, though the latter would later appropriate Poe's claim to the contrary. Richard was a good pupil, having been taught by a private tutor. He later claimed to have studied in Cambridge, although the registration records provide no evidence of his enrolment. Instead of employment on the family estate, Locke became a journalist, writing for many London newspapers before becoming the inaugural editor of a newly launched paper in Somerset. Because of his unpopular republican views, he lost the post and, seeing little future in England, emigrated with his small family to New York in late 1835.[37] Locke quickly made a name for himself there in journalism, and he caught the eye of a young Benjamin Day, founding owner of the *Sun*. As a result, Locke became the editor of Day's paper in May 1835.[38]

Day had launched the *Sun* as the city's first penny paper (except for another, very short-lived enterprise). Unlike the other dailies in circulation that were aimed at a more affluent, better-educated audience and charged six cents a copy, the *Sun* went for just a penny a piece. This was Benjamin Day's strategy to reach a wider public and high circulation, which was largely successful, with the *Sun* reaching a daily run of 15,000 copies by mid-1835.[39] Other newspapers based on the same model soon followed – including, for example, the *New York Herald*, Bennett's paper that was mentioned earlier – and the penny press was born. These papers differed from the established press not only in terms of price and a more compact format but also in terms of style. They avoided boring their readers with nuanced political analyses and the international despatches that were so common in the more upscale papers. Instead, they occupied themselves with more appetizing and regional fare. They did not shy from sensationalist pieces and spared no effort to reach a wide readership.[40]

As a sensationalist story that aimed at maximizing circulation without concern for truth, Locke's elaborate moon hoax fits comfortably in the contemporary journalistic style of the penny press, even though Locke himself claims to have intended 'Great Astronomical Discoveries' as a satire.[41]

Connections and non-connections

Readers' reactions varied widely. Many media expressed their incredulity in various ways almost immediately following the publication of the first spectacular discoveries. Some, like the *Journal of Commerce*, evinced scepticism in their articles about whether the reports were true and suspected a hoax. The *Transcript*, a penny paper in direct competition with the *Sun*, responded satirically to the lunar discoveries and came up additional information from a correspondent of its own. With their deliberate and exaggerated absurdity, these replies cast the *Sun*'s reports in a ridiculous light.[42] But no one took a more aggressive stance towards the articles than Bennett's *New York Herald*. As soon as 31 August – the day on which the final episode appeared in the *Sun* – Bennett printed a trenchant text on the front page of the *Herald* bearing the title 'The Astronomical Hoax Explained', where he stated clearly and with characteristic bluntness that the story must be a hoax. Moreover, as mentioned before, he raised the possibility of Richard Adams Locke's authorship and spread all manner of half-truths about the latter's life. However, Bennett did seem to admire Locke's talent as a storyteller: 'Mr. Locke, however, deserves great credit for his ingenuity – his learning – and his irresistible drollery. He is an original genius.'[43] Locke replied to Bennett's revelations in an open letter, repudiating the claims of his authorship at every turn. Locke slyly claimed: 'I did not make those discoveries.'[44] Locke's refusal to admit to the ruse annoyed Bennett, who launched many more attacks against the *Sun* in the following days, but the New York public took little notice. Even those who doubted the veracity of the story were difficult to rile. According to Mario Castagnaro, many readers and journalists were indifferent about the truth of the reports, holding the opinion, 'wonderful if true, entertaining if not'.[45] This might explain why so many other papers jumped on the bandwagon and reprinted the moon story themselves. Asa Greene, editor of the *Transcript* at the time, published a travel guide for New York two years later, which contained, among other things, a comment on the moon hoax:

All New York rang with the wonderful discoveries of Sir John Herschell [*sic*]. Every body read the Sun, and every body commented on its surprising contents. There were, indeed, a few sceptics; but to venture to express a doubt of the genuineness of the great lunar discoveries, was considered almost as heinous a sin as to question the truth of revelation.

Nor was it only among the populace in general, that the moon story was believed. Certain of the sixpenny editors also gave into it, and copied the account, with flaming notices of the very wonderful and important discoveries of Sir John Herschell at the Cape of Good Hope. The papers in this city, which were thus caught, were the Daily Advertiser and the Mercantile Advertiser. The Daily Advertiser of Newark, and the Daily Gazette of Albany, were also among the ready believers of the great discoveries. How many papers, in other places, swallowed the hoax, we do not know.

Most of the editors, we believe, prudently kept their minds suspended as to the truth or falsehood of the account; though most of them copied it, as a capital story, whether it should turn out true or false.[46]

Greene, thus, followed a line of pragmatic disinterest as to the veracity of the story while simultaneously stressing how many of his colleagues were taken in by the tale. Writing retrospectively in the biographical piece on Richard Adams Locke mentioned earlier, Edgar Allan Poe was even more candid:

Not one person in ten discredited it, and (strangest point of all!) the doubters were chiefly those who doubted without being able to say why – the ignorant, those uninformed in astronomy, people who would not believe because the thing was so novel, so entirely 'out of the usual way'. A grave professor of mathematics in a Virginian college told me seriously that he had no doubt of the truth of the whole affair! The great effect wrought upon the public mind is referable, first, to the novelty of the idea; secondly, to the fancy-exciting and reason-repressing character of the alleged discoveries; thirdly, to the consummate tact with which the deception was brought forth; fourthly, to the exquisite vraisemblance of the narration.[47]

Both kinds of reactions – belief in the trustworthiness of the discoveries as well as the relative disinterest in it – depended on at least a sheen of authenticity. That is, the report needed a modicum of credibility to induce the credulity of some and to entertain the others. In the quote given earlier, Poe identified four main factors that, according to him, contributed to the credibility of the moon hoax. Besides the story's novelty and the way it tickled the audience's fancy, he also mentions the 'consummate tact', but the fourth factor in his list, the *vraisemblance* of the tale, was probably decisive. With this reference to a literary concept drawn from French classicism, Poe accorded the moon hoax a considerable degree of plausibility and probability. As many contemporary assessments of the text confirm, it fit almost seamlessly into the horizons of scientific and aspirational possibilities of the time. Take, for example, an anonymous letter to the editor printed in a Stralsund newspaper that had previously published translated excerpts of the observations:

As to the overall character of the reports, from the German translator all the way to the reputed observer himself, we can come to no other conclusion than that what a report based on perception would profess outweighs that which a report based on fantasy would betray.[48]

This begs the question as to what method Richard Adams Locke used to lend his fiction *vraisemblance* and let it pass as a 'report based on perception'.

Along with his skill as a storyteller and his scientific erudition, his cunning manipulation of global connections and non-connections were the primary ingredients, as will be shown.

Recent research on seafaring has solidly established that oceans not only have served as partitions in human history but have also been binding elements.[49] The so-called 'Atlantic world', which bound much of Europe to North America and the Caribbean, is but one example.[50] Since the intensive colonization of North America there has been a bustling exchange of people, goods and information – including scientific knowledge – among these regions. Hence, Sir John Herschel (as was the case with his father William) was a recognizable personality among educated New Yorkers in the early nineteenth century. In fact, the English scientist was also considered in North America to be one of the most renowned scientists of his time. His expedition to South Africa to conduct celestial observations in the southern hemisphere, which began in 1833, was no secret. Even in the relatively provincial city of Cincinnati, a notable newspaper reported in April 1834 (a delay of five months) on Herschel's journey to the Cape:

> The long projected voyage of sir John Herschel to the southern hemisphere is at length proceeded in. [...] To the learned of all countries, the voyage of our astronomer may be regarded as an event of unusual interest.[51]

Herschel's works were also of interest to educated and passionate amateurs in America. Richard Adams Locke had read Herschel's *A Treatise on Astronomy* shortly after its 1834 American printing. Edgar Allan Poe was also very familiar with Herschel's views, so familiar, in fact, that one of his stories, 'Hans Phaall – A Tale', relies on Herschel's book for many passages.[52] The events around the figure and work of David Brewster, who was pressed into service as the expert witness in support of the improvements to Herschel's telescope, tell a similar tale. Brewster was a famous Scottish physicist who had made a name for himself principally in the field of optics.[53] The rediscovery of the kaleidoscope and the so-called 'stereoscope' are among his most prominent accomplishments, which together led Brewster to be considered an authority on optics in the early nineteenth century. Moreover, he had founded the influential *Edinburgh Philosophical Journal* in 1819 with Robert Jameson and was one of its leading lights until 1824. As an encore, he launched the *Edinburgh Journal of Science*, which he edited until 1832. Brewster's direct connection to the journal, which was supposedly the *Sun*'s source in reporting the lunar observations, redoubled the story's *vraisemblance*. The news snippet that appeared on 21 August 1835 and was reportedly drawn from the *Edinburgh Courant* referred to its source as an 'eminent publisher in this city'.[54] Even though Brewster had left the helm of the *Edinburgh Journal of*

Science in 1832, on the other side of the Atlantic this phrase aroused obvious suspicions. Could David Brewster himself be the source?

The North American intelligentsia paid close attention to germane British science journals, including the *Edinburgh Journal of Science* and the *Edinburgh Philosophical Journal*, despite receiving them with some delay relative to European readers. One implication is that, by claiming to reproduce text that had appeared in the *Edinburgh Journal of Science*, Locke was able to bask in the journal's scientific prestige. The success of this tactic becomes clear in the following quote, where British writer Harriet Martineau describes the reaction to Herschel's supposed discoveries:

> I happened to be going the round of several Massachusetts villages when the marvellous account of Sir John Herschel's discoveries in the moon was sent abroad. The sensation it excited was wonderful. As it professed to be a republication from the Edinburgh Journal of Science, it was some time before many persons, except professors of natural philosophy, thought of doubting its truth.[55]

Beyond raising the report's credibility, the circulation of European scholarly journals in North America also meant that their North American readers were widely familiar with debates conducted in these journals. One popular discussion being carried out there (and elsewhere) for many years treated the question of whether there was life on the moon and what indications there might be to that effect.[56] One clear strand in the debate of the late eighteenth and early nineteenth centuries is that several clerics and scholars (sometimes with both unified in one person) were convinced of the existence of intelligent extraterrestrial (especially lunar) life. In an article on 'The Moon and its Inhabitants' that appeared in 1826 in the inaugural issue of the *Edinburgh New Philosophical Journal*, successor to the *Edinburgh Philosophical Journal*, German astronomers Franz von Paula Gruithuisen, Wilhelm Olbers and Carl Friedrich Gauss published their thoughts on the subject. It covered Gruithuisen's claim to have seen traces of massive constructions (including a temple), Olbers's hypotheses about lunar vegetation and Gauss's proposal to communicate with the moon people by way of basic mathematical principles.[57] There is evidence of Richard Adams Locke having read the article.[58]

The short article in the *Edinburgh New Philosophical Journal* – at least the one preserved in the collection of the Harvard Library – includes the handwritten addition of 'Thomas Dick, LL.D. of Dundee' as author.[59] Dick, a Scottish astronomer and priest, was also convinced on religious grounds alone that there had to be extraterrestrial life, which he proclaimed to the world in several works, including *The Christian Philosopher* (1823) and *The Philosophy of Religion* (1826).[60] Apparently, Richard Adams Locke could not take Dick's ideas or, indeed, the entire debate about life on the moon seriously. Fifteen years after the publication of the Great Moon Hoax, he wrote that the story was a parody of this controversy and, in particular, of Thomas Dick.[61] In fact, the text does contain hints of this satirical intent that most contemporaries overlooked. For example, the discovery of the temple structure in the fifth episode could be taken as a send up of Gruithuisen's lunar observations.[62] Further, Locke's Dr Grant said about the discovery of the temple, 'It was a temple – a fane of devotion, or of science, which, when consecrated to the Creator is devotion of the loftiest order',[63] which can be read as Locke mocking Thomas Dick's conflation of religion and science. But Dick was not the only one for whom the question of extraterrestrial life carried a strong religious dimension, as these words of Harriet Martineau reveal:

> A story is going, told by some friends of Sir John Herschel (but whether in earnest or in the spirit of the moon story I cannot tell), that the astronomer has received at the Cape a letter from a large number of Baptist clergymen of the United States, congratulating him on his discovery, informing him that it had been the occasion of much edifying preaching and of prayer-meetings for the benefit of brethren in the newly-explored regions; and beseeching him to inform his correspondents whether science affords any prospects of a method of conveying the Gospel to residents in the moon.[64]

Other versions also related the story that clerics were already pondering the proselytization of lunar inhabitants,[65] which further exemplifies the ubiquity of the debate about extraterrestrial life and the common practice of mixing revelation with experimentation.

There was a broad array of global – mostly transatlantic in this particular case – connections and patterns of exchange that Richard Adams Locke employed, whether deliberately or not. For instance, newspaper and magazine articles from Europe crossed the Atlantic in the early nineteenth century as easily as noteworthy scientific works did. Within a few weeks, the North American public was as well informed about John Herschel's trip to the Cape, his new telescope and his ongoing work as attentive Europeans were. Those Americans interested in science had access to the relevant European publications, knew their editors and followed the important contemporary debates. In short, North American and European actors (especially the British, of course) were closely connected to each other in spite of an ocean's remove; knowledge and ideas, not just people and goods, crossed the pond.[66] Richard Adams Locke made extremely cunning use of these existing global connections and used the horizon of his readers' experiences to inform his narrative. Thus did he create new, equally effective kinds of connections: expectations, hopes and global possibilities.

But the hoax also profited from the obverse of transregional connections described earlier: delays and interruptions. This, too, is apparent in the figure of Herschel and in the circulation of the journals already mentioned. At the turn of the twentieth century, Frank O'Brien studied the history of the *Sun* and wrote about the moon hoax, among other topics. He related how two Yale professors made their way to New York shortly after the fraudulent reports had been published. Once at the offices of the *Sun*, they demanded to see the original copy of the *Edinburgh Journal of Science*, from which the story had reportedly been drawn. Benjamin Day responded with indignation that the professors would dare to doubt the report's authenticity, but he nonetheless referred them to Locke. For his part, Locke received them cordially and explained that the issue in question was at a print shop in William Street, where it was naturally available for perusal.

> As the Yale men disappeared in the direction of the printery, Locke started for the same goal, and more rapidly. When the Yalensians arrived, the printer, primed by Locke, told them that the precious pamphlet had just been sent to another shop, where certain proof-reading was to be done. And so they went from post to pillar until the hour came for their return to New Haven.[67]

While there is reason to doubt whether these events really transpired as reported, they still show to what degree reference to the Scottish journal not only enhanced the observations' credibility but also led many readers to want to verify them in the original. By accident or design, however, Locke had made verification impossible, given that the *Edinburgh Journal of Science* had been merged with another journal, the *London and Edinburgh Philosophical Magazine and Journal of Science*, in 1832. It might well be the case that Locke, who had left England in 1831, was simply unaware of the change,[68] or that he actually meant the *Edinburgh New Philosophical Journal*, in which Thomas Dick had published his 1826 article.[69] Whatever the case, direct verification of the *Sun*'s claims was impossible. No one on the American east coast could access the relevant issue, as the journal in question was no longer in print in 1835. Moreover, the *Sun* claimed that the original account had appeared in a supplement to the journal, not in a regular issue, which further hindered its verification. By referring to a recently discontinued journal, existing journals with similar titles and the red-herring supplement, Locke docked onto existing knowledge while simultaneously fomenting uncertainty and confusion about the article's pedigree. This opened a window of opportunity that could only be closed by requests of information sent to Britain whose reply would take several weeks.

A similar non-connection pertained to the accessibility of John Herschel himself. During the tumult about his alleged discoveries, Herschel was on a trip lasting several years to the Cape of Good Hope in order to conduct astronomical research in his own observatory. Such geographical isolation added more difficulty and delay in questioning him about the reports than would have been the case had he been in England. Even more importantly, only very few people were appraised of his progress, and they were on location with him. As a result, no one was able to verify the authenticity of the dubious reports – no one, that is, beside Dr Grant, whom Locke had invented, or David Brewster, who was an unwitting background actor. Thus, the isolation of Herschel and his team, too, contributed considerably to the window of opportunity in which the story maintained some fleeting plausibility. Locke drew on existing knowledge while preventing it from being updated.

John Herschel did not learn of his own amazing discoveries until late 1835. Caleb Weeks, proprietor of an animal sideshow from Long Island, sailed to South Africa soon after the *Sun* had published the hoax in order to stock up his menagerie with exotic animals. He used the opportunity to inform Herschel of the moon hoax, and the scientist initially reacted with surprise and amusement.[70] After a while, though, he started to receive numerous requests from around the world sent by those who wanted confirmation of the reports or merely to hear his opinion of the story. Predictably enough, the correspondence did start to irk Herschel, who wrote to his aunt Caroline, 'I have been pestered from all quarters with that ridiculous hoax about the Moon – in English French Italian & German!!'.[71] Herschel eventually wrote an open letter directly to the *Athenaeum* journal in London, thanking them for the correction that had been published in April 1836. Evidently, he was still able to look on the affair with good humour: 'Since there are people silly enough to believe every extravagant tale which is set before them, we ought to hope that these tales may be as harmless as that now in question.'[72]

In light of the effect of Locke's fabricated report, there were more factors at play than merely Locke's invocations of prevailing scientific knowledge and the range of expectations this knowledge induced in the entangled transatlantic world. Indeed, denying the audience any ability to immediately verify or falsify the information was equally important. Couching the story cleverly in a network of transregional connections and non-connections allowed for people's imaginations and interpretations to romp freely.

Conclusion: Connections in global history

What became of Richard Adams Locke after his deception was exposed? In autumn 1836, a little more than a year after the publication of the moon hoax, Locke left the *Sun* and became the editor of *New Era*, a newly launched penny paper with loftier journalistic ambitions. The new paper found it difficult to compete in the New York market, driving Locke to see no other prospect by winter 1838 than to venture another hoax in order to boost circulation. In 'The Lost Manuscript of Mungo Park' he claimed that the lost journals of Mungo Park, an explorer who had vanished without a trace on an 1806 mission to the Niger River, had turned up. *New Era* promised that the journals would finally shed light on Park's disappearance. This time, however, the ruse failed. The public knew exactly who was behind the story: the very same man who had staged the Great Moon Hoax three years prior.[73]

Locke's name has been associated with the moon hoax ever since. That first con profited greatly from the complexity of global processes of exchange, from the assemblages of manifold unique connections of widely varying forms and intensities. Thus, as a historical case study the moon hoax exemplifies a key point to consider in conceptualizing connections analytically. Namely, the character and efficiency of global interrelationships result from cross-fertilization of particular connective links, from their tensions and mutual references. The spatial distance between Europe, North America and South Africa, along with the impediments to communication that went with it, created a certain context in which certain connections were more effective than others. There was sufficient reciprocal interest and enough rough, somewhat outdated knowledge in North America about events in Europe and South Africa to cultivate a space of expectations, possibilities and cognitive associations. However, there were no means of immediate verification or clarification, which allowed the space to persist for a reasonable amount of time. This assemblage of connections, some of which were more open and others fairly closed, an assemblage of connections and non-connections, results from the distance that must be overcome and the borders that must be crossed. A more local context would have required a very different assemblage. The moon hoax could only have succeeded in a particular configuration of simultaneously occurring connections and non-connections. This particular case accentuates the multiplicity of global connections, which is also of substantial importance to research in global history more broadly. The significance of global connections is always catalysed through interaction with other connections or explicit non-connections.

Such phenomena are a clearly recurring theme throughout all the case studies in this book. For example, the section on the concept of transit, which tackles the second yawning gap in the current understanding of connections and explains their significance as discrete historical phenomena, uses the flight and capture of Dr Crippen in 1910 on suspicion of murder in order to investigate the topic further. While concentrating on the pivotal stage of the transit, the circumstances around the hunt for Crippen simultaneously reemphasize the diversity of global connections. More specifically, the fugitives in this case were travelling between two continents on a steamship, which itself was tied into a worldwide communication network by radio-telegraph. Only through the partially countervailing relations between such connections and non-connections could this story's historical context emerge. The same goes for the cases selected to elucidate space and time. As they will describe, global networking processes created new spaces and altered existing ones, but these alterations did not manifest themselves until they interacted with still other spaces and temporal structures. In the end, the multiplicity of spaces and times is a function of the diversity of connections described here. This is the case even in the two sections that deal with the role of actors and structures – perhaps most obviously in the example of how traversing the Alps brought various lines of communication between Europe and Asia into play.

Notes

1 Bayly, *The Birth of the Modern World, 1780–1914*.

2 This is a direct translation from the German original: 'grenzüberschreitende Prozesse, Austauschbeziehungen, aber auch Vergleiche im Rahmen globaler Zusammenhänge'. Conrad, *Globalgeschichte*, 9. In Conrad's English-language introduction, the passage has been translated without the reference to comparisons. Conrad, *What Is Global History?*, 5.

3 O'Brien, 'Historiographical Traditions', 3–39, 4.

4 There is, by the way, a lively debate about the utility of comparison as a method in the entangled contexts of global history. Advocates of the *histoire-croisée* approach argue, for example, that mutually entangled objects cannot be adequately analysed with comparative methods. See Michael Werner and Bénédicte Zimmermann, 'Beyond Comparison: Histoire Croisée and the Challenge of Reflexivity', in: *History and Theory* 45 (2006): 30–50.

5 See Michel Espagne and Michael Werner (Hrsg.), *Transferts. Les relations interculturelles dans l'espace franco-allemand* (xviii\ᵉ–xix\ᵉ siècles). Paris 1988.

6 See Shalini Randeria, 'Geteilte Geschichte und verwobene Moderne', in: Jörn Rüsen, Hanna Leitgeb and Norbert Jegelka (Hrsg.), *Zukunftsentwürfe. Ideen für eine Kultur der Veränderung*. Frankfurt am Main, 1999, 87–95; Sanjay Subrahmanyam, 'Connected Histories: Notes towards a Reconfiguration of Early Modern Eurasia', in: *Modern Asian Studies* 31/3 (1997): 735–62; Shalini Randeria and Sebastian Conrad, 'Geteilte Geschichten. Europa in einer postkolonialen Welt', in: dies. (Hrsg.), *Jenseits des Eurozentrismus. Postkoloniale Perspektiven in den Geschichts- und Kulturwissenschaften*. Frankfurt am Main, 2002, 9–49; Angelika Epple, Olaf Kaltmeier and Ulrike Lindner (Hrsg.), *Entangled Histories: Reflecting on Concepts of Coloniality and Postcoloniality*. (Comparativ, Bd. 21/1.) Leipzig, 2011, 7–104.

7   On the concept of contact zones, see Mary Louise Pratt, *Imperial Eyes: Travel Writing and Transculturation*. London, 1992.

8   Charles Wentworth Dilke, 'Extraordinary Discoveries by Sir John Herschel', in: *Athenaeum* 440 vom 2. April 1836, 244.

9   In referring to the *Granada Free Press*, the *Athenaeum* editor most likely meant the *Grenada Free Press* from the eponymous colony in the British West Indies.

10 Matthew Goodman, *The Sun and the Moon: The Remarkable True Account of Hoaxers, Showmen, Dueling Journalists, and Lunar Man-Bats in Nineteenth-Century New York*. New York, 2008, 136.

11 Richard Adams Locke, 'Celestial Discoveries', in: *The Sun* vom 21. August 1835, 2.

12 Richard Adams Locke and Joseph Nicolas Nicollet, *The Moon Hoax; or, a Discovery that the Moon Has a Vast Population of Human Beings*. New York, 1859.

13 Richard Adams Locke, 'Great Astronomical Discoveries: Lately Made By Sir John Herschel, L. L. D. F. R. S. &c. At the Cape of Good Hope [From Supplement to the Edinburgh Journal of Science.]', in: *The Sun* vom 25. August 1835, 2.

14 Ibid., 1.

15 Ibid.

16 'We are assured that when the immortal philosopher to whom mankind is indebted for the thrilling wonders now first made known, had at length adjusted his new and stupendous apparatus with the certainty of success, he solemnly paused several hours before he commenced his observations, that he might prepare his own mind for discoveries which he knew would fill the minds of myriads of his fellow-men with astonishment, and secure his name a bright, if not transcendent conjunction with that of his venerable father to all posterity'. Ibid.

17 Ibid.

18 See Michael J. Crowe, 'A History of the Extraterrestrial Life Debate', in: *Zygon* 32/2 (1997): 147–62.

19 Locke, 'Great Astronomical Discoveries', in: *The Sun* vom 25. August 1835, 1.

20 Locke, 'Great Astronomical Discoveries [continued from yesterday's Sun]', in: *The Sun* vom 26. August 1835, 1.

21 Ibid.

22 Ibid.

23 Locke, 'Great Astronomical Discoveries. [continued from yesterday's Sun]', in: *The Sun* vom 27. August 1835, 1.

24 Locke, 'Great Astronomical Discoveries. [continued from yesterday's Sun]', in: *The Sun* vom 28. August 1835, 1.

25 Ibid.

26 Ibid.

27 Locke, 'Great Astronomical Discoveries. [continued from yesterday's Sun]', in: *The Sun* vom 29. August 1835, 1.

28   Ibid.

29   Locke, 'Great Astronomical Discoveries. [Concluded.]', in: *The Sun* vom 31.
     August 1835, 1.

30   Ibid.

31   Ibid.

32   Ibid.

33   Ibid.

34   See Paul Maliszewski, 'Paper Moon', in: *Wilson Quarterly* 29/1 (2005):
     26–34, 29.

35   See Goodman, *The Sun and the Moon*, 209 ff. Auch Mario Castagnaro,
     'Lunar Fancies and Earthly Truths. The Moon Hoax of 1835 and the Penny
     Press', in: *Nineteenth-Century Contexts: An Interdisciplinary Journal* 34/3
     (2012): 253–68.

36   Edgar Allan Poe, 'Richard Adams Locke', in: ders., *The Literati of New York
     City: Some Honest Opinions at Random Respecting Their Autorial Merits,
     with Occasional Words of Personality*. (Bd. 6.) o.O. 1846, 159–61, 161.

37   See Goodman, *The Sun and the Moon*, 49–62.

38   Ibid., 81–2.

39   Castagnaro, 'Lunar Fancies and Earthly Truths', 254.

40   See Castagnaro, 'Lunar Fancies and Earthly Truths'.

41   Goodman, *The Sun and the Moon*, 274–5.

42   See ibid., 204–5.

43   James Gordon Bennett, 'The Astronomical Hoax Explained', in: *New York
     Herald* vom 31. August 1835, 1.

44   Richard Adams Locke, 'To the Editor of the Evening Star', in: *New York
     Herald* vom 1. September 1835, 1.

45   Castagnaro, 'Lunar Fancies and Earthly Truths', 256.

46   Asa Greene, *A Glance at New York: The City Government, Theatres, Hotels,
     Churches, Mobs, Monopolies, Learned Professions, Newspapers, Rogues,
     Dandies, Fires and Firemen, Water and Other Liquids &C. &C.* New York,
     1837, 245–6.

47   Poe, *The Literati of New York City*, 161.

48   Translation from German original: 'Was nämlich den allgemeinen Charakter
     der Berichte betrifft, von dem deutschen Uebersetzer an bis zu dem
     angeblichen Beobachter selbst, so können wir nicht anders urtheilen, als daß
     das, was einen Bericht aus der Wahrnehmung bekundet, in ihnen durchaus
     überwiegend sey, gegen das, was einen Bericht aus der Phantasie verräth.'
     O.A., O.T., in: *Literatur- und Intelligenzblatt für Neu-Vorpommern und Rügen.*
     (Beilage zur Sundine.) 1836, 12.

49   See, for example, the notion of a 'seascape' in Brigitte Reinwald and Jan-
     Georg Deutsch (Hrsg.), *Space on the Move: Transformations of the Indian
     Ocean Seascape in the Nineteenth and Twentieth Centuries.* (Arbeitshefte
     Zentrum Moderner Orient, Bd. 20.) Berlin, 2002; Jeremy H. Bentley, Renate

Bridenthal and Kären Wigen (Hrsg.), *Seascapes: Maritime Histories, Littoral Cultures, and Transoceanic Exchanges.* (Perspectives on the Global Past.) Honolulu, 2007.

50 See the range of variations on the Atlantic world in Kevin O'Rourke and Jeffrey Williamson, *Globalization and History: The Evolution of a Nineteenth Century Atlantic Economy.* Cambridge, 1999; Peter Linebaugh and Marcus Rediker, *The Many-Headed Hydra: Sailors, Slaves, Commoners, and the Hidden History of the Revolutionary Atlantic.* Boston, 2000; David Armitage and Michael Braddick (Hrsg.), *The British Atlantic World, 1500–1800.* Basingstoke/New York, 2002; Paul Gilroy, *The Black Atlantic: Modernity and Double-Consciousness.* 3. Aufl. London, 2002; Marcus Rediker, *Villains of All Nations: Atlantic Pirates in the Golden Age.* Boston, 2004.

51 O.A., O.T., in: *Cincinnati Mirror & Western Gazette of Literature and Science* vom 5. April 1834, 199.

52 Goodman, *The Sun and the Moon,* 159–61.

53 Alison D. Morrison-Low, 'Brewster, Sir David (1781–1868)', in: *Oxford Dictionary of National Biography 2004.* Version Januar 2014, in: URL= http://www.oxforddnb.com/view/article/3371 (accessed: 15 June 2016).

54 Locke, 'Celestial Discoveries', 1.

55 Harriet Martineau, *Retrospect of Western Travel.* (Bd. 3.) London, 1838, 22–3.

56 See Michael J. Crowe, *The Extraterrestrial Life Debate 1750–1900: The Idea of a Plurality of Worlds from Kant to Lowell.* Cambridge, 1986; Crowe, 'A History of Extraterrestrial Life Debate'; Roger Hennessey, *Worlds without End.* Gloucestershire, 1997.

57 Franz von Paula Gruithuisen, Wilhelm Olbers and Carl Friedrich Gauss, 'The Moon and Its Inhabitants', in: *Edinburgh New Philosophical Journal* 1 (1826): 389–90.

58 See Goodman, *The Sun and the Moon,* 187–8.

59 See Paula Gruithuisen, Olbers and Gauss, 'The Moon and Its Inhabitants', 390.

60 See Crowe, 'A History of the Extraterrestrial Life Debate', 156.

61 See Goodman, *The Sun and the Moon,* 274–5.

62 See Ibid., 200.

63 Locke, 'Great Astronomical Discoveries', in: *The Sun* vom 29. August 1835, 1.

64 Martineau, *Retrospect of Western Travel,* 23.

65 See Goodman, *The Sun and the Moon,* 183.

66 Matthew Goodman claims to detect another subtle literary cross reference that would give educated readers a hint about the falsity of the report in the *Sun.* He holds the fact that Herschel first discovered red poppies on the moon to be a wink and a nudge from Richard Adams Locke, taking poppies to be a cloaked reference to Thomas De Quincey's *Confessions of an English Opium Eater,* which appeared in 1821 and was very popular. The subsequent colourful safari across the moon is to be read in the light of De Quincey's pipe dreams. However, this interpretation is perhaps a bit strained, especially since the report in the *Sun* explicitly mentioned *papaver rhoeas*, the common red poppy, not *papaver somniferum*, the opium poppy, and the former has no intoxicating properties (see Locke, 'Great Astronomical Discoveries', in: *The Sun* vom 26. August 1835, 1; also see Goodman, *The Sun and the Moon*, 165–6).

67 Frank O'Brien, 'The Story of the Sun: Part 2', in: *Munsey's Magazine*, Juni 1917, 99–115, 108.

68 See Goodman, *The Sun and the Moon*, 210.

69 Ibid.

70 William Griggs, *The Celebrated "Moon Story," Its Origins and Incidents*. New York, 1852, 37–9.

71 David S. Evans, *Herschel at the Cape: Diaries and Correspondence of Sir John Herschel, 1834–1838*. Cape Town, 1969, 282.

72 Sir John Herschel, 'Extracts of a Letter from Sir J. Herschel to M. Arago', in: *Athenaeum* 478, 24. Dezember 1836, 908. A letter buried in Herschel's estate until 2001 also supports his lighthearted attitude towards the story. He composed the missive, which was also addressed to the editor of *Athenaeum*, on 21 August 1836 (exactly one year after the brief initial announcement in the *Sun*) in Feldhausen near Cape Town, but he never sent it. It shows that he was able to preserve his sense of humour: 'Now I should be sorry, for my own sake as well as for that of truth, that the world or even the most credulous part of it, should be brought to believe in my personal acquaintance with the man in the moon – well knowing that I should soon be pestered to death for private anecdotes of himself and his family.' (Steven Ruskin, 'A Newly-Discovered Letter of J.F.W. Herschel Concerning the "Great Moon Hoax"', in: *Journal for the History of Astronomy* 33/1 (2002): 71–4, 73.)

73 See Goodman, *The Sun and the Moon*, 265–9.

3

Space:

Connectivity and isolation

Space in global history

'**G**lobal' is a spatial term. According to one reading, its referent comprises the entire planet, implying that global events are only those of planetary significance. Following this tack has immediate consequences for the study of global history, which would then have to verify and determine that its objects, in as many contexts as possible, do in fact affect the entire world. Global space would, then, constitute the frame of reference that requires maximal saturation. As Sebastian Conrad established, there are indeed branches of global history that subscribe to interpretations like this and hope to achieve their goal through historiographical synthesis.[1] The approach to global history described here, which stresses the importance of global connections, is based on a different, relational understanding of 'global'. Here, the term describes phenomena that are directly connected to each other over vast distances, and for which, to add a further qualification, this bridge distance is a defining feature. These connections, the fundamental units of observation in global history, are what create global spaces.

That space as a category is not stable or objective, one that cannot be made stable or objective, is not news to postmodern theory. On the contrary, it assumes that space is constantly being socially and culturally (re) negotiated.[2] The so-called 'spatial turn', which is often invoked in the social sciences and humanities, also proceeds from such a dynamic concept of space.[3] Space emerges from social action, from the ascription of meaning and position as well as their constant reaffirmation and reproduction. Accordingly, geographical space is but one kind of space among many, a kind that, like all spaces, comprises the sum of relations between its objects. The particularity is that geographical distance is the decisive relation. For our spatial purposes, geographical space has pride of place because of its predominance in human sensory perception. That is, our senses situate the information they provide us predominantly in geographical space, and as a result, it is the decisive category in our spatial imagination. There are, however, alternatives to geographically localizing our sensory inputs, as the increasing use of digital media,[4] which are based on dissimilar spatial principles, would indicate. Even this simple example reveals to what extent our spatial imagination, as informed by our senses, depends on geographical space, even though the actual networks of relations are products of society and culture that are not strictly congruent with geographical space.

To grasp a concept of space of this kind, the British geographer Doreen Massy includes several suggestions of how to conceptualize space in her book *For Space*. First, space is the product of reciprocal relationships in that it does not antecede identities/entities, as Massey calls subjects and objects in space, or their relationships. Rather, identities/entities, their relationships and their spatiality are co-constitutive,[5] implying that they cannot be conceived of in absence of each other. Another necessary implication for Massey is that, to the extent space is the product of reciprocal relationships, it must also draw on diversity.[6] Though Massey generally has space in mind that can accommodate many kinds of relations, it remains analytically helpful to assume the existence of diverse spaces for the purposes of global history. As the historian Karl Schlögel put it, the 'diversification of spaces is in itself perplexing', but it restores to us a 'sense of the complexity that makes up the world'. 'Generally speaking', wrote Schlögel, 'there are as many spaces as there are domains, issues, media and historical actors.'[7] Thoroughly abstracting this approach and combining it with the research interests of global history, it is reasonable to assume that each kind of connection entails its own space.[8] Thus conceptualized, individual spaces automatically become very dynamic, as does space as such. Massey confirms this view in her third proposed conceptualization of space, when she states that space is constantly transforming: 'It is never finished; never closed. Perhaps we could imagine space as a simultaneity of stories-so-far.'[9]

In summary, the most important qualities of the present concept of space are as follows. Space is not a given; it is socially constructed. It emerges out of connections between subjects and objects. There is no single, all-encompassing space; rather there are as many spaces as there are kinds of connection. And as patterns of connections change, so too do spaces. Finally, spaces share subjects and objects, which connect them to each other.

Historical actors are bound into a vast array of diverse spaces simultaneously, as will be demonstrated later in discussing the mutiny on the *Bounty*. This is one reason why a dynamic, multifaceted concept of space, like this one, is such an excellent analytical instrument to trace processes of globalization and their socio-cultural meanings. To the extent that globalization is to be understood as an increase in the density of connections in global networks, it also represents a change in global spaces. A broad consensus has developed in history that globalization is not a homogeneous, unidirectional macro-process but rather an assemblage of micro-processes operating at different speeds, in different directions and at different intensities.[10] Hence, different kinds of global connection develop in different ways, and in doing so they also change the attendant spaces in the most diverse ways.

In spite of catchy metaphors, like 'the shrinking of the world' and 'global village', which suggest a comprehensive spatial change in the wake of globalization, some spaces have changed dramatically in the course of this process, others have changed less and some have hardly changed at all. Whatever differences spaces display in their development, the principal change has come in their relations to each other. Since historical actors are embedded in multiple spaces simultaneously, a new spatial configuration results whenever some spaces change and others do not. Shifts of this kind make the qualitative changes induced by processes of globalization visible and tangible. To draw an analogy from physics, if all spaces surrounding a particular actor moved along the same trajectory, the actor would be unable to detect the change at all. Only when there are differential rates of change across the various spaces does the shift become manifest, imbuing processes of globalization with qualitative meaning for the actors involved.

Telegraphy provides an especially clear example of the diversity of spaces, their dynamics and the resulting shifts, as it played a vital role in the great burst of globalization in the nineteenth century. Telegraphy has been compared with the internet in terms of its significance and mode of operation.[11] Although this comparison does not bear close scrutiny,[12] it does provide a sense of how contemporaries apprehended the technology. Both technologies represent a massive 'flattening of the world' or even for the 'annihilation of space and time', but the telegraph was no more able to flatten the world or compress time and/or space then than the internet can today. Instead, it accelerated only a few select types of communication. The telegraph created new potential connections, which in turn created new spaces that could communicate with other spaces through their actors. The novel and momentous qualities of telegraphy become apparent precisely in these altered spatial configurations, as the following examples will now demonstrate.

The telegraph and the ostensible
annihilation of space

Inventors had started playing with the idea of using electricity to transmit information already in the mid-eighteenth century. An anonymous author described a practicable method of such transmission in *Scots' Magazine* in 1753, signing the piece only with the initials 'C.M.'. The device described therein built on the contemporary state-of-the-art: it was well known that electrostatic generators could generate static electricity, which then could attract very light objects, like paper shavings. C.M. proposed to erect a dedicated circuit for each letter of the alphabet, and each one would correspond to a slip of paper bearing the designated letter. As current flowed out of the generator over a particular circuit, it would attract the slip at the receiving end with the corresponding letter.[13] Given how cumbersome and unreliable this design must have been, it is no surprise that it failed to catch on, but the idea came at a time when knowledge about electricity and its principles was blooming rapidly. Scientists like Luigi Galvani, Alessandro Volta and, somewhat later, Hans Christian Ørsted and Michael Faraday made notable contributions to the process of taming electricity, and others soon began to develop and test new means of transmitting information electrically in the early nineteenth century. Some, like Samuel Thomas von Soemmering, Francis Ronalds, Carl Friedrich Gauss, Wilhelm Eduard Weber, Carl August von Steinheil and Paul Schilling von Canstatt, were indeed quite successful. However, their inventions usually lacked the technological refinement to be of practical use outside the laboratory.

Others quickly began building on the ground thus laid. Functional telegraph prototypes were successfully demonstrated independently of each other in Great Britain and the United States in 1837. The two designs differed considerably, but they both used electromagnets to make the electrical signals visible. Samuel Morse demonstrated his device in a New York classroom, and he continued to develop it together with Alfred Vail. He needed years, though, to convince Congress to finance the first telegraph line between Washington, DC, and Baltimore. In London, Charles Wheatstone and William Fothergill Cooke demonstrated their needle telegraph along a stretch of the London and Birmingham railway. Although their technology was able to help coordinate the trains, convincing the railway companies of the telegraph's practicality and to grant a concession for construction also took quite a while.

Congress finally agreed to finance Morse's line between Washington, DC, and Baltimore in 1842, and the line opened two years later. Almost simultaneously, Cook was finally able to convince the Great Western Railway Company to let him erect a telegraph line between London-Paddington and

Slough at his own expense. Both ventures soon proved successful and profitable. The railway companies gradually came to see how useful telegraphy could be in helping to coordinate the trains and began erecting telegraph lines along the tracks. Soon thereafter, a veritable telegraph mania swept through the United States[14] and Great Britain[15] that continued through the 1840s and 1850s, during which the first national telegraph networks appeared in both countries as well as much of the Continent. The first attempts to connect these national networks with each other came at an early stage. Several telegraph cables connected Great Britain to the Continent, with the first being a cable laid across the English Channel to connect Great Britain and France in 1851. From the mid-1850s there were a number of attempts to lay a transatlantic cable between Ireland and Newfoundland, which would, by extension, connect Great Britain with the United States. With the exception of a short-lived connection in 1858, these attempts failed. Europe and India were connected in 1865, and the first functioning cable across the Atlantic was not finally laid until the following year,[16] which marks the inception of a genuinely global telegraph network that would reach every corner of the world in the ensuing decades.[17]

The reason for this rapid growth of national and, later, global telegraph networks lay in its extraordinary utility for many purposes. Naturally, businesspeople were among the first to develop an enduring taste for the new technology, but the military and the British colonial administration also found it very useful. However, the railway companies provided the greatest impetus, at least in Great Britain, after some initial hesitation. Once Cooke finally managed to wrestle a concession to build his line to Slough from Great Western Railway, the telegraph's benefits quickly became clear, especially in coordinating rail traffic on single-track routes. This new means of communication allowed trains to be coordinated safely and efficiently on such lines.[18]

With the rail's rights-of-way facilitating the construction of telegraph lines, there was a natural symbiosis with railways that primed telegraphy's rapid expansion. It also highlights the innovation's disruptive potential in terms of the dematerialization of information flows. Transmitting information by means of electrical current reached technological maturity with the telegraph. Information could now be encoded in electrical impulses and sent along a wire to be decoded at the receiving end. The telegraph decoupled communication from transportation.[19] Electrical transmission was immune to many of the obstacles that the transportation of material faced over very long distances. The distance the information had to cross affected the duration of the process only negligibly. Once a functioning line was in place, the physical distance between its nodes was virtually irrelevant, with the upshot that communication accelerated greatly. Whereas a letter sent by steamship across the Atlantic would need about ten days to reach its destination, a telegraph message could be sent and answered within a few hours under favourable conditions. Of even greater importance than the compression of absolute transmission times was the relative acceleration that the telegraph made possible. There was now a communication medium faster than rail or – for intercontinental transmission – steamship. The telegraph's relative advantage meant that it could be used to efficiently control and coordinate rail and steamship travel. Telegraphy's outstanding characteristic was its ability to overtake and interact with established modes of transport and communication.

The dematerialization of information flows by telegraphic means not only was of great importance for speeding up communication (not only but most importantly concerning transportation) but also had an effect on the associated means of communication. The telegraph transmitted information as a series of electrical impulses, and given that the data was encoded as current either flowing or being suspended, this has been viewed as an early form of binary coding. However, both the Morse telegraph and the Cooke-and-Wheatstone needle telegraph in fact had and used three possible states. The former's code included a short signal, a long signal and periods of no signal. As for the latter, there was either no signal or the current could flow in one of two directions at a given moment. In each case, these three basic possibilities were combined into codes that allowed for the transmission of complex information. Both the Morse and the needle code were based on the Latin alphabet, but the initial version of the needle telegraph's code could not even accommodate all the letters. Each individual character corresponded to a certain combination of pulses, and only letters, digits and certain punctuation were susceptible to transmission. All other information, such as handwriting, handwritten corrections or the type of paper used, to name a few kinds, were lost in transmission.

Another deficiency was that encoding characters into electrical pulses led to relatively long series of pulses, even when transmitting only short messages. Telegraph cables were expensive to lay and to maintain, and their transmission capacity remained quite low for many years. Consequently, communication by telegraph was an expensive luxury, and the expense rose in step with the length of the message. Telegraphy rewarded brevity and concision. The information to be transmitted was best left unadorned, getting directly to the point without embellishing diction or superfluous remarks. Grammar and punctuation were negotiable. A number of special abbreviations became popular in international business correspondence, and they were recorded in official codebooks to encrypt as well as to shorten messages. For example, in the widely used *ABC Telegraphic Code*, the word 'Aigulet' meant 'Is not likely to affect you in any matter',[20] and 'Bluster' was to be read as 'The boxes were delivered in bad order.'[21] Such techniques allowed complex messages to be transmitted relatively quickly and cheaply by using few words. However, any meaning beyond this kind of standardized content was lost. A popular handbook with tips and guidelines on composing telegraphs put its finger at the heart of the matter:

> Naturally, there is a right way and a wrong way of wording telegrams. The right way is economical, the wrong way, wasteful. If the telegram is packed full of unnecessary words, words which might be omitted without impairing the sense of the message, the sender has been guilty of economic waste.[22]

The demands of syntactical economy led to the development of a particular style of expression in telegrams, which itself was subject to still other socio-cultural norms. Thus, brevity was more highly valued than proper grammar, courtesy or protocol, as demonstrated by a brief exchange of telegrams between the prince of Wales and the king of Portugal upon the opening of the first submarine connection between Europe and India in 1870. Since the submarine cable also landed in Portugal, the prince congratulated the king by official telegram, thanking the Portuguese government for its support. Disregarding established rules of protocol, the king replied: 'Thanks for the good wishes you expressed me in your telegram. Equally I congratulate myself for the completion of the Telegraph. LUIZ.'[23]

Due to the value of brevity and concision in telegraphic communication, whether real or affected, individual snippets and factoids were often transmitted without any kind of qualifying context. Telegrams were for only the most important messages, and everything else was relegated to letters. Still, telegraphy neither displaced other means of communication, nor did it overwrite their spaces. Rather, the new technology insinuated itself into the existing system of media, assuming a certain role in this system and interacting with other media.[24]

Instead of overcoming or annihilating space, as some contemporary observers were given to prophecy,[25] telegraphy created a new, dynamic space of communication that was embedded in a number of similar spaces. The interaction between these mutating spaces yielded telegraphy's real novelty, which made this technology so important to macro-processes like industrialization and globalization. The following section will demonstrate this new quality in the context of concrete examples that show the diversity and interaction of communication media in the lives of historical actors. The goal is to identify situations where the simultaneity of different connection patterns and, along with them, different spaces are especially distinct. The key questions relate to global connection and isolation as well as the role of telegraphy in demarcating these.

Fanning and Cocos: On the variety of spaces of communication

'That sounds as if I were away down at McMurdo Sound with a South Pole expedition doesn't it!!!' – thus apologized a British telegrapher in March 1914 in a letter to his friend and colleague Hollingworth in Montreal for the haste with which he had had to compose the missive. The supply ship that would take his letter was to leave a day earlier than planned, leaving him just an hour to answer his friend's last correspondence. It was almost as bad as the South Pole: the postal service was a scandal, driving him to distraction, continued the telegrapher. This letter, along with two others donated to the Porthcurno Telegraph Museum from private collections,[26] exemplifies the remoteness of the outposts where telegraphers did their duty in the late nineteenth and early twentieth centuries. The letters were authored by a telegrapher who simply signed his alias, 'Napoleon', and was stationed on Fanning Island from 1913 to 1915. The tiny atoll lies about 1,450 kilometres south of Hawaii in the middle of the Pacific and had belonged to the British Empire since 1889.[27] From 1902, the island served as a relay station along the first transpacific telegraph line, which was run by the Pacific Cable board and connected British Columbia to Australia and New Zealand via Fanning, Fiji and Norfolk Island. Together with the Commercial Pacific Cable Company's cable from San Francisco to Manila via Honolulu, the line closed the last major gap in the worldwide telegraph network at the beginning of the twentieth century.[28] Therefore, these two Pacific cables represent the contemporary apotheosis of the world's communicative connectivity, though the personnel stationed along these routes were embedded in a more complex web of connection and isolation. Even in the middle of the Pacific, the telegraphic connections between these remote stations and the rest of the world were tremendous. Hundreds of telegrams arrived through the cable daily before being transcribed in the relay stations. Tasked with receiving and forwarding messages from around the world, the personnel – especially the telegraphers – had their fingers on the pulse of the world in a nearly literal sense. Despite this direct connection with the rest of the world, many of the relay stations were as geographically isolated as could be, as indicated by the quote given earlier. Supply ships would call on stations like Fanning only every few weeks or months. The first difficulty was that the seclusion inhibited private communication with friends and family, which was a postal rather than telegraphic affair. The second was that it complicated the provision of food supplies and adequate medical care. Thus, these telegraph stations exemplify to what degree various global spaces of communication overlapped and to what extent tensions resulted from the interrelations among such spaces.

Tension is a recurrent theme in the letters from Fanning mentioned previously. Three letters from Napoleon to his colleague Hollingworth survive. The first is dated 17 March 1914, the second two months later on 17 May and the third, most sweeping letter, 8 January 1915. The tension between connection and isolation experienced by the Fanning crew is tangible in many passages of the final letter. For example, the author repeatedly laments how cumbersome correspondence by letter was – in the passage quoted earlier as well as in several others. Napoleon opens the second letter by apologizing to Hollingworth for not having thoroughly answered the latter's letter from 21 November 1913. While he admits to procrastinating, he also offers the excuse of having to write long letters to his wife Josephine, which is probably an allusion to his namesake's wife: 'But I've had my work cut out in keeping Josephine satisfied with the promised lengthy Epistle.'[29] He closes the letter with renewed reference to her (among other ubiquitous nods towards French history): 'If Josephine knew I have given you eleven pages she would have you guillotined!!! Am 167 pages up to her and still unfinished, so must away to do so.'[30] These facetious remarks emphasize how intermittent postal correspondence was between the captives on Fanning Island and the rest of the world, especially their families. Long letters would incubate over weeks and months before being loaded in heaps onto the supply ship. Although these texts could be very rich and detailed, especially those addressed to family members, the sporadic postal pick-ups and deliveries made really meaningful, responsive communication very difficult.

Beyond the hardships in communicating with the outside world that resulted from the post's remote location, Napoleon also repeatedly deplores the meagre provisions and mediocre medical care. Delays in the arrival of the supply ships meant tight rations for the station's personnel. One such situation is vividly described in the first letter from March 1914:

Completely out of flour, therefore no bread, but we substituted with those thick square ship's biscuits which they feed the natives on, and for which I have to thank them for leaving me a Souvenir in the shape of a broken tooth! No dentist here, so what you going to do about it!!! For the first fortnight we were on famine rations. We were allowed one potatoe and one onion for dinner!!! But the last week we were completely out of these and existing on the fish we could catch, rice and these biscuits.[31]

And he recounts very similar circumstances two months later in his second letter:

When our provision boat was some weeks overdue and we were reduced to famine rations!!! This time we were worse off than before [...]! A week before the boat arrived we were absolutely out of everything except tinned soup. No tinned meat, vegetables, fruit, milk or butter, and no fat to fry the fish in; so we had the enviable experience of getting boiled fish from Monday to Saturday. [...] When the last famine occurred we had a few fowls left in the run and were able to provide a poultry dinner for Sunday and an occasional egg for breakfast, but this time we had no such luxuries as that![32]

Even if the personnel at the station were not in mortal danger, Napoleon's descriptions do indeed illustrate how tenuously it was tied into the larger supply network. His remarks about the postal service and especially about the shortages indicate that the supply ships, which did not come very often at the best of times, were regularly delayed. Such delays left the personnel to fend largely for themselves while messages from the other side of the world would be forwarded at lightning speed.

The peculiarity of the interaction between connection and isolation is perhaps clearest in Napoleon's third surviving letter to Hollingworth. Dated 8 January 1915, in this letter the writer addresses his friend after a long silence. Accordingly, he opens the message with an apology: 'It is with a blush of shame (and it's a long time since I blushed) that I sit down to write you, because I have neglected you so long that you will by now, almost be wondering if I have got you out of focus as one of my friends.'[33] In addition to the typical excuses for the delay that Napoleon lists, he also mentions how the outbreak of war had changed circumstances at the station in the form of palpable tension and exhausting double shifts. War made the worldwide telegraph network a vital strategic interest, and the personnel on Fanning Island were not immune to its turmoil:

But altho' we are only a mere handful of 14 Britons, we fully recognised each day, more + more, that the Empire depended on us standing up to the pressure of traffic and rendering her all assistance we could by metaphorically sticking to our guns.[34]

The longest section of the letter, however, was devoted to describing how patriotic service demanded more than mere metaphorical contact with arms. 'You must be dying to hear a true version of the German invasion of [Fanning Island],' wrote Napoleon at the beginning of the letter, referring to the arrival of German light cruiser *Nürnberg* at Fanning on 7 September 1914. The SMS *Nürnberg* was part of the Imperial Navy's 'East Asia Squadron', which was founded shortly after the German seizure of Kiautschou (now Jiaozhou) Bay in order to protect the empire's colonial and commercial interests in East Asia with a permanently stationed fleet.[35] Upon the outbreak of the First World

War, the squadron operated principally in the South Pacific, to attack among other things the enemy's communications infrastructure.[36] It was part of these activities what brought *Nürnberg* to Fanning Island on 7 September. Owing to the squadron's frightful reputation, the island's staff had received some warning. Word had come a few days prior that the *Nürnberg* and the *Leipzig* had left Honolulu and must have been in the immediate vicinity.[37] Napoleon was understandably apprehensive when a ship was sighted slowly approaching the island on the morning of 7 September. At first, it was unclear whether the callers were friends or foes:

> Personally I was of opinion that if she were a German man o' war they would commence bombarding us as soon as they reached our anchorage and [...] that within a few minutes we might all be blown to Kingdom Come[.][38]

The station's superintendent was not as circumspect and was fooled by the false French flag that the *Nürnberg* was flying. Without firing a shot, the *Nürnberg* sent a landing party, which the superintendent, believing them to be Frenchmen, welcomed with open arms. Napoleon described in his letter how this grave error came to light:

> The marines floundered out of their whaler + stood on the beach until their officer landed from the stern, + the next thing we knew was that the same officer's revolver was levelled at us with the command in a stentorian, but rather excited voice 'Hands ub, you are my brizoners!' With lightning precision, of course, we all obeyed + we all fully expected to hit the beach in less than a few seconds, especially as the marines had surrounded us and stood with the rifles half way up to the shoulder in readiness to bring their weapons up upon the word of command being given.[39]

For their part, the German marines were only interested in the communication facilities. They promptly took the prisoners captive and began to destroy all the technical devices and facilities that they could find (Figure 4). They had the superintendent lead them to the telegraph room: 'Then the marines got busy with their axes + rifles and soon made an unholy mess of that instrument room.'[40] The German officers then checked that all instruments had been disabled and confiscated all available code books and official documents, before moving on to their final measure:

> Nothing would convince them that our engineroom was not in connection with a wireless plant on the island + they sent aboard for cases of dynamite + on its arrival proceeded to blow up the engineroom + then did the same

with the two shore-ends of our cables. After blowing up the engineroom
the officer was again told by someone that it was only our electric light
plant + he profusely apologized + said 'very sorry Gentlemen, but this
is war; personally we take no delight in destruction, but we must obey
orders'.[41]

Once all the communication systems had been destroyed and all remaining
instruments commandeered (Figure 5), the Germans released their captives
and sailed off on the *Nürnberg*. The British remained on the island alone,
without electricity and badly shaken. Napoleon poignantly describes how
the night watches were doubled after the incident and how someone was
always claiming to see lights in the distance, which invariably proved to be
mere stars or other chimera.[42] Due to their utter isolation resulting from the
telegraph equipment's destruction, the mood among the crew was tense.
Once the Germans had left, there was no longer any connection to Fiji or
British Columbia; both lines were down and out. According to Napoleon, they
also assumed that the *Nürnberg* had laid underwater mines around the cable
landing points, but no one was willing to go out and survey the damage to the
cables until 11 September.[43] Although the damage was severe, there were
at least no mines to be found, so the station's electricians could set to work,
repairing the cable to Fiji and a few instruments. After a few false starts, the
station finally managed to restore communication with the Suva station on Fiji
on the evening of 22 September.[44]

FIGURE 4 *British telegraphists and German soldiers of* Nürnberg *auf Fanning.
Courtesy of the Australian War Memorial P02564.002.*

FIGURE 5 *The destroyed generator room on Fanning. Courtesy of the Australian War Memorial P02564.003.*

They were naturally very relieved. The superintendent was able to telegraph a report about what had transpired to Suva, and the members of the crew were able to send short messages to relatives around the world as to their well-being. Beyond that, however, headquarters ordered silence on the Fiji cable, banning messages both to and from Fanning, aside from a test signal to be transmitted every fifteen minutes to confirm that the cable was still operational. As long as the connection to British Columbia remained cut, the Fanning station had no practical use, and every message transmitted could have fallen into German hands. Still, this further and seemingly unnecessary exacerbation of their isolation was a heavy blow to the crew:

> This nearly broke us up and we were all very much disgusted, but as it was the Admiralty's instructions we afterwards resigned ourselves to the bad luck with the consolation that no doubt it was for our ultimate good in baulking the enemy.[45]

The men on Fanning were not just geographically isolated; they were also communicatively cut off for over three weeks. Napoleon himself claimed credit for ending their desolation:

> It was not until 30th Sept. that Suva's observance of 'Strict Silence' to us was removed by the Governor there + I fancy I was responsible for this, as, when on duty that afternoon I remarked to Suva that the monotony of this exchanging signals every 15 minutes + being forbidden any news of the outside world was <u>worse</u> than prison-life, and I also added that even the Nurnberg people were generous enough to give us their wireless news!!! The fellow on duty must have felt sympathetic for us + spoken to the Supt: who, shortly afterwards interviewed the Governor + we were supplied with a morning + evening bulletin daily, after that.[46]

The three surviving letters that Napoleon sent to his friend in Montreal between March 1914 and January 1915 vividly display the diversity and simultaneity of spaces, especially spaces of communication. Located in the middle of the Pacific, the Fanning islet was a virtual laboratory in which the effects of being simultaneously embedded in very different spaces could be observed. The spatial discrepancy initially appears in Napoleon's many comments on the scant supplies and the poor state of the postal service, which were in stark contrast to his privileged access to the latest news from everywhere. However, its clearest depiction is in the course and aftermath of the *Nürnberg* assault, first in the circumstances prior to the arrival of the German ship. At that time, the personnel on Fanning had access to the latest information about the whereabouts of the two light cruisers, the *Nürnberg* and the *Leipzig*, without any ability to take practical steps in reaction to the looming threat. Second, the moment when the different spaces were realigned after the two undersea cables had been cut dramatically revealed their simultaneity. Fanning was cut off from global telegraphic communication twice in short succession: first by the Germans and second by the silence order from Suva. Their isolation was complete – the geographic and communicative spaces became congruent. The crew's frustration at losing their connectivity shows to what extent the diversity of spaces had affected their lives and how keenly they felt its loss.

There are other, similarly evocative examples of such diversity. In his long third letter, Napoleon told of a message from their counterparts on the Cocos Islands that had arrived shortly after their connection to Suva had been restored: 'The next day the Staff at Cocos sent us one saying: "Congratulations, our turn next, what!" And whether they really anticipated it or not, their turn came true enough on 10th Nov.'[47] The British Eastern Extension, Australia and China Telegraph Company, a subsidiary of John Pender's Eastern and Associated Telegraph Company, had operated a telegraph station on Direction Island, one of the Cocos Islands, since 1901. Three undersea cables converged there: one from the African east coast via Mauritius and Rodrigues, one from Batavia and one from the Australian west coast. The installation of a radio station on Direction Island in 1910 increased its strategic value, which enticed a German cruiser to attack on 9 November 1914 (and not on the following day, as Napoleon wrote).

The SMS *Emden* was detached from the East Asia Squadron once war broke out, and its captain Karl von Müller was to prosecute the war independently with his cruiser in the South Pacific and the Indian Ocean. This mission led them to the Cocos Islands, where von Müller wanted to strike at the British communications infrastructure. The captain sent out a landing party under the command of Captain Lieutenant Hellmuth von Mücke to destroy all telegraphic equipment and cables, just as had been done on Fanning. This time, though, the *Emden* was spotted from the island, and its personnel were

FIGURE 6 *British telegraph operators on the Cocos Islands are following the battle between the* Emden *and the* Sydney. *Sea Power Center Australian Navy.*

able to radio for help. An Australian ship, the HMAS *Sydney* was in the vicinity, received the call and engaged the *Emden* while the landing party was still on the island. The German cruiser was so badly damaged in the fray that Captain von Müller was forced to ground her (Figure 6).[48]

After having destroyed the communication infrastructure (Figure 7), the landing party under von Mücke managed to escape capture and to leave the Cocos Islands on the *Ayesha*, a schooner that had been laying at anchor off the coast. The convoluted situation provided both sides with plenty of material for tall tales of heroism, which the telegraph crew and the landing party continued to embellish in the following years. One story goes that the crew had briefly fallen into German captivity, as on Fanning, but endured it with sangfroid. Once the landing party had absconded on the *Ayesha*, the electricians and telegraphers were able to repair the worst of the damage to the cables and equipment and resume transmission on the undersea cable in no time. This event reinforced the legend of the intrepid British telegrapher like no other. Even at the moment of greatest peril, the telegraphers of Eastern and Associated maintained their British stiff upper lip and acted coolly and efficiently – or so they perceived and represented themselves in subsequent years.[49] The company's in-house magazine The *Zodiac* reported on the incident at length and did what it could to uphold the image of the dauntless telegraphers:

> The men who perform these unostentatious miracles [...]. On desolate little islands, in remote alien cities, they lead the loneliest of lives. For conversation, they must talk across the wires to colleagues, possibly equally lonely, a thousand miles away. They know as soon as kings and mighty ones what is happening in the great world from which they are exiles; but they keep the charge with an honour as strict as their devotion.[50]

Indeed, the central theme in this representation is the very interplay between connection and isolation – and the telegraphers' concomitant immersion in very different spaces simultaneously. Its role is not diminished in Captain Lieutenant von Mücke's reports about the events on the island and his subsequent journey on the *Ayesha*. Following the defeat of the *Emden*, von Mücke and his landing party undertook an extraordinary journey to Sumatra, then up the Arabian Peninsula and finally returning to Germany via Constantinople. He and his men received a heroes' welcome, and he actively tried to maintain that status by writing two books about his adventures in the following years. In his second book, which was published in 1915 and is mostly concerned with his perilous journey back to Germany, he described the peculiar encounter even before the *Sydney* opened fire on the *Emden* of the German landing party with the British telegraphers on Direction Island:

> We quickly found the telegraph building and the wireless station, took possession of both of them, and so prevented any attempt to send signals. Then I got hold of one of the Englishmen who were swarming about us, and ordered him to summon the director of the station, who soon made his appearance, – a very agreeable and portly gentleman.
>
> 'I have orders to destroy the wireless and telegraph station, and I advise you to make no resistance. It will be to your own interest, moreover, to hand over the keys of the several houses at once, as that will relieve me of the necessity of forcing the doors. All firearms in your possession are to be delivered immediately. All Europeans on the island are to assemble in the square in front of the telegraph building.'
>
> The director seemed to accept the situation very calmly. He assured me that he had not the least intention of resisting, and then produced a huge bunch of keys from out his pocket, pointed out the houses in which there was electric apparatus of which we had as yet not taken possession, and finished with the remark: 'And now, please accept my congratulations.'
>
> 'Congratulations! Well, what for?' I asked with some surprise.
>
> 'The Iron Cross has been conferred on you. We learned of it from the Reuter telegram that has just been sent on.'[51]

Although this passage from Mücke's book also touches on the celebrated imperturbability of British telegraphers, the real gem relates to the decoration of the Iron Cross. Hellmuth von Mücke had been decorated with an Iron Cross, 2nd Class[52] in early November 1914, but, as he was stationed on the *Emden*, he himself had yet to hear the news. The remote Cocos Islands were, thanks to their geographic isolation, the last place one would expect him to receive the information – had they not been tightly connected to the worldwide telegraph network. Von Mücke's surprise at hearing the news, which he

FIGURE 7 *The blasted radio system on the Cocos Islands. Sea Power Center Australian Navy.*

naturally used to good narrative effect in his book, reflects the discrepancy between communicative space and geographical space. Hence, this oft-cited anecdote serves as yet another example of the diversity of spaces and their meaning in the context of global history.

Conclusion: Space in global history

The episodes described in this chapter are especially fruitful examples of the simultaneity of various spaces. Fanning Island and the Cocos Islands are effectively laboratories in which the relations and interactions among these spaces are most recognizable as a result of the discrepancy between communicative connection and geographic isolation, which the islands' extraordinary role in the worldwide telegraph network further accentuated. In fact, telegraphy is an apt means to show the diversity of spaces and their meaning for historical actors beyond these remote settings. Telegraphy dematerializes flows of information, and new spaces emerge when transport is decoupled from communication, spaces that operate according to an utterly new communicative logic and differ sharply from existing spaces. That is why examples from the history of telegraphy, like those presented here, are so helpful. This theme recurs in the next chapter, which, in spite of its focus on the relation between time and global history, cannot avoid returning to questions of space. Many examples in the next chapter treat the malleable relation between various spaces of transportation and communication, like con men in colonial India sending fraudulent information by telegraph and thus locating themselves in a different space than the steamship that was simultaneously en route, or gamblers trying to get their hands on telegrams from the sites of the horseraces. Telegraphy creates a new space in both examples that looks and operates differently than those previously known.

Although telegraphy brings the significance of spatial concepts for global history into particularly sharp relief, the principle can be generalized well beyond this one communication medium. In the course of globalizing processes, new spaces emerge and existing spaces evolve and mutate. Every space is always dependent on the other spaces in which historical actors are also situated. Indeed, the relations between the various spaces are of paramount interest because the changes they induce provide the people acting in them with new constellations, opportunities and constraints. These interstices render consequences of globalization and its processes for people's lives and experiences tangible. As the aforementioned example of the Great Moon Hoax makes clear, transatlantic connections and processes of exchange introduced a new epistemic space that Locke instrumentalized in his story. However, the residual uncertainty preserved by non-connections fragmented the space enough to prevent immediate verification of his claims. The analytical quality of thinking in terms of spaces will become even more obvious in the coming discussion of transit as a concept. Various spaces and their interrelations are also manifest in the case of the flight, pursuit and eventual capture of Dr Hawley Harvey Crippen, especially the peculiar space of transit and a nearly global mediatized space, both of which play important roles.

A complex, flexible concept of space allows us to produce more nuanced analyses of the processes of globalization and to distance ourselves from simplifications and clumsy metaphors that obscure more than they reveal, like that of a 'shrinking' world. It allows us to recognize what in the history of globalization is genuinely new and how it affected the experience of historical actors.

Notes

1 Conrad, *What Is Global History?*, 6–11.

2 See, for example, Henri Lefebvre, *La Production de l'Espace*. Paris, 1974; Edward W. Soja, *Postmodern Geographies: The Reassertion of Space in Critical Social Theory*. London/New York, 1989; Ders., *Thirdspace: Journeys to Los Angeles and Other Real and Imagined Places*. 18. Aufl. Malden, 2014; David Harvey, *Social Justice and the City*. London, 1979; David Harvey, *The Condition of Postmodernity: An Enquiry into the Origins of Cultural Change*. Cambridge, 1990; Doreen B. Massey, *Space, Place and Gender*. Cambridge, 1994; Dies., *For Space*. Los Angeles u.a., 2005.

3 See, for example, Matthias Middell and Katja Naumann, 'Global History and the Spatial Turn: From the Impact of Area Studies to the Study of Critical

Junctures of Globalization', in: *Journal of Global History* 5/1 (2010): 149–70; Jörg Döring and Tristan Thielmann (Hrsg.), *Spatial Turn. Das Raumparadigma in den Kultur- und Sozialwissenschaften*. 2. Aufl. Bielefeld, 2009.

4   Martina Löw, *Raumsoziologie*. Frankfurt am Main, 2001, 93–4.

5   Massey, *For Space*, 10.

6   Ibid., 10–11.

7   Translation from German original: 'Man könnte summarisch sagen: es gibt so viele Räume, wie es Gegenstandsbereiche, Themen, Medien, geschichtliche Akteure gibt.' Karl Schlögel, *Im Raume lesen wir die Zeit. Über Zivilisationsgeschichte und Geopolitik*. 3. Aufl. Frankfurt am Main, 2009, 69.

8   Roland Wenzlhuemer, *Connecting the Nineteenth-Century World: The Telegraph and Globalization*. Cambridge u.a., 2013, 42.

9   Massey, *For Space*, 9.

10 See Isabella Löhr and Roland Wenzlhuemer, 'Introduction: The Nation State and Beyond. Governing Globalization Processes in the Nineteenth and Early Twentieth Centuries', in: dies. (Hrsg.), *The Nation Sate and Beyond: Governing Globalization Processes in the Nineteenth and Early Twentieth Centuries*. Berlin/Heidelberg, 2013, 1–26.

11 Tom Standage, *The Victorian Internet: The Remarkable Story of the Telegraph and the Nineteenth Century's On-Line Pioneers*. 2. Aufl. New York u.a., 2014.

12 Wenzlhuemer, *Connecting*, 7–9.

13 Anton A. Huurdeman, *The Worldwide History of Telecommunications*. Hoboken, 2003, 48.

14 For a comprehensive history of telegraphy in the United States, see Richard John, *Network Nation: Inventing American Telecommunications*. Cambridge u.a., 2010; David Hochfelder, *The Telegraph in America, 1832–1920*. Baltimore, 2012.

15 The most useful survey of the history of telegraphy in Great Britain remains Jeffrey Kieve's, although others have examined particular phases of its development more closely. Jeffrey Kieve, *The Electric Telegraph: A Social and Economic History*. New Abbot, 1973; Steven Roberts, 'Distant Writing. A History of the Telegraph Companies in Britain between 1836 and 1868. Version 2012', in: URL = http://distantwriting.co.uk/index.htm (accessed 23 June 2016); Roger N. Barton, 'Brief Lives: Three British Telegraph Companies 1850-56', in: *The International Journal for the History of Engineering and Technology* 80/2 (2012): 183–98; Charles Perry, 'The Rise and Fall of Government Telegraphy in Britain', in: *Business and Economic History* 26/2 (1997): 416–25.

16 See Simone Müller-Pohl, 'The Transatlantic Telegraphs and the Class of 1866: Transnational Networks in Telegraphic Space, 1858–1884/89', in: *Historical Social Research* 35/1 (2010): 237–59; Christian Holtorf, *Der erste Draht zur Neuen Welt. Die Verlegung des transatlantischen Telegrafenkabels*. Göttingen, 2013.

17 See Dwayne R. Winseck and Robert M. Pike, *Communication and Empire: Media, Markets and Globalization, 1860–1930*. Durham/London, 2007; Peter

J. Hugill, *Global Communications since 1844:* Geopolitics and Technology. Baltimore/London, 1999; Wenzlhuemer, *Connecting*.

18   Kieve, *Electric Telegraph*, 33.

19   Credit for this observation goes to James Carey. James Carey, 'Technology and Ideology: The Case of the Telegraph', in: ders., *Communication as a Culture: Essays on Media and Society*. Boston, 1989, 201–30.

20   William Clauson-Thue, *The ABC Universal Commercial Electric Telegraphic Code*. 4. Aufl. London, 1881, 13.

21   Ibid., 41.

22   Nelson E. Ross, *How to Write Telegrams Properly*. (Little Blue Book Bd. 459.) Girard, 1928.

23   Commemoration of the Opening of Direct Submarine Telegraph with India, John Pender, Souvenir of the Inaugural Fête held at the House of Mr John Pender vom 23. Juni 1870, 21–2.

     Waiving courtesy in telegraphic communication did, however, have its limits, as an excerpt from Nelson Ross's manual aptly shows: 'A man high in American business life has been quoted as remarking that elimination of the word "please" from all telegrams would save the American public millions of dollars annually. Despite this apparent endorsement of such procedure, however, it is unlikely that the public will lightly relinquish the use of this really valuable word. "Please" is to the language of social and business intercourse what art and music are to everyday, humdrum existence. Fortunes might be saved by discounting the manufacture of musical instruments and by closing the art galleries, but no one thinks of suggesting such a procedure. By all means let us retain the word "please" in our telegraphic correspondence.' Ross, *How to Write Telegrams Properly*.

24   This is a common phenomenon in the history of technology that David Edgerton discusses at length. David Edgerton, *The Shock of the Old: Technology and Global History since 1900*. Oxford u.a., 2007.

25   On the origin of these metaphors, see Iwan R. Morus, 'The Nervous System of Britain: Space, Time and the Electric Telegraph in the Victorin Age', in: *The British Journal for the History of Science* 33/4 (2000): 455–75; Jeremy Stein, 'Annihilating Space and Time: The Modernization of Fire-Fighting in Late Nineteenth-Century Cornwall, Ontario', in: *Urban History Review* 24/2 (1996): 3–11; Ders., 'Reflections on Time, Time-Space Compression and Technology in the Nineteenth Century', in: John May and Nigel Thrift (Hrsg.), *Timespace. Geographies of Temporality*. (Critical Geographies, Bd. 13.) London u.a., 2001, 106–19.

26   Porthcurno Telegraph Museum, DOC//5/107/1-3, Letters from the Fanning Islands.

27   The atoll bears the names Tabuaeran or Tahanea in Gilbertese and belongs to the island state of Kiribati.

28   Wenzlhuemer, *Connecting*, 118.

29 Porthcurno Telegraph Museum, DOC//5/107/2, Letters from the Fanning Islands, 1.

30 Ibid., 11.

31 Porthcurno Telegraph Museum, DOC//5/107/1, Letters from the Fanning Islands, 1–2.

32 Porthcurno Telegraph Museum, DOC//5/107/2, Letters from the Fanning Islands, 5–6.

33 Ibid., DOC//5/107/3, Letters from the Fanning Islands, 1.

34 Ibid., 3.

35 On the history of the East Asia Squadron, see Heiko Herold, *Reichsgewalt bedeutet Seegewalt. Die Kreuzergeschwader der Kaiserlichen Marine als Instrument der deutschen Kolonial- und Weltpolitik 1885 bis 1901.* (Beiträge zur Militärgeschichte, Bd. 74, zugleich Phil. Diss. Heinrich-Heine-Universität Düsseldorf 2010.) München, 2013; Heinrich Walle, *Deutschlands Flottenpräsenz in Ostasien 1897–1914. Das Streben um einen ‚Platz an der Sonne' vor dem Hintergrund wirtschaftlicher, machtpolitischer und kirchlicher Interessen.* (Jahrbuch für europäische Überseegeschichte 9.) Wiesbaden, 2009, 127–58; Andreas Leipold, *Die deutsche Seekriegsführung im Pazifik in den Jahren 1914 und 1915.* Wiesbaden, 2012.

36 Herold, *Reichsgewalt*, 384.

37 Porthcurno Telegraph Museum, DOC//5/107/3, Letters from the Fanning Islands, 4.

38 Ibid., 7.

39 Ibid., 10.

40 Ibid., 13.

41 Ibid., 13–14.

42 Ibid., 18.

43 The courageous soul was not, however, a member of the station's crew. Rather, he was a man by the name of Hugh Greig, the grandson of a British captain who had settled on Fanning in the 1850s and married an indigenous woman. Occasional Papers of Bernice P. Bishop Museum 15/17, Kenneth P. Emory, *Additional Notes on the Archaeology of Fanning Island.* 1939, 179–89, 179, footnote 1.

44 Porthcurno Telegraph Museum, DOC//5/107/3, Letters from the Fanning Islands, 18–20.

45 Ibid., 21.

46 Ibid., 26–7.

47 Ibid., 30.

48 Wenzlhuemer, *Connecting*, 88–9.

49 On this legend and the role of the incident in the Cocos Islands, see also Wendy Gagen, 'Not Another Hero: The Eastern and Associated Telegraph Companies: Creation of the Heroic Company', in: Stephen McVeigh and

Nicola Cooper (Hrsg.), *Men After War*. London, 2013, 92–110 und Dies., 'The Manly Telegrapher: The Fashioning of a Gendered Company Culture in the Eastern and Associated Telegraph Companies', in: Michaela Hampf and Simone Müller-Pohl (Hrsg.), *Global Communication Electric: Business, News and Politics in the World of Telegraphy*. New York, 2013, 170–96.

50 O.A., 'The Emden's Fatal Visit to Cocos', in: *The Zodiac* 8 (1915): 62–8.

51 Hellmuth von Mücke, *The 'Ayesha': Being the Adventures of the Landing Squad of the 'Emden'*. Boston, 1917, 3–6.

52 Upon his return to Germany, he was awarded the Iron Cross, 1st Class, for his exploits in 1915.

4

Time:

Telegraphy and temporal structures

Time in global history

Remarking that history as a process and as a discipline deals with time is, as Reinhart Koselleck has put it, trivial.[1] Historians gaze on the past from the present. They retrace human development, try to find connections and causes, and they order events chronologically to relate them to each other in some meaningful fashion. No scholarly endeavour in history can make do without time, chronology or temporality. Moreover, the actors and phenomena that historians investigate are themselves temporal; they exist in time, they have beginnings and endings. As Jörn Rüsen observed, time is one of the 'primal experiences of humanity': 'Nothing is more natural than the becoming and passing of all things, but, at the same time, nothing demands more of us, challenges our culture to cope with it, not to simply let it be what it is.'[2] It may be the case that both relations, that of time to the discipline of history as well as to history as a process, are trivial in the sense of being obvious. In terms of finding a sophisticated approach to dealing with the idea of time, though, these relations are anything but self-evident.

Recent years have seen a plethora of studies treating various aspects of these relations.[3] However, the widely divergent semantic fields associated with time are difficult to keep separate and distinct. Time as a term often refers to temporality as a fundamental condition of human existence. That is, time is hardly susceptible to human perception since all that we know exists in time – even if this law is claimed not to obtain in a given exception (like God), our apprehension of such things remains coloured by temporal terms (like 'eternity'). Like space, time becomes tangible through the temporal relations between people, things and events. Dealing with time historiographically often raises metaphysical questions about time as a fundamental category of human existence, even though history's curiosity is really to dissect and analyse temporal relations precisely as well as their manifestations and the socio-cultural means of dealing with them.[4] In fact, the imperceptibility of time as such begs some of history's most productive questions, namely, how people have dealt with time in light of this dilemma, where time has made itself visible and tangible to them, how they apprehend and represent it, and, of course, how people thus create time. To the extent that history deals with time, it cannot approach the object directly; rather, it must focus on time's socio-cultural interpretation, the perception, representation and measurement of time.

For historians, time is foremost a socio-cultural phenomenon of scholarly interest. Time emerges from the temporal relations between actors, objects, ideas and events. Just as space was shown to be a dynamic socio-cultural phenomenon produced by social relations, the same applies to time. As the temporal relations between entities change, so too does time change in terms of its perception, representation and measurement. The clichéd lament that time passes ever faster is a helpful illustration. From the perspective of absolute time as a fundamental condition of existence, this statement is nonsense (which does not preclude its utterance). Since we exist in time along with all our points of reference, it is impossible to perceive any acceleration of time as such. In terms of socio-culturally created time, however, this old chestnut can express a relatable observation and describe the acceleration of one or more pursuits in life. The German sociologist Hartmut Rosa wrestled with just such accelerating phenomena in a path-breaking book, defining acceleration broadly as a quantitative increase over time.[5] This is to say that certain experiences, actions or events occur in ever-shorter intervals, which can change how time is perceived and used. Thus is socio-cultural time shaped and warped.

While Koselleck might hold this little illustration to be trivial, it does clearly indicate that temporal change amounts to nothing more than changing temporal relations. According to Rosa, then, acceleration equates to an increase in temporal density. Since global history inquires into the meaning of global networks and their densities as well as how transregional connections become historically efficient, time's immediate relevance to this kind of research should be obvious. Global connections of these kinds leave traces in temporal relations, which in turn makes them perceptible for individual actors and even for entire societies. Consequently, changes in the perception, usage, representation and measurement of time are immanently relevant to global history.[6]

Processes of globalization and modernization can be understood spatially, as was sketched in the previous chapter and intimated in the 'shrinking world' metaphor. They can also be understood in terms of temporal shifts, as the idea of 'the great acceleration'[7] in the nineteenth century expresses. Thus, the temporal and the spatial approaches, which are not really separable, as this chapter will show, both relate to changes in patterns of relations. However, only friction with other patterns make such changes visible, as was clear in the previous chapter. Indeed, shifts in the relations between different times and temporal layers are also the source of changes in socio-cultural time.[8] Hartmut Rosa expands on this point by discussing the relatively common phenomenon of time running short. Shortages arise, according to Rosa, when one growth rate increases more rapidly than corresponding rates of acceleration;[9] that is, when growth in the quantity of tasks outpaces the ability to complete them. Hence, shortages of time indicate a change in temporal structures that results from the ratio between two levels – growth and acceleration – shifting.

Focusing on the relations between different temporal levels also helps to grasp global network processes analytically and not to lose sight of their qualitative effects. As in the previous chapter on space, telegraphy provides apt examples to illustrate these effects. Using this new technology brought new spaces into existence, transformed existing ones and deeply affected relations between spaces in the process, but it also caused similar disruptions with respect to time and temporal structures. I will now explain this in more detail in addition to the inseparable connection between space and time.

Telegraphy and time

A compendium of anecdotes entitled the *London Anecdotes for all Readers* was published in London in 1848, and it became quite popular. The publisher used the first few pages to explain the criteria according to which the stories and anecdotes had been selected: 'The subject will be chosen with especial regard to living interest, and the prime movers of these eventful times.'[10] The *London Anecdotes* were classified along three themes, and the first section contained over 100 crisp and often witty *Anecdotes of the Electric Telegraph* spread over 120 pages. Appearing barely ten years after the first successful public demonstrations of electric telegraphs in Great Britain and the United States, this collection displays with its extent and contents just how quickly and deeply the telegraph had come to pervade the societies, cultures and everyday routines in these countries, especially those of their wealthier inhabitants.

Many of the scenes sketched in the compendium centre around the inconceivable speed with which the telegraph could transmit information over vast distances. Such rapid communication allowed for one of the most staggering innovations of the age: the ability to reroute trains by telegraph.[11] One stranded traveller ordered a horse and carriage by telegram, drastically reducing his delay.[12] Telegraphy enabled authorities to nab a deserter before he got the least wind of their pursuit.[13] Perhaps the most impressive instance of the telegraph's unimaginable speed, however, was presented to the readers in the following anecdote entitled *Less Than No Time*:

By the electric telegraph on the Great Western Railway has been accomplished the apparent paradox of sending a message in 1845, and receiving it in 1844! Thus, a few seconds after the clock had struck twelve, on the night of the 31st of December, the superintendent at Paddington signalled his brother officer at Slough, that he wished him a happy new year. An answer was instantly returned, suggesting that the wish was premature, as the year had not yet arrived at Slough! The fact is – the difference of longitude makes the point of midnight at Slough a little *after* that at Paddington; so that a given instant, which was after midnight at one station, was before midnight at the other. Or, the wonder may be more readily understood, when it is recollected that the motion of electricity is far more rapid than the diurnal motion of the earth.[14]

The anecdote continues to detail later on how people in other locations, too, had been able to 'get the better of time':

We hear of similar feats in the United States. Thus, a letter from Indiana says, 'That wonderful invention, the magnetic telegraph, passes through our country from the eastern cities, communicating intelligence almost instantaneously.' News has been transmitted from Philadelphia to Cincinnati, a distance of 750 miles, on one unbroken chain of wires. Of course, as Cincinnati is 13 degrees west of Philadelphia, or 40 minutes of time later, the news is that much ahead of the time.[15]

The story about the premature New Year's greetings, which played masterfully off the experiences and expectations of contemporary readers, proved especially contagious in Great Britain and its colonies. Supposedly originating in an unspecified report in the *Reading Mercury*, in 1845 the text was also printed in the *New Zealander*[16] and the *Journal of the Franklin Institute*[17] in Philadelphia. Three years later in 1848, when the *London Anecdotes* were published, the tale reappeared with some deviation under the headline *Facts Connected with the Electric Telegraph* in the *New Zealand Spectator and*

Cook's Strait Guardian.[18] It is noteworthy both that the story spread so rapidly throughout the Anglophone world and that it appeared in the *Journal of the Franklin Institute*, which was otherwise concerned with rigorous scientific studies. These two facts testify to the broad public and scientific interest telegraphy generated in the mid-1840s by seemingly overcoming time.

Dematerialising the information to be transmitted freed it from material transportation. The communicative distance between two points was no longer strictly a function of their geographic-spatial proximity. Although this is typically read as the transcendence of space (see previous chapter), the relationship between space and telegraphy is far more complex. As described more thoroughly in the previous chapter, telegraphic communication created new spaces, restructured existing ones and transformed the relations between different spaces, and time underwent much the same process. Contemporary talk of overcoming time reflects the fascination with a virtually instantaneous connection. The telegraph, however, was both a timeless and time-dependent medium; it was both immediate and mediated.[19] Of course, contemporaries were aware that telegraphy was not an instantaneous medium, at least not in practical application, and that it could not outstrip time, as the anecdotes given earlier might suggest. Nonetheless, the reconfiguration of temporal relations may have given many the impression that time's divisive effects had been overcome, implying the potential 'annihilation' of time itself. In the middle of the nineteenth century, the telegraph represented a temporal revolution. It was fast and immediate enough to, for instance, connect people in different time zones (*avant la lettre*) in a way that allowed them to actually notice the chronometric difference, and that in practical application, and that in the mid-nineteenth century.

With his typically critical stance, Karl Marx also doubted the easy metaphor of time's annihilation. In 1857/58 he wrote in the *Grundrisse*:

> While capital must, first, strive to tear down every local barrier to traffic and exchange, conquering the entire planet as its market, it also strives to annihilate space through time; that is, to minimize the time expended in the motion from one place to another.[20]

This passage is often read merely as a lightly modified version of the postulate that time and space are undergoing annihilation,[21] but that is decidedly not the case. Capital, according to Marx, annihilates or, more accurately, replaces space with time by means of new transportation and communication technologies. With the annihilation of space, time becomes decisive. This interpretation implies that two points in space are no longer separated by the geographic distance between them, but rather only by the time that it takes to communicate between them. Telegraphy and other technologies do indeed compress this interval, but it remains important because the total duration of the dialogue yet depends on the length of the delay between sending and receiving between two places. Advantages gained through informational arbitrage are still very perishable. Interlocutors expect quicker replies. Markets know no interval in their constant reactions to the steady flow of information from all quarters. In a letter to his brother Carl written in 1870, Werner von Siemens explains just how central the acceleration of communication processes was for his contemporaries:

> A man can speak as quickly as he pleases, but London and Teheran still ruin much through slow work. That proves with great certainty that we will soon speak directly to Calcutta, as only three transfers are regularly required to Teheran. Make a proper fuss now and beat the British Indian's 10 to 12 hours with our one minute to Teheran and 28 minutes to Calcutta. One would have a hard time overpaying for that.[22]

The letter refers to the magnificently successful test of the so-called 'Siemens line' (*Siemenslinie*) that had just recently connected London to Calcutta telegraphically. A telegram managed to arrive in Calcutta in only 28 minutes, and the answer from India arrived in London a mere one hour and five minutes after the message had been sent. This record had been previously unimaginable, and Siemens wanted to leverage this clear competitive advantage with 'a proper fuss' ('*tüchtig Geschrei*'). Rather than overcoming or annihilating it, telegraphy instead condensed time, concentrating its importance. More and more was happening in ever-shorter intervals, which is why it became increasingly important for all interlocutors in an exchange to know exactly when each message had been sent and received.[23]

Clearly, the telegraph did not herald the annihilation of time in any form. Rather, telegraphic communication led to a transformation of temporal structures, a change in the importance of temporal units and similar developments that – as was the case with space – represented a shift in the relations among various temporal levels. Illustrating these claims with concrete historical examples is the task of the next section. First, I will sketch the relation between space and time in somewhat more detail to show how telegraphy permanently altered it. Second, I will show how the spread of telegraphy was able to dramatically remould the perceptions, sensations and usages of time among communicating subjects.

Telegraphy, space and time

The terms 'time' and 'space' are often deployed together in critiques of the present. The annihilation of space and time that many sensed in the nineteenth century effectively addressed the same notion as the more current terms 'time-space compression'[24] and 'time-space distanciation'.[25] Such conceptions bind time and space inseparably to one another in an interdependent relationship. By contrast, Marx postulated that time annihilates space – an act of destruction that, however metaphorical, nonetheless implies two clearly separable concepts. From the perspective of global history, which is primarily concerned with the preconditions and effects of transregional networks through history, both conceptions of the relation between space and time are too mechanical and, as a result, of only limited use. Although it is also in need of modification, Reinhart Koselleck provided a better starting point in his volume entitled *Zeitschichten* ('Layers of Time'), which opens as follows:

> One cannot avoid metaphors in speaking about time because time only becomes perceptible in motion through certain units of space. The distance covered from here to there, development, progressing and even progress itself contain illustrative images from which insights can be derived. […] Every historical space constitutes itself thanks to time, which allows its traversal and makes it susceptible to political and economic rule.[26]

The sociologist Manuel Castells follows a similar tack with his 'space of flows' concept, which he contrasts with conventional space, the 'space of places'.[27] Castells writes:

> Space and time are related, in nature as in society. In social theory, space can be defined as the material support of time-sharing social practices. […] The space of flows refers to the technological and organizational possibility of practicing simultaneity (or chosen time in time-sharing) without contiguity.[28]

For both Koselleck and Castells, then, spaces are principally functions of time. Koselleck describes them as being constituted 'thanks to time', while for Castells they specifically represent practices of sharing time. Although both conceptions leave room for space and time to be separated analytically, they remain connected to each other in a certain sense. The generalizability of this relationship is debatable, especially the implication that time conversely cannot be a function of space.[29] For the purposes of global history with its focus on connections, however, this approach is analytically useful if supplemented by the postulate that not every space is necessarily a function of time but can also represent other kinds of connection.[30] To summarize the relation of space and time from the perspective of global history, whenever new and altered temporal structures result from transregional networks in a certain area, their spaces change as well, which in turn change their own relationships to still other spaces, as described in the previous chapter. Networking processes reveal their qualities precisely in these interstitial points of contact.

I will illustrate this with concrete examples from the history of telegraphy in which such altered space-time configurations become tangible. In a nutshell, the telegraph decoupled communication from transport, pivotally affecting issues of coordination and control. Then, and to a lesser degree now, information tended to move in combination with people, animals and things, making communication and transport virtually inseparable. Through the spread of telegraphy, though, these two processes became decoupled. Rapid telegraphic communication allowed for transport to be controlled effectively along with the mobility of people and things, including the information travelling with them. Here lies the fissure in which telegraphy with its stronger, faster connection was able to generate a new kind of connection, and this new connection fed back into the connected societies, reshaping the horizons of thought and action available to historical actors.

In order to make the transformation as clear as possible, the following examples derive from a clearly defined historical context. They all relate to how telegraphy created new opportunities for illegal activity by modifying the relation between space and time. All cases related here stem from a period relatively early in the social history of the telegraph. They are all instances where the telegraph, though already well known, opened up new opportunities and uses in the respective socio-cultural contexts. Thus, the cases provide a glimpse into a phase when a technology, along with its transformative potential, had to adapt to existing socio-cultural relations. Of course, this also entailed plenty of friction with several bumps and scrapes along the way. The layers did not fit together perfectly at first, leaving temporary cracks of which the actors in these examples made cunning use, and tracing their actions and intentions illuminates these crannies. This can thus help us to develop a feel for what is genuinely novel about a certain technology, in this case telegraphy. In the concrete cases discussed here, our gaze keeps returning to the relation between transport and communication, which is always changing and redefining itself. It becomes apparent that the functional shift induced by the opportunities telegraphy opened up also changed contemporary perceptions of space and time.[31]

The first example is a spectacular case of fraud that occurred in the mid-nineteenth century in British India in which the electric telegraph was used to manipulate market prices, and it offers valuable insights about the value of telegraphy in the British colonies. The first experiments with telegraphy in India began just a few years after the first lines had entered operation in Europe, and the initial steps towards a telegraph network on the subcontinent began in the early 1850s. However, the expansion of the British-Indian network suffered from two obstacles: the sheer size of the colony and structural differences compared to the European exemplars. While the European networks included many lateral connections and alternate routes, the growing Indian network was foremost conceived to cover vast distances. It was very loosely woven in the 1850s and 1860s with very few alternate routes or backup lines, which is one reason why the telegraph was rapidly disabled as an asset of British power during the Indian Rebellion of 1857, remaining practically irrelevant to the conflict.[32] Once they had quelled the revolt, the British authorities drew lessons from it and began to expand the network incrementally over the following decades. But in 1861, when the swindle took place, the planned expansion was not very far along. As a result, the con men had the advantage of a relatively slow and inefficient network that was virtually without alternate routes. Reporting on the phenomenon, *Lloyd's Weekly Newspaper* quoted a report on 31 March 1861 that had originally appeared in the *Bombay Gazette* in late February:

> For some time past frauds on an extensive scale have been practiced on the electric telegraph wires. A few speculators in opium have caused messages to be most grossly falsified whilst passing through the wires between Galle and Bombay.[33]

More specifically, the report was referring to opium prices in China, the biggest importer of Indian opium. Larger Indian cities usually received pricing information via *The China Mail*, which arrived via steamships that typically stopped over in the port city of Galle in southern Ceylon. The most important pricing information was then relayed to Bombay by telegraph in order to expedite its dissemination, which was possible because Ceylon had been connected to the Indian network since 1857/58.[34] However, the steamers would simultaneously continue their journey to India carrying the mail, but at a much more leisurely pace. The delay between the arrival of the telegram and the arrival of the steamship opened a window of opportunity that the con artists used for their fraudulent arbitrage.

In the early 1860s, the British-Indian telegraph network not only was loosely knit but also suffered from a serious shortage of qualified personnel.[35] As a result, its hiring practices were initially not very selective, which is likely why George Pecktall and William Allen, two men of dubious character, came to work in the Indian Telegraph Department only to be fired shortly thereafter. An Indian merchant from the region of Marwar saw an opportunity and hired them both for his own purposes. After managing by hook or by crook to obtain a telegraph terminal and a battery, Pecktall and Allen sought a suitably secluded spot to tap the telegraph line and to interpose their equipment. This set-up allowed the two telegraphers to hijack messages in transit and to forward them along with their employer's desired modifications. As mentioned earlier, they usually manipulated information relating to opium prices, which was virtually a licence to print illicit money: 'Enormous sums of money were alleged to be made by the parties in secret.'[36] The dealers in Bombay were none the wiser until the steamers arrived in Bombay with the accurate information. Pecktall and Allen were quickly apprehended and ratted out their employer, who was sentenced to two years of hard labour.[37]

This short con was not designed to last. The speculator had only little time to commit his fraud in the window between the receipt of the telegram and the arrival of the steamer. Indeed, the decoupling of communication and transport, which allowed information to travel at different speeds, is what made the fraud possible in the first place. That window, while offering many opportunities for fraudulent arbitrage, stayed open only as long as verification was impossible. The tampering at the root of the scam was only possible due to the decontextualization of the messages' contents, which itself was a side effect of telegraphy's dematerialization of communication, as I described in the previous chapter in relation to space. While information encoded in electrical signals could travel very quickly, the transmission rates typically remained fairly low, and unit prices for telegrams were commensurately high. These economic constraints led to the so-called 'telegram style', which attended little to courtesies or grammar, focusing instead on communicating only the most essential information to keep telegrams short, fast and cheap. Consequently, telegrams contained hardly any context or background relative to letters and as their recipients did not expect such information. At the same time, the lack of context also made telegrams easy to forge, provided one had access to the necessary equipment. Finally, one had only to alter individual characters. There was no need to emulate another's penmanship, to forge an author's signature or to reconstruct a suitable context in order to prevent detection. A few marginal tweaks sufficed to falsify the contents of a message imperceptibly. Of course, this kind of fraud also benefitted from the social status of telegraphy as a technology. Even though hardly anyone in British India had much practical experience with the telegraph in the 1860s, it carried certain connotations. Any message worthy of a relatively expensive telegram had to be urgent and important and would be accorded a certain respect and pertinence. Virtually no one doubted the accuracy of the Chinese opium prices. The con artists profited from the cultural value ascribed to the technology.

But the telegraph's early history includes more than just transmitting stock quotes and pricing information. The particularities of telegraphic communication and its capacity to transform the relation of space and time also played a notable role in an entirely different branch of economic activity: gambling, specifically horse races. The British are inveterate fans of horse racing. Not only were the races able to attract hordes of spectators to the tracks, monitoring their results was also a popular pastime, especially since they would decide how enormous sums would change hands. In the mid-nineteenth century, the race results from the famous tracks of Ascot, Epsom, Newmarket and Doncaster reached major cities by rail. Distant off-track bookmakers would typically accept bets until the respective train had arrived, so anyone who managed to obtain the requisite information before the arrival of the train would obviously have had a great financial advantage. Not surprisingly, the telegraph was a godsend for cheats. As a result, telegraphers and rail operators were prohibited from transmitting race results over their wires in the early days of telegraphy (until in later years race results were officially disseminated by telegraph). Where there are rules, though, one can also expect attempts to circumvent them, and the collection of aforementioned anecdotes reported on a few:

> It was not to be supposed that the advantages of the exclusive obtainment of intelligence on such topics by its possessor would for a moment be overlooked by the turfites; and accordingly, we have to relate a few instances of the manœuvres of the sporting fraternity, which redound much to their ingenuity, but very slightly to their credit. [...] The consequence was, that the 'knowing ones' resorted to a variety of *ruses*, one of which, in sporting phraseology, would probably be called – NO GO![38]

That the compilation related such stories at length under the heading *The Telegraph and the Turf* testifies to the pervasiveness of such fraud attempts already in the 1840s, when telegraphy in Britain was still in its infancy. The practised response of the switch operator in the first detailed description of an attempt at cheating corroborate that these were not seldom occurrences. One episode tells of a Londoner who had bet on the horses in an important race in Doncaster and sought the aid of a switch operator of the East Counties Railway the same day in Shoreditch:

> 'Hangit! I'm heartily glad your're here, for I'm in a most awful fix. A friend I left at Doncaster, first thing this morning, not being able to let me have it when I left him, has promised to transmit by the next train a very valuable parcel, to be placed in one of the first-class carriages. Will you be kind enough to inquire for me the number of the carriage it is placed in, so that on the arrival of the train I may have no difficulty, as every moment is of consequence, in at once finding it there.' So far so good; but the clerk was too cunning for his customer, and explained to him that the object was rather too transparent for him to be gulled; and our disappointed turfite was compelled to retire, 'grinning horrible a ghastly smile' at the miscarriage of his manoevre. The fact was, as is known to all sportsmen, the horses when placed are *numbered*: of course, the number to be returned by the

correspondent in concert at Doncaster, to the inquiry of the telegraph, would have been the number of the 'winning horse', the consignment of the parcel being the means of a cunningly devised end. Added to this, the turfite was informed, to his unutterable anguish, that the carriages on the Eastern Counties, by which route the intelligence could then only come [...], were *not numbered*, though the carriages on other lines were.[39]

Thus, this clumsy attempt to use the telegraph to obtain information prematurely would have failed due to the lack of numbers on the carriages even if the operator had not immediately seen through the ruse. Some con artists were more adept, as the next example shows:

A clerk on another occasion met with a redoubtable defeat. It was Derby day. An enterprising individual entered the office at Shoreditch in great agitation, saying he had left his luggage and a shawl behind him, and wished them to be sent on instanter, that he might take the north train at night. The request was one of an everyday description, and there seemed such truthfulness about it, that the telegraph clerk was taken off his guard, and he sent on the required message, which was thus answered by an accomplice at the other end: 'Your luggage and tartan will be safe by the next train.' This was enough – the *ruse* had succeeded, our worthy had won, and he, doubtless, made the best use of his information, by betting bravely and clearing largely, upon the strength of information some hours in advance of all London besides. Of course, had the winning horse been any other colour, it would have been your '*pink*' shawl, or your '*yellow*' shawl, is all right. The information thus gained by a ruse for a shilling was, probably, productive of many pounds.[40]

Here, the identity of the winning horse could be communicated by associating it with a particular colour or pattern, and the ordinariness of the request duped the operator. It is reasonable to assume that the operators were willing accomplices in countless other cases and received a portion of the profits. However, the ability to use the technology to obtain an inter-temporal advantage lasted only a few years before the telegraph became the official medium to transmit results. Important tracks even had their own telegraph offices installed on the premises.[41] As long as an interval remained, cheats used the same style of con as displayed in the previous example, which was based on generating opportunities for action by obtaining information sooner. When the ruses worked, the cheats gained a few hours in which to bet inconspicuously on the horses that had already won, as only they knew. Again, this window of opportunity was a product of how the telegraph decoupled communication and transport.

In summary, it is clear that decoupling, and the acceleration of certain flows of information that accompanied it, changed temporally dependent spaces. Together with other spaces, like communication by steamship or rail, new chronologies emerged that were foreign and obscure to many contemporaries. The con artists in these examples made use of this disorientation. Telegraphic communication, as an example of a transregional network, contributed significantly to the shift of prevailing space-time relations. In essence, the underlying logic is very similar to the claims about space in the previous chapter. Some temporal structures change (e.g. processes of acceleration), while others do not. They each have their own spaces, and their relations change, which is exactly where the qualitative change from transregional networks manifests itself.

Telegraphy and the sense of time

Changing temporal structures can also make themselves felt beyond spatial notions. They can often do without space as a manifestation. In many cases they affect historical actors' temporal perception and how they use time directly (while never being completely free of space as subtext, as is the case with the examples in the following section). The use of telegraphic communication – and sometimes just the possibility of it – directly affected socio-cultural, quotidian and work routines of those connected by telegraph as well as their personal senses of time. The following examples have been selected to show how the technical and practical innovations that followed in the wake of telegraphy began to matter.

After successfully completing his education at the Royal Engineering College in Cooper's Hill, Surry, Eustace Alban Kenyon was appointed assistant superintendent of the British-Indian telegraph administration on 26 September 1860 and stationed in Calcutta. Kenyon held various posts in the administration in the subsequent years, supervising the construction and upgrade of many telegraph lines throughout the colony. Until at least 1898, he corresponded regularly with his family in England, and his letters contained thorough descriptions of his life and work in British India. The letters are accessible in the archive of the Centre of South Asian Studies in Cambridge University. His writing often deals with telegraphy, and it is obvious to what extent Kenyon's privileged position in the worldwide telegraph network changed his personal sense of space and time. For instance, he wrote to his sister Tizie on 9 March 1891. Earlier he had received orders to report to Ellore in order to supervise the construction of a telegraph line there. Work on the commissioned section of the line had just been completed, when he wrote his letter:

I have just finished all work up to a little north of this, as far as the route is sanctioned and I am now just waiting for a boat – which ought to have been here long ago to take me off to Coconada from where I go on by sea on Friday to Vizagapatam; always supposing that I don't meanwhile get a telegram saying that the remainder of the line is sanctioned & that I am to go on with that. I shall be very annoyed if I do get any such telegram, as I have now broken up my working party and sent the men off to their homes, over 100 miles away.[42]

The boat that was to bring Kenyon to Coconada on the east coast of India arrived even before he had finished his letter. Neither this letter nor any that followed indicate whether he indeed received a telegram en route ordering him back to Ellore, but his trepidation about the possibility of one coming betrays a rapidly changing sense of time. Travelling along a telegraph line for the duration of the journey on the boat meant that he could be contacted at almost any time. Compared to the constant and total accessibility provided by mobile internet, social media and cellular networks nowadays, his misgivings might seem quaint. From a contemporary perspective, however, this marks the advent of utterly new temporal structures and rhythms. Had there not been a telegraph line nearby, Kenyon might well have continued on in peace to Coconada, Vizagapatam and, eventually, all the way to Calcutta before receiving new orders. He would have been able to plan the coming days and weeks, or he would have at least had a rough idea of what they would contain. The presence of a telegraphic connection, though, meant that new orders could arrive at any minute. Kenyon was, in effect, on call, and he does not sound very pleased about it.

His changing sense of time is also apparent elsewhere in the letter. Although the text mentions it nowhere explicitly, Kenyon most likely learnt of the boat's imminent arrival by telegram. Were the information to have arrived through a different medium, it would hardly have been possible to state precisely when the boat was to arrive; instead, he would have simply mentioned a wider interval or general term, like 'soon' or 'any day now', as a leisurely flow of information would have allowed little more. It was only because he had received a relatively precise appointment that he could be disappointed by the boat's delay in the first place. Thus, the telegraph also created a pattern of tight temporal sequences and associated expectations that reality could not fulfil. While the source does not state so explicitly, one would assume that Kenyon's impatience was just as much a product of the precision of information as was the boat's delay.

Although Eustace Alban Kenyon seems mostly to have been annoyed by the constant accessibility that telegraphy provided, some of his contemporaries celebrated the newly achieved connection to the world. A caricature that David

Hochfelder included as an illustration in an article about of how 'common people' originally became involved in finance provides an apt example.[43] Charles Dana Gibson drew it in 1903 (Figure 8),[44] and it shows a businessman in the garden of his vacation house who is obviously 'unwilling to forgo his stock quotations even while on vacation'.[45] Dressed in a suit in the spacious garden of the country house, in his right hand he holds a newspaper and the ticker tape that the telegraph terminal beside him is spewing out. The lawn is littered with old newspapers and stock quote telegrams, and his secretary is sitting at a desk typing on a typewriter. Two messenger boys doze next to her in the shade of a tree in whose trunk a telephone has been installed, which is currently in use by another man. The telling caption of the cartoon goes: *Mr. A. Merger Hogg is taking a few days' much-needed rest at his country home.*

The protagonist of this cartoon, who was clearly meant to portray a new breed of businessman, had a sense of time similar to Kenyon's as he waited for his boat in Ellore, but with the poles reversed. While Kenyon adamantly resisted changing the rhythm of his life to suit the telegraph's clock, A. Merger Hogg was in his element. Not only is he constantly accessible, he is actively communicating (as illustrated through the secretary, the messenger boys

FIGURE 8 *Charles Dana Gibson, 'Mr. A. Merger Hogg Is Taking a Much-Needed Rest at His Country Home', in: Life 41, 4 June 1903, 518–519. Courtesy of the Library of Congress, Prints and Photographs Division.*

and the telephone). The new rhythm has permeated his life, and through the telegraph wire he taps this rhythm to his interlocutors.

A letter to the editor printed in *The Times of London* echoes this sense of time.[46] The letter's anonymous author took the staff of the British telegraph administration to task and facetiously described his odyssey through London by night. He starts with a thorough description of how he wanted to send a telegram from London to Calcutta and how the dismal cooperation among the various telegraph companies and administrations nearly doomed his enterprise. His vividly described escapades[47] cast an interesting light not only on the fissures between local and global communications structures but also on the customers' transformed sense of time. Although the anonymous author emphasizes with much flowery prose how difficult it was to send a telegram to Calcutta in all haste on an evening in the City of London, he never questions whether doing so is necessary in the first place. After an introductory paragraph, he starts the tale with a fairly blasé sentence: 'I had occasion to telegraph to Calcutta between 9 and 10 in the evening.' This shows to what extent many users were already taking the telegraphic connection to India and the ability to access it at any time for granted, and this just a few years after it had begun operation. Of course, the time difference between London and Calcutta was one reason for the author's zeal. A new day – indeed a new *work*day – was breaking in eastern British India, and having the telegram from London waiting on the recipient's desk in the morning would surely have been advantageous. This desire presupposed access to a globally effective medium at all (local) hours.

The time difference between England and British India could also cause confusion, though, when the apparent spatial and temporal proximity conjured by the telegraph led users to forget, or at least ignore, the sizeable difference between the respective local time zones. Out of the plethora of telegrams exchanged on the opening day of the submarine line between England and India on 23 June 1870, two examples stand out. John Pender, chairman of the British-Indian Submarine Telegraph Company,[48] hosted a party for the occasion in his glamorous residence in Arlington Street in London. A telegraph line had been installed directly into his house for the soiree in order for the dignitaries in attendance to send celebratory greetings and congratulations. One of the well-wishers was none other than Sir Henry Bartle Frere, former governor of Bombay, who sent a cheery telegram to his successor William Vesey Fitzgerald and received confirmation of receipt after only four minutes and fifty seconds. However, the confirmation came only from the superintendent of the British-Indian Submarine Telegraph Company in Bombay, who forwarded the message to the governor's residence. The governor's reply did not arrive for a full 36 minutes, as Vasey Fitzgerald was still in bed, as was to be expected given that it was yet daybreak locally.[49] Lady Mayo, wife of the governor general and viceroy of India, had a similar experience when she tried to send greetings to her husband in Shimla. Though receipt of the telegram in Shimla, high in the Himalayas, was confirmed after only fifteen minutes, there was no word from Lord Mayo himself for an hour and a half. Of course, 'the explanation of delay in the reply from India received on the following day is, that Lord Mayo had arranged to be in his office at 5 a.m., and her Ladyship's message arriving at 4.7 a.m., found his Lordship still in bed'.[50]

Conclusion: Time in global history

As a perennially beloved topic in history, time has been approached from many directions in recent decades. Despite the persistent attention, the relationship between time and history continues to suffer from imprecision due to the overlap of very different semantic and analytical facets of the term. Historiographically speaking, the socio-cultural aspects of time are the most interesting. How do people perceive time? What meaning(s) do they ascribe to it? How do they measure it? And, lastly, what do these answers imply for how people and societies create their own time? As with space, the relations between various times and temporal structures play a key role. Time is especially palpable when these relations shift, as the common observation about the acceleration of life would suggest, itself being the result of various temporal flows shifting relative to each other. This also explains why global history – understood here as a history of connections – is particularly concerned with investigating temporal structures and how they change. Global history asks how global and transregional connections affect the relations among various temporal structures and how they can shift in light of global networks. Telegraphy, for example, shows how the decoupling of transport and communication became so pivotal. Just as this example illustrated the diversity of spaces and the significance of the relations between them, telegraphy also illuminates temporal regimes and their development. The scams described earlier show how a new medium (i.e. a new kind of connection) permanently changes the relationship between time and space. Other case studies show how telegraphic connections changed perceptions of time and its usage patterns. The exemplary cases of tension between connection and isolation in the previous chapter similarly relate to time in that their spaces are often functions of time and represent these spatially. Let us recall Hellmuth von Mücke, who learnt of his Iron Cross by telegraph nearly as quickly on a remote island as he would have at home in Europe.

Taken together, these case studies, among many other possible ones from the history of telegraphy, show how dramatically transregional connections can affect temporal structures as well as how people apprehend and comprehend them. However, telegraphic connections are just an evocative example of a wider phenomenon that also obtains in other contexts. A later chapter on structures in global history treats the conglomeration of various parts of a global transport network, which sought to achieve better temporal coordination among its component parts and modes of transportation. The Crippen case in the chapter on transit also deals with different, but parallel, temporalities whose interrelations produced a particular tension when the slowness and monotony of an oceanic passaged collided with the haste and insatiability of global news media.

By examining temporal changes, global history can better perceive where and how global connections manifest themselves and become significant for historical actors. At the same time, how people deal with such momentous changes in their everyday lives is also of great interest to global history because it shows how local actors coped with the concrete consequences of globalization and how they tried to make good use of them.

Notes

1 Reinhart Koselleck, *Vergangene Zukunft. Zur Semantik geschichtlicher Zeiten.* (Suhrkamp Taschenbuch Wissenschaft, Bd. 757.) 8. Aufl. Frankfurt am Main, 2013, Klappentext.

2 Translation from German original: 'Nichts ist natürlicher als das Werden und Vergehen aller Dinge, und zugleich fordert nichts mehr den Menschen dazu heraus, sich kulturell deutend damit auseinanderzusetzen, es nicht einfach als das zu lassen, was es ist.' Jörn Rüsen, 'Einleitung. Zeit deuten – kulturwissenschaftliche Annäherungen an ein unerschöpfliches Thema', in: ders. (Hrsg.), *Zeit deuten. Perspektiven, Epochen, Paradigmen.* Bielefeld, 2003, 11–22, 11.

3 To name just a few examples, Aleida Assmann, *Ist die Zeit aus den Fugen? Aufstieg und Fall des Zeitregimes der Moderne.* München, 2013; Stephen Kern, *The Culture of Time and Space, 1880–1918.* With a new Preface. 2. Aufl. Cambridge/London, 2003; Achim Landwehr, *Geburt der Gegenwart. Eine Geschichte der Zeit im 17. Jahrhundert.* (S. Fischer Geschichte.) Frankfurt am Main, 2014; Chris Lorenz and Berber Bevernage (Hrsg.), *Breaking up Time: Negotiating the Borders between Present, Past and Future.* (Schriftenreihe Der FRIAS School of History, Bd. 7.) (Schriftenreihe Hartmut Rosa, *Beschleunigung. Die Veränderung der Zeitstrukturen in der Moderne.* (Suhrkamp Taschenbuch Wissenschaft, Bd. 1760.) 9. Aufl. Frankfurt am Main, 2012.

4 For a good review of scholarly treatments of socio-cultural time, see Nancy D. Munn, 'The Cultural Anthropology of Time: A Critical Essay', in: *Annual Review of Anthropology* 21 (1992): 93–123; Peter Burke, 'Reflections on the

Cultural History of Time', in: *Viator. Medieval and Renaissance Studies* 35 (2004): 617–26.

5 Rosa, *Beschleunigung*, 115.

6 See Hunt, 'Globalisation and Time'.

7 Bayly, *The Birth of the Modern World, 1780–1914*, 451–87.

8 Reinhart Koselleck, *Zeitschichten. Studien zur Historik.* (Suhrkamp Taschenbuch Wissenschaft, Bd. 1656.) Frankfurt am Main, 2003.

9 Rosa, *Beschleunigung*, 118–119.

10 New Anecdote Library (Hrsg.), *The London Anecdotes for All Readers. Part 1: Anecdotes of the Electric Telegraph.* London, 1848.

11 Ibid., 68.

12 Ibid., 100.

13 Ibid., 46–7.

14 Ibid., 55–6.

15 Ibid., 56.

16 O.A., 'We Have Heard of Things Being Done', in: *New Zealander* vom 1. November 1845, 4.

17 Thomas P. Jones (Hrsg.), *Journal of the Franklin Institute of the State of Pennsylvania and American Repertory of Mechanical and Physical Science, Civil Engineering, the Arts and Manufactures and of American and Other Patented Inventions.* Philadelphia, 1845, 203.

18 O.A., 'Facts Connected with the Telegraph', in: *New Zealand Spectator and Cook's Strait Guardian* vom 26. Juli 1848, 4.

19 See Florian Sprenger, 'Between the Ends of a Wire: Electricity, Instantaneity and the Globe of Telegraphy', in: Michaela Hampf and Simone Müller-Pohl (Hrsg.), *Global Communication Electric: Actors of a Globalizing World.* Frankfurt am Main, 2013, 355–81, 356.

20 Translation from German original: 'Während das Capital also einerseits dahin streben muß, jede örtliche Schranke des Verkehrs, i.e. des Austauschs niederzureißen, die ganze Erde als seinen Markt zu erobern, strebt es andrerseits danach den Raum zu vernichten durch die Zeit; d.h. die Zeit, die die Bewegung von einem Ort zum andren kostet, auf ein Minimum zu reduciren.' Karl Marx, *Ökonomische Manuskripte 1857/58* (Grundrisse der Kritik der politischen Ökonomie). (Marx-Engels-Gesamtausgabe [MEGA], Abt. 2/Bd. 1.) 2. Aufl. Berlin, 2006, 438.

21 Z.B. auch von Jeremy Stein, 'Reflections on Time', 106–19, 108.

22 Translation from German original: 'Man hätte beliebig schnell sprechen können und London und Teheran verderben viel durch langsames Arbeiten. Das beweist, dass wir künftig sehr sicher nach Kalkutta direkt werden sprechen können, da der Regel nach nur drei Translationen bis Teheran nötig sind. Macht jetzt nur tüchtig Geschrei und schlagt die 10 bis 12 Stunden der British Indian mit unserer einen Minute bis Teheran und 28 Minuten bis Kalkutta. Da wird sie schwer über renomieren können.' Werner von Siemens, *Brief an Carl von Siemens* vom 12. April 1870, zitiert nach: Hans Pieper and

Kilian Kuenzi, in: Museum für Kommunikation (Hrsg.), *In 28 Minuten von London nach Kalkutta. Aufsätze zur Telegrafiegeschichte aus der Sammlung Dr. Hans Pieper im Museum für Kommunikation, Bern.* (Schriftenreihe des Museums für Kommunikation, Bern.) Zürich, 2000, 209.

23 Consider, for example, the practice of striking telegraphers in British India who, in the course of the massive telegraph strike of 1908, sought to impose their demands by forwarding telegrams without dates or times, which allowed them to render the communication useless without formally neglecting their duty. Deep Kanta Lahiri Choudhury, 'Treasons of the Clerks. Sedition and Representation in the Telegraph General Strike of 1908', in: Crispin Bates (Hrsg.), *Beyond Representation: Colonial and Postcolonial Constructions of Indian Identity.* Oxford, 2006, 300–21, 312; Dies., 'India's First Virtual Community and the Telegraph General Strike of 1908', in: Aad Blok and Greg Downey (Hrsg.), *Uncovering Labour in Information Revolutions, 1750–2000.* (IRSH. Supplements, Bd. 11.) Cambridge/New York/Melbourne, 2003, 45–71, 66–7.

24 David Harvey, 'Between Space and Time: Reflections on the Geographical Imagination', in: *Annals of the Association of American Geographers* 80/3 (1990): 418–34; Stein, 'Reflections on Time', 106.

25 Anthony Giddens, *A Contemporary Critique of Historical Materialism. Bd. 1: Power, Property and the State.* London, 1981; Anthony Giddens, *The Constitution of Society: Outline of the Theory of Structuration.* Cambridge, 1984.

26 Koselleck, *Zeitschichten*, 9.

27 Manuel Castells, 'Informationalism, Networks, and the Network Society: A Theoretical Blueprint', in: ders. (Hrsg.) *The Network Society: A Cross-Cultural Perspective.* Cheltenham, Northampton, 2004, 3–45, 36–8.

28 Castells, 'Informationalism', 36.

29 See, for example, Doreen Massey, 'Politics and Space-Time', in: *New Left Review* 196 (1992): 65–84, 80.

30 One of many possible examples and of particular importance for global history and the history of globalization is cost spaces. See, for example, Roland Wenzlhuemer, 'Globalization, Communication and the Concept of Space in Global History', in: ders. (Hrsg.), *Global Communication. Telecommunication and Global Flows of Information in the Late 19th and Early 20th Century.* (HSR 35/1. Special Issue: Global Communication.) Köln, 2010, 19–47, 27–9; Hunt, 'Globalisation and Time', 201–2.

31 I have explained this phenomenon in more detail elsewhere: Roland Wenzlhuemer, 'Verbrechen, Verbrechensbekämpfung und Telegrafie. Kriminalhistorische Perspektiven auf die Entkoppelung von Transport und Kommunikation im langen 19. Jahrhundert', in: *HZ* 301/2 (2015): 347–74.

32 Nonetheless, a legend later arose, which was very popular among the more progress-minded colonial rulers, to the effect that the telegraph had saved India for the British. See O.A., 'How the Electric Telegraph Saved India', in: *Daily News* vom 29. September 1897, 6.

33 O.A., 'The Telegraph Frauds in India', in: *Lloyd's Weekly London Newspaper* vom 31. März 1861, 2.

34 Paul Fletcher, 'The Uses and Limitations of Telegrams in Official Correspondence between Ceylon's Governor General and the Secretary of State for the Colonies, circa 1870–1900', in: Wenzlhuemer (Hrsg.), *Global Communication*, 90–107, 90–1.

35 British Library. Oriental Collections IOR/V/24/4284, Administration Report of the Indian Telegraph Department for 1862–1863, 1863, 4.

36 O.A., 'Telegraph Frauds', 2.

37 British Library. Oriental Collections IOR/V/24/4284, 9.

38 New Anecdote Library, Anecdotes of the Telegraph, 29–30 (emphasis in original).

39 Ibid., 30–1 (emphasis in original).

40 Ibid., 31–2 (emphasis in original).

41 House of Commons. Parliamentary Papers C. 304. Telegraphs. Report by Mr Scudamore on the Re-Organization of the Telegraph System of the United Kingdom. Presented to the House of Commons by Command of Her Majesty. London, 1871, 34.

42 Eustace Alban Kenyon, 'Letter to Tizie, Cambridge 1891', in: *Cambridge South Asian Archive*, Centre of South Asian Studies, University of Cambridge.

43 David Hochfelder, '"Where the Common People Could Speculate": The Ticker, Bucket Shops, and the Origins of Popular Participation in Financial Markets, 1880–1920', in: *JAH* 93/2 (2006): 335–58, 337.

44 Library of Congress. Prints & Photographs Division, Reproduktion (LC-USZ62-61482) von Charles Dana Gibson, 'Mr. A. Merger Hogg is Taking a Much Needed Rest at His Country Home, Zeichnung', in: *Life 41* vom 4. Juni 1903, 518–19.

45 Hochfelder, 'Common People', 337.

46 O.A., 'The Post Office and the Telegraphs', *Times of London* vom 7. Dezember 1870, 6.

47 I have described and analysed the twists and turns in more detail elsewhere. Roland Wenzlhuemer, '"I had occasion to telegraph to Calcutta". Die Telegrafie und ihre Rolle in der Globalisierung im 19. Jahrhundert', in: *Themenportal Europäische Geschichte*. Version von 2011, in: URL= http://www.europa.clio-online.de/2011/Article=513 (accessed: 23 June 2016).

48 British-Indian Submarine Telegraph Company was but one of the companies invested in the submarine cable between England and India. Pender founded four separate firms for this purpose between 1868 and 1870: the Falmouth, Gibraltar, and Malta Telegraph Company; the Anglo-Mediterranean Telegraph Company; the Marseilles, Algiers, and Malta Telegraph Company; and the British-Indian Submarine Telegraph Company. The Eastern Telegraph Company was the product of the merger of these four companies in 1872, and it dominated the market for many decades thereafter. Daniel R. Headrick, *The Invisible Weapon: Telecommunications and International*

Politics, 1851–1945. New York/Oxford, 1991, 35–6; Winseck and Pike, *Communication and Empire*, 37–8.

49 Cable and Wireless Archive. British-Indian Submarine Telegraph Co Ltd DOC/ BISTC/6/2. Souvenir of the Inaugural Fête to Celebrate the Opening of Direct Submarine Telegraphic Communication to India, 2. Juni 1870, 18.

50 Ibid., 19.

5

Actors:

Mutiny on the *Bounty*

Actors in global history

The concept of historical actorhood has become an indelible part of historical scholarship. Most recent historiographical works invoke historical actors sooner or later along with the promise to give them pride of place. The nearly rote invocations of actors in history do not, however, always reflect a common historiographical paradigm or particular analytical perspective. More often than not, the term 'historical actor' is simply used as shorthand for the people present in some historical context or other. That is, the term refers merely to the human furniture of a certain scenario to be investigated – the dramatis personae, so to speak. Beyond this loose usage, the word 'actor' has little analytical purchase in most studies, which does not do justice to a valuable scholarly term. Basically, the notion of actor is grounded in human activity, which in its sum shapes history. Actors – historical actors for the purposes of historical research – perceive their surroundings and circumstances in a particular way because they constrain and enable certain actions. Actors' deeds are meant to realize certain intentions, which may have little to do with their actual consequences. Taking history to be the sum of human actions privileges a focus on actors, their agency, historical opportunities, responsibility and the interaction between humans and their world, as these would be particularly revealing.

Building on the social theories of, for example, Pierre Bourdieu[1] and Anthony Giddens,[2] historical anthropology[3] was one of the first genuinely historical approaches to engage with human activity seriously and precisely. For historical anthropology, which emerged in English- and French-language scholarship in the last quarter of the twentieth century and has since gained a foothold in German historical circles, the human subject and subjectivity are the keystones of historical writing.[4] This approach also produced the preferred research objects that seem to attract the most passionate discussion: the body, clothing, disease and labour, for example.[5] Topics like these emerge naturally, but not inevitably or exclusively, from the actor centricity of historical anthropology. Indeed, the focus on humans as actors can bear fruit in relation to other questions, especially on how to grasp the historical significance of interactions between agents and structures. Historical anthropology is generally concerned with plumbing the constraints and opportunities open to the actors involved, which are a product of the various structures in which the actors are embedded. By contrast, structures, which will be covered in more detail in the following chapter, are more or less congealed patterns of human activity. This leads to the basic claim that, in analytical terms, actors rarely face a single, compelling course of action.[6] To focus on people as historical actors endowed with agency is to survey and grasp their alternatives and opportunities. Doing so illuminates not only the actors' perspectives on the circumstances of their activity, which is synonymous with their world views, but also the opportunities and constraints they face within these circumstances.

An actor-based approach behoves history as a whole because it concentrates on the feelings, thoughts and actions of the people involved, making history a humanities discipline. That is, it is a mode of scholarly inquiry into conditions of humans' existence in the world. Adopting such a perspective commits history to remaining 'grounded' in human experience. Further, it allows historians to be socially active, to make judgements based on their historical perspective and to take a principled stand. Strictly speaking, only historical work informed by anthropology and that takes people and their sensibilities seriously can really do so. Moreover, reflecting on historical actors also raises deeper philosophical questions about the relation between human subjects and history as such, and investigating historical actors' freedom of action inevitably leads to considering concepts like contingency, determinism and free will. While these actor-centric aspects penetrate right to the quick of historical writing, concentrating on humans as actors coping with the structures that guide and constrain them helps to unveil the cloaked machinery behind human history. In the process, history gains tools with which it can ponder questions about how human activity acquires the property of historicity and how this activity creates the very world that provides the setting for such activity.

Thanks to these analytical qualities, the actor-based perspective has become a vital component of global history. With its interest in global connections and processes of exchange, global history seeks to understand the emergence of such connections, how they obtain in local contexts and how they produce certain effects in combination with other factors. Therefore, global history is basically concerned with the historical efficiency of global and inter-regional connections, which themselves arise from the opportunities human actors actually face and realize. Focusing on humans as acting subjects, on people who create, use change or disrupt connections, goes a long way towards unpacking the concept of 'global connections'. It reveals the diverse components that comprise such connections. Historical actors are the loci where these individual strands converge and realize their potential. They are the fulcrums on which constellations of global connections turn, and they are where the multiplicity of existing connections intersect. Alternatively, building on the ideas in the chapter on space in global history, one could also say that a wide range of spaces converge within actors. Historical actors belong simultaneously to several spaces; they are at once embedded in many different kinds. Hence, they are also translators between spaces and among various kinds of connections, and the shifting relations among multiple spaces that result from processes of globalization become substantial for the actors involved.

For the purposes of researching global history, focusing on connecting and connected human subjects is doubly relevant. Actors lend substance to the connections, make them effective and grant them agency. At the same time, the meaning of global connections and shifts in spatial relations become manifest in precisely these actors. How these connections emerge, how they operate and how they affect the thoughts and actions of historical actors remains invisible without an actor-centric perspective. Actor centricity allows global history to directly examine the hubs of a networked world as well as its horizons and opportunities.[7] Rather than demanding explanations, global entanglements become explanatory factors, and global connections can be locally grounded. I will illustrate this utility using a historical example whose fame extends well beyond archives and academic discourse.

Huzza for Otaheite

On 23 December 1787, the *Bounty* sailed from Portsmouth Harbour under the command of William Bligh and in service of the British Admiralty. The destination of the voyage was the island of Otaheite, which is now known as Tahiti. About sixteen months later, not far from the island in the middle of the South Sea, a mutiny occurred,[8] the infamy and popular fascination of which is reflected in a number of extravagantly casted films and countless literary treatments.[9] With a number of the crew following him, Fletcher Christian, master's mate on the *Bounty*, mounted a revolt against Bligh and took control of the ship. Bligh related in many later documents, but always in similar terms, how the mutineers overcame him in his sleep. The following passage from a letter he wrote to his wife Elizabeth serves as an example:

> On the 28th. April at day light in the morning Christian having the morning watch, He with several others came into my Cabbin while I was a Sleep, and seizing me, holding naked Bayonets at my Breast, tied my Hands behind my back, and threatened instant distruction if I uttered a word. I however call'd loudly for assistance, but the conspiracy was so well laid that the Officers Cabbin Doors were guarded by Centinels, so that Nelson, Peckover, Samuels or the Master could not come to me. I was now dragged on Deck in my Shirt & closely guarded – I demanded of Christian the cause of such a violent act, & severely degraded him for his Villainy but he could only answer – 'not a word Sir or you are Dead'. I dared him to the act & endeavored to rally some one to a sense of their duty but to no effect.[10]

Along with eighteen loyal crewmen, Bligh was transferred to the dinghy and left behind in the South Sea with few provisions and little equipment. With an unparalleled stroke of navigational mastery, Bligh managed against all odds to pilot the overburdened boat to Coupang on the island of Timor, reaching the Dutch trading post there after several weeks and 3,600 nautical miles (c. 6,700 kilometres). There he wrote back to his wife in England on 19 August 1789 to the effect that he was in a part of the world he had never expected to see, but that it had saved his life. He assured Elizabeth that he was in the best of health before describing in the following lines the perils he had overcome. Then, even before sketching out the details described earlier, he wrote the most essential sentence in the entire letter, which tersely and bluntly expresses the state of its author's spirits: 'Know then my own Dear Betsy, I have lost the Bounty.'[11]

Apart from his wife, Bligh also wrote to his patrons Duncan Campbell and Joseph Banks from Coupang. It is fair to assume that these letters were not intended to inform their recipients about Bligh's location and well-being for, as Bligh himself remarks in several places, he was likely to arrive in England around the same time as his correspondence. A more reasonable suspicion is that the commander of the *Bounty* instead sought to record his narrative of events as early as possible in writing in order to secure the supremacy of his own version of the unfortunate events. In addition to the letters, he also began to compose a detailed report about the voyage and mutiny of the *Bounty* while still on his passage from Batavia to England.[12] In these letters and reports, Bligh could hardly conceal his outrage and fury about the mutineers. As he saw it, Fletcher Christian and his followers were nothing more than unruly traitors who had opted for a carefree life in the South Sea over serving king and country, stopping not even at mutiny:

What a temptation is it to such Wretches when they find it in their power (however illegally it can be got at,) to fix themselves in the midst of Plenty in the finest Island in the World, where they need not labour, And where the allurements of disipation are more than equal to any thing that can be conceived.[13]

Upon returning to England in March 1790, Bligh had to answer in court for the loss of the *Bounty*, but the Admiralty shared his assessment of the motivation behind the mutiny, and Bligh was acquitted of any guilt. Still, doubts about the events on the ship appeared early on in the public discourse. For example, the *Times* pointed out some dubious claims in his version about how the mutiny had occurred, and that only two weeks after his return. In a short passage reprinted here in its entirety, the paper wrote:

There are three circumstances in the case of the disaster which happened to Captain BLIGH, that are, perhaps, unparalleled in the annals of mutiny.

The first is, that out of forty-five men eighteen should suffer themselves to be pinioned and put on board a boat, at the almost certainty of death, without the least resistance.

Second, that the secret of the conspiracy should be so well kept by twenty-seven men (most of them very young) as not to give the least suspicion to the rest of the crew.

And, thirdly, that after having carried through this successful mutiny–the question might be asked *cui bono?* As in those seas there was no possibility of plunder, or committing the smallest act of piracy.[14]

Although the *Times* article did not impugn Bligh's abilities or integrity directly, it did raise some initial questions about the reasons for and circumstance of the mutiny, which would become more insistent in the following months. Bligh remained adamant and justified his actions in his own very detailed narrative of the events. Before the year 1790 was out, he published *A Narrative of the Mutiny, on Board His Majesty's Ship Bounty*.[15] The *Times* published an excerpt of his story on 7 September 1790 that relates Bligh's take on the reasons for the mutiny:

It will very naturally be asked, What could be the reason for such a revolt? in answer to which, I can only conjecture, that the mutineers had assured themselves of a more happy life among the Otaheitans, than they could possibly have in England[.][16]

William Bligh had no doubt that the mutineers sought to return to Tahiti, where the crew of the *Bounty* had just spent five months. Although the *Bounty* tacked northwest and away from Tahiti once the commander and those loyal to him had been abandoned in their skiff, Bligh suspected – correctly, as it happens – this apparent course to be a ruse. In recollecting the sight of the *Bounty* distancing itself from the skiff in his *Narrative*, Bligh wrote:

> While the ship was in sight she steered to the WNW, but I considered this only as a feint; for when we were sent away – 'Huzza for Otaheite' was frequently heard among the mutineers.[17]

He remained adamant in his opinion that the selfish pursuit of a more pleasurable life was the mutineers' sole motivation. Public opinion, however, deviated increasingly from Bligh's estimation, questioning instead his own role in the chain of events. The shift of opinion against Bligh certainly had several reasons, many of which can only be partially reconstructed, but his righteous indignation and glaring arrogance likely contributed to his sinking popularity. One could also conjecture that the revolutionary atmosphere in neighbouring France, which was also widely known and discussed in England, may have cast a different light on this case of toppled superiors. The most important factor, though, was probably the testimony of the mutineers' relatives, friends and supporters, who tried as best they could to vouch for them and to justify their deeds. The endorsement of these supporters carried considerable weight in eighteenth-century England. Fletcher Christian and Peter Heywood, for example, whom Bligh identified as the mutiny's ringleaders, were from wealthy and influential families, and their relatives had considerable interest in preserving their good names. In 1792 some of the surviving mutineers were returned to England and brought before court, where they had the opportunity to present their own version of the story in which Bligh did not always acquit himself well. Six mutineers were sentenced to death in October 1792, but only three of these were eventually executed. One of the condemned was released because of faulty court procedure, and two more, including Peter Heywood, were pardoned by the king.

After his pardon, Heywood continued his career in the Royal Navy and was even promoted to the rank of captain in 1803. That he achieved this rank as a convicted mutineer testifies both to his family's connections and to the devaluation of William Bligh's reputation. Despite remaining in the navy and even becoming a rear admiral, Bligh never managed to overcome the stain of the mutiny. His public image was increasingly that of a miserly, sadistic slave driver who treated his crew with undue cruelty, which gave the mutineers the moral advantage, though not a legal one. This reinterpretation of events was due in no small part to Edward Christian – Fletcher's brother and a Cambridge-educated lawyer. In order to protect his family's good name, he attacked Bligh directly. Christian published a text in 1794 asserting that, while the mutiny and his brother's conduct were unjustifiable, they should be viewed in light of Bligh's cruelty.[18] To this end he provided a detailed account of how the commander accosted and abused his crew, thus depicting the mutiny as a sort of uprising against a tyrant. Bligh reacted with a public defence,[19] to which Christian promptly replied.[20]

Bligh's reputation never recovered from the public revelations and doubts about his conduct and leadership practices on board the *Bounty*, and many reassessed their views of the mutiny. The popularity of this version of events endured and became a recurring theme in the literary and cinematic treatments of the story of the *Bounty*. Bligh usually comes off in the films as a sadistic tyrant who practically forced the fairly noble Fletcher Christian to mutiny against him. The antagonism between Bligh and Christian is presented in greatest relief in the 1962 film with Trevor Howard as Bligh and Marlon Brando as Christian.[21]

The breadfruit mission

This condemnation of Bligh's character does not withstand scholarly scrutiny. In this case historians enjoy an unusually high quantity of sources produced in the course of the *Bounty*'s voyage and even more in reaction to the mutiny. Bligh recorded his impressions and perspectives in the ship's log, in his letters and in his several attempts to vindicate himself, and the surviving mutineers were subjected to a lengthy trial and recorded their own versions of events in writings of their own, on which Edward Christian's account rests. One must also not forget reports in contemporary media. When this vast range of sources is taken into account, William Bligh becomes a more complex character. For example, Greg Dening, whose *Mr Bligh's Bad Language* is one of the most insightful works about the mutiny on the *Bounty*, determined that Bligh was one of the most lenient commanders of his time in terms of his readiness to inflict corporal punishment on his crew.[22] At the same time, though, he seems to have had trouble inspiring others to recognize his authority on board.[23] While this difficulty may have been due in part to Bligh's personality, the extraordinary conditions on board the *Bounty* were the most important factor, and they presented Bligh's command with significant challenges.

Explaining the mutiny with reference to Bligh himself is inadequate. His difficult character certainly influenced the course of events indirectly, but the causes of the mission's failure are indelibly marked by its circumstances. William Bligh took command of the ship in 1787 in order to sail to the South Sea and load great quantities of breadfruit saplings at the behest of the British

Admiralty. When the mutiny occurred, the *Bounty* was leaving Tahiti loaded with nearly a thousand saplings that the crew had collected there. King George III, who was called 'Farmer George' for his great interest in agricultural reforms, had ordered the mission himself. He had instructed the Admiralty to collect breadfruit in the South Sea, its native habitat, and transplant it to the British colonies in the Caribbean.[24] The Royal Navy then sought the most efficient and cost-effective means of carrying this order out, for which the navy purchased the *Bethia*, a commercial coaler, and retrofitted her in the naval dockyards in Deptford for the demands of its new purpose. The coaler was converted into a floating greenhouse and rechristened the *Bounty*. All available space was devoted to protecting and cultivating breadfruit trees. The Great Cabin, which typically held generous bunks for the commander or officers, was sacrificed entirely along with the refuge it would have provided, serving instead as an arboretum. In addition to other modifications, this decision drastically reduced the space available to the crew on an already small ship (Figure 9). The conditions were extremely snug for the commander, officers and sailors alike.

Cramped conditions and a lack of refuge are really nothing new for sailors, but the conversion not only reduced the available space but also disturbed the

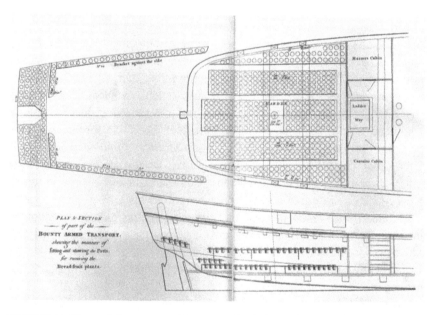

FIGURE 9 *Plans of the converted* Bounty, *which shows how much space on board was provided for the seedlings. William Bligh,* A Voyage to the South Sea, Undertaken by Command of His Majesty, for the Purpose of Conveying the Bread-Fruit Tree to the West-Indies, in His Majesty's Ship the Bounty, Commanded by Lieutenant William Bligh. *London 1792.*

social organization of that space. Rather than reflecting the ship's hierarchy and nautical routines, the ship's design was subordinated to the demands of botanical functionality. The accommodations for Bligh and his sailing master, John Fryer, were reduced to a small cabin below decks. Eight crewmen, including Fletcher Christian and Peter Heywood, had to share a small room amidships that was adjacent to an open room with a stove that was to house more than thirty seamen. That room would have ordinarily served as the petty officer's cabin, which instead was relocated below decks to the cargo area. As Greg Dening notes, this move isolated the very officer most responsible for the crew's discipline from his charges.[25] The general-purpose quarterdeck provides another example of how the retrofit altered social space on the *Bounty*. Located above the main deck, this space was raised, corresponding physically to the hierarchy prescribed by the ship's social institutions, and was usually reserved for the commander, officers and important guests. On the *Bounty*, however, the distinctions in this spatial organization were sacrificed in favour of botanical needs, and even common sailors were to be found on the quarterdeck.

These are but a few examples of how converting the ship led to spatial changes that corroded the social order on the ship. As commander, it was properly William Bligh's duty to restore the ship's symbolic order on board by commanding confidently and decisively, but here is exactly where he seems to have failed. One might suppose that a firm hand, including sufficient corporal punishment, would have probably been a more fruitful – though not necessarily more civilized – approach. As mentioned earlier, however, Bligh was one of the more lenient commanders of his time and tended to spare the lash. He also undermined the ship's hierarchy in other ways. His behaviour often reflected a combination of high standards and insecurity.[26] His insecurity was likely due in large part to the fact that Bligh did not hold the rank of captain, even though cinematic portrayals typically depict him as *Captain* Bligh. As the ship and its crew were not large enough to justify promotion to captain, Bligh was in fact only a commanding lieutenant during the mission, which hardly fostered the establishment of a clear hierarchy on the ship. The Admiralty was not necessarily averse to this circumstance, as it also capped Bligh's pay, which he supplemented by serving as the ship's quartermaster in addition to his duties as commander. Having commanding officers fill both roles was not without precedent in the British navy, but this combination was famously troublesome in that it demanded two very different behavioural patterns of one person.[27] A good commander looks after his crew, but a quartermaster, on the other hand, had to watch the bottom line and was financially liable to the Admiralty. Not surprisingly, quartermasters tended not to be very generous towards the crew. Bligh had to attempt to reconcile these two antithetical roles, though without much success. He would regularly accost and accuse his crew of random infractions. For example, just prior to the mutiny he had accused Fletcher Christian and a few others of having stolen a few coconuts from the ship's stores.[28]

The atmosphere on board was tense before long due to these unfortunate circumstances. The Admiralty's decision to take the shortest route to the South Sea by circumnavigating Cape Horn aggravated this already anxious situation. The motivation here was to minimize the expense of the unpopular mission, and Bligh dutifully tried to follow this order. However, the *Bounty*'s departure from England was plagued by extended delays with the consequence that the ship reached the cape just as the storm season was setting in. Bligh was undeterred and continued, risking his ship and crew. Included in a letter to Joseph Banks, Bligh described the situation in morose terms:

> [I] met with such dreadfull, tempestuous Weather and mountainous Seas, with Hail and Snow Storms, that altho I tryed it for 30 Days I could not accomplish it. I therefore (as my people were getting ill, and I had the Honor to have the most discretionary Orders to do as I thought best for the good of the Voyage,) determined to bear away for the Cape of Good Hope on the 22d of April.[29]

The *Bounty* did not reach Tahiti until October 1788 – months behind schedule. Upon arrival, the crew discovered that the breadfruit trees were in a spell of seasonal dormancy, during which saplings would not take. It took another five months to stock the *Bounty* with the requisite quantity of saplings, and, owing to the cramped conditions on board and against standard practice, the crew spent the greater part of these five months on land. The native population received the crew warmly, even integrating them to a certain extent in their community. Relative to the conditions on board, food and water were plentiful, and sexual encounters with Tahitian women were also not uncommon. Some of the sailors even married native women and fathered children in this short time. In short, this sojourn was a heavenly respite from the hardships of the voyage and the impoverished backgrounds of most of the crewmen. Some tried to desert, which did not particularly surprise Bligh, as desertion was a common temptation on South Sea voyages. A local leader did, however, help to retrieve the deserters.[30]

When the *Bounty* departed Tahiti on 4 April 1789, conditions were even more cramped than before. The ship's carpenter had adapted the Great Cabin and other parts of the ship to house saplings, which cost further space. The saplings also demanded a share of the fresh-water stores, meaning that after Tahiti the *Bounty* was constantly on the lookout for opportunities to replenish its provisions. Given these circumstances, it is little surprise that many crewmen wanted to return to their paradise, and they found a leader in Fletcher Christian, who was among those who had married there. Mutiny broke out three weeks after they had left Tahiti, and Bligh and those loyal to him were abandoned to their fate in the skiff (Figures 10 and 11). In a pointed gesture, the crew tossed the entire stock of saplings overboard and set course back to Tahiti (and then on to Pitcairn).

This section has shown how the outbreak of mutiny was deeply enmeshed with the *Bounty*'s unusual mission. The cramped conditions, the ambiguous hierarchy, the inadequate supplies and, of course, the promise of a life in paradise sowed the seeds of the revolt against Bligh. Even the mission to transplant breadfruit was embedded in an array of global ties that converged in the actors involved, and I will examine two of these ties that were directly related to breadfruit in more detail in the next section. The following discussion treats the idealized European vision of the South Sea in the eighteenth century and the need to supply Caribbean sugar plantations with cheap sustenance for the slaves. The breadfruit plays a key role in both contexts, though in very different ways.

FIGURE 10 *A painting of the suspension in the dinghy made shortly after Bligh's return to England. Robert Dodd,* The Mutineers Turning Lieut. Bligh and Part of the Officers and Crew Adrift from His Majesty's Ship the *Bounty* 1790. *Courtesy of the State Library of New South Wales, Austrialia.*

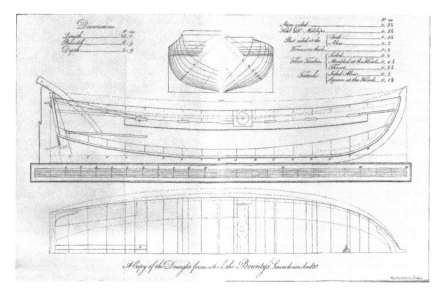

FIGURE 11 *Plans of* Bounty's *dinghy. William Bligh,* A Voyage to the South Sea, Undertaken by Command of His Majesty, for the Purpose of Conveying the Bread-Fruit Tree to the West-Indies, in His Majesty's Ship the *Bounty*, Commanded by Lieutenant William Bligh. *London 1792, folding 164–5.*

The South Sea and the Caribbean

From its terminological advent as *El Mar del Sur* in the early sixteenth century, through its Anglicization as the 'South Sea' in the eighteenth century and even to today, the region has never had clear borders. The term originally referred to the entire Pacific Ocean, later only its southwestern portion and the islands located there. Starting with Magellan, Europeans sailed these waters only irregularly until the mid-eighteenth century, when the voyages of Samuel Wallis, James Cook, Louis Antoine de Bougainville and others heralded the beginning of serious European exploration in the area. The reports of their travels and (for Europeans) discoveries shaped Europeans' image of this exotic region, but this image was composed of very different views, leading to a complex and sometimes incoherent result.[31] The natives, for instance, were often portrayed as uncivilized, godless savages in chilling reports of cannibalism. Other descriptions of Tahiti in particular recalled the wistful, idealized visions of the South Sea that remain popular in Western representations of it. The natives in this particular caricature were 'noble savages' who lived in harmony with their heavenly natural surroundings,[32] and it was the idealized image of the South Sea that most readily resonated with the Enlightenment ideas that were percolating in Europe.

From the outset, reports of the natural bounty and uninhibited sexuality of the native women played a starring role in these visions of an earthly paradise. The Admiralty commissioned author John Hawkesworth to compose a multivolume travelogue, which he wrote in the first-person voices of his sources: John Byron, Samuel Wallis, Philip Carteret, James Cook and Joseph Banks. The behaviour of the islands' female inhabitants, which was wanton by European standards, was a recurring motif of the adapted reports. Hawkesworth gives Captain Wallis to report how, shortly after arriving in Tahiti in 1767, he feared for the physical integrity of his ship due to a certain peril:

> While our people were on shore, several young women were permitted to cross the river, who, though they were not averse to the granting of personal favours, knew the value of them too well not to stipulate for a consideration: the price, indeed, was not great, yet it was such as our men were not always able to pay, and under this temptation they stole nails and other iron from the ship. The nails that we brought for traffick, were not always in their reach, and therefore they drew several out of different parts of the vessel, particularly those that fastened the cleats to the ship's side. This was productive of a double mischief; damage to the ship, and a considerable rise at market.[33]

Wallis himself was ill on arrival in Tahiti, though he was summoned on land by Queen Oberea a few days later for special treatment:

> As soon as we entered the house, she made us sit down, and then calling four young girls, she assisted them to take off my shoes, draw down my stockings, and pull off my coat, and then directed them to smooth down the skin, and gently chase it with their hands.[34]

Queen Oberea plays an even bigger part in James Cook's account than she does in Wallis's. Rather than restrict himself here to Cook's own notes, Hawkesworth also consulted the records of Joseph Banks, a London gentleman-botanist who accompanied Cook on his voyage and went on to be a key player in the saga of the *Bounty*. In his journal, Banks made no secret of his enthusiasm for the enticement of the Tahitian women,[35] and he described his encounter with Oberea in similarly frank terms. One episode, which he described and Hawkesworth repeated, attracted particular attention in England: one night, after having slept disrobed in Oberea's canoe, he awoke to find that his clothes had been stolen while he slept.[36]

These portrayals, among many others in Hawkesworth's book, made Oberea into 'the conduit of new and ancient fantasies of exotic femininity'.[37] Hawkesworth's choice to include numerous innuendos and explicit scenes in his adapted anthology attracted harsh criticism from many contemporaries, including the cleric John Wesley.[38] However, these were precisely the passages that made a lasting impression on his audience, and satirical treatments of the adventurers' romantic exploits in Tahiti, especially those of Joseph Banks, soon began to appear. Anonymous authors composed fictional correspondence between Banks and Oberea,[39] one of which alludes directly to Hawkesworth:

> One page of *Hawkesworth*, in the cool retreat,
> Fires the bright maid with more than mortal heat;
> She sinks at once into her lover's arms
> Nor deems it vice to prostitute her charms
> 'I'll do', she cries, 'what Queens have done before';
> And sinks, *from principle*, a common whore[40]

The explicit language and, in particular, the racy subject matter of the travelogues found their way into popular media, which contributed to Europeans associating visions of nudity and sexual abandon with the South Sea. Naturally, they also stimulated sailors' fantasies and channelled their expectations in a certain direction, making it difficult to maintain discipline among European visitors there. For example, Louis Antoine de Bougainville, who circumnavigated the globe for the French two years before James Cook, also spent a relatively long spell on Tahiti and remarked:

> I ask you how to keep four-hundred young, French sailors at work in the face of such a spectacle, when they have not even glimpsed a woman for six months?[41]

Bougainville mentions one of his cooks as an example of the abandon. The cook reportedly quit the ship to heed the explicit invitations of the natives, but he soon returned to seek refuge from the overwhelming local inclinations.[42] Other elements informed the European image of the South Sea beyond the preoccupation with sexuality and lasciviousness. The topos of nudity was especially thought to typify a lifestyle in harmony with nature. Idealized perceptions of the humanity's relation to nature in the South Sea appear in nearly all contemporary travel reports, but Bougainville's *Voyage autour du monde*, which was published in 1771 and sold magnificently, presents perhaps the most definitive and poetic example. Bougainville's descriptions of Tahiti in particular assumed great significance in the history of ideas after having been directly taken up by Denis Diderot and Jean-Jacque Rousseau. Not only does Bougainville describe Tahiti as the *Île de la Nouvelle Cythère* ('Island of New Kythira') in direct allusion to the island where Aphrodite, goddess of love, beauty and sexuality, resided, he also compares it unequivocally with the Garden of Eden:

> I ventured several times into the interior, with one or two others, and I believed myself transported to the Garden of Eden. We traversed a grassy field covered in beautiful fruit trees and coupled with small rivulets that exuded a marvellous freshness without any of the nuisances that humidity entails. The many people enjoyed the treasures that nature heaps upon them with full hands.[43]

Nature provided the islanders with all they required, disbursing her treasures onto the people from her full hands, so the narrative. The breadfruit played a key role in the European notion of a society blessed by nature and at peace with itself. Breadfruit trees were ubiquitous on Tahiti, they needed hardly any care, and the fruit of just two trees could feed a person for an entire year. When baked, the flesh of the fruit tasted of freshly baked bread – hence the name.[44] From the European perspective, the breadfruit seemed to be a cornerstone of the South Sea islanders' lifestyle and society, which for many Enlightenment thinkers presented a promising alternative to the pre-revolutionary European order. In the words of Emma Spary and Paul White, the breadfruit thus became a heavily loaded ideological symbol, a 'food of paradise' and an 'autocritique of European consumption'.[45] Consequently, the *Bounty*'s mission to transfer the breadfruit from the South Sea to the Caribbean and on to Kew Gardens is inseparably tied to contemporary Enlightenment discourse.

Another more mundane and less panegyric explanation for the significance of the breadfruit is also available. In 1775 John Ellis, a member of the Royal Society and – more importantly – a colonial agent for the West Indies, published a treatise addressed to the Earl of Sandwich, who was first lord of the Admiralty at the time. The title gives an accurate image of the contents: *A Description of the Mangostan and the Bread-Fruit: The First, Esteemed One of the Most Delicious; the Other, the Most Useful of All the Fruits in the EAST INDIES*. Ellis described both plants in botanical terms, but his main purpose was to bring considerable expertise to bear in a vigorous campaign for the mangosteen and breadfruit to be transplanted from the South Sea to the Caribbean (Figure 12). His book thus carries the appropriate subtitle of *DIRECTIONS to VOYAGERS, for bringing over these and other Vegetable Productions, which would be extremely beneficial to the Inhabitants of our West India Islands*. Ellis refers to a host of explorers who had described the breadfruit as a miracle food while refraining from colouring it ideologically himself. Rather, he was strictly interested in the breadfruit's economic potential, and he made no secret of what he considered to be the tree's primary advantage:

The Bread-fruit affords a most necessary and pleasant article of subsistence to many. This, likewise, might be easily cultivated in our West India islands, and made to supply an important article of food to all ranks of their inhabitants, especially to the Negroes.[46]

Thus, Ellis remarked already in the opening lines on the potential utility of the breadfruit for British plantation owners in the West Indies. Since the mid-seventeenth century a plantation economy had been growing in the Caribbean that was based almost exclusively on cultivating sugar cane, and African slaves were used to labour on the giant plantations. Devoting the sugar islands to monoculture meant that large quantities of food for the slaves had to be

FIGURE 12 *John Ellis,* A Description of the Mangostan and the Bread-Fruit: The First, Esteemed One of the Most Delicious; the Other, the Most Useful of All the Fruits in the EAST INDIES. *London 1775, between 10 and 11.*

imported. Cheap grain from North America was long the chief food source, but when conflict between the North American colonies and their British metropole conflagrated in the 1770s, these imports ground to a halt. Instead, food had to be imported from more distant sources and at higher prices. Ellis and many others in the sugarcane business saw the transfer of the breadfruit as a relatively practicable solution to their problem. The tree needed little space, it did not compete with sugarcane, and – most importantly – it would not draw labour off the sugar plantations. From a strictly fiscal perspective, transferring the breadfruit tree seemed like an ideal solution to the woes of the Caribbean economy.

Although Ellis's tract did not bear any fruit itself, it constituted the first expression of a West Indian lobby group that was gaining sway and that would soon compel the British government to launch a breadfruit mission. Their pressure cumulated in King George III's order to the Admiralty, commanding that the breadfruit tree be transplanted to the Caribbean. The *Bounty*'s voyage, then, was not just embedded in the Enlightenment and perceptions of the South Sea; it was also tightly intertwined with the 'Caribbean plantation complex'. This also provides the bridge to the global context of the Age of Revolution in which the voyage took place. Just as impending American independence necessitated transplanting the breadfruit in the eyes of the plantation lobby, the French Revolution and its aftermath were providing a frame of reference in which to interpret the mutiny.

The mutiny doomed the first attempt to transfer breadfruit. After his return to England and his acquittal, Bligh was reassigned to another such mission, which succeeded on the second attempt. The HMS *Providence* arrived in the West Indies in 1792 loaded with many saplings, and cultivation began immediately. However, the cultivators were dismayed to find that the slaves initially refused to eat breadfruit despite their malnutrition,[47] and the European plantation owners refused to touch it. Even though the geographical transfer of breadfruit succeeded on the second attempt, its socio-cultural status also underwent a change, dropping from 'food of paradise' to peasant food.[48]

Global actors

The brief description of the background of the breadfruit mission presented here yields various historical contexts and conceptual connections in which the voyage of the *Bounty* and the mutiny were embedded. One such context was the so-called 'second age of exploration' that included the voyages of Wallis, Bougainville and Cook along with the emergence of the South Sea image and its many variants. Enlightenment and, later, revolutionary discourses of freedom and equality also fed into this image depicting South Sea societies as an alternative to Europe and the breadfruit as a key component in them. However, these revolutionary ideals directly contradicted the fundamental principles of the Caribbean slave economies, where the plantation lobby saw in the breadfruit another, no less decisive, kind of salvation. Therefore, the *Bounty*'s mission was enmeshed in the intercontinental system of transatlantic triangular trade along with all its tributaries, like the collapsing grain trade with North America. This supplements the larger historical context of the Age of Revolution, integrating North America, the Caribbean and France.

As different as these interpretative contexts might be in terms of their content and geographical positions, together they provide the historical framework in which the voyage of the *Bounty* took place. Understanding these contexts and the connections and interactions between them is essential to grasping the mutiny as a historical event. The mere existence of such interactions and influences has already been sufficiently established, but the bland conclusion that everything is somehow connected to everything else yields little scholarly or analytical satisfaction from a global-history perspective. Indeed, global history seeks to identify the preconditions, mechanisms and effects of global connections in order to explain their historical efficiency. In other words, global history does not ask *whether* historical phenomena and contexts affect each other; rather, it asks *how* they do so and what it means. This approach entails inquiring into the kinds of connection and their concrete manifestations, which leads inevitably to historical actors.

Taking actors literally as those who act and who shape history with their actions equates the desire to understand history with the need to understand actors' thoughts and deeds. And these thoughts and deeds take place in overlapping contexts that connect individual actors with each other, not in clearly delimited, isolated circumstances. The acting subjects serve as conduits between different settings and frameworks of meaning. In the particular case of the *Bounty*, the events' authors weave together the spaces and contexts mentioned earlier and relate them to local opportunity structures, like the location of the ship, the living conditions on Tahiti, the fiscal miserliness of the Admiralty and the ambiguity of William Bligh's role on board. The combination of all these circumstances, as different as they might appear as first, composes the frame and horizon of what the actors could do.

Several examples clarify these ideas in relation to the specific example of the mutiny. For instance, the mutineers' actions must be considered in the context of the ship with its cramped conditions and privations, which were the diametric opposite of the five-month sojourn on Tahiti. Moreover, the expectations and fantasies that the sailors developed in the course of their journey influenced their actions. That Fletcher Christian and Peter Heywood

FIGURE 13 *Painting of Joseph Banks. Joshua Reynolds,* Sir Joseph Banks, *1772. Courtesy of the Public Domain Review.*

both came from respectable families on the Isle of Man, meaning that they were embedded in similar social networks, must also be taken into account.

The conduit function performed by the actors in an entangled history is apparent in the mutineers themselves, but it is perhaps most visible in the characters of Joseph Banks and William Bligh, so the opportunity structures they faced will be treated in more detail. Joseph Banks (Figure 13) is an apt starting point, as the idea to send Bligh and the *Bounty* on a breadfruit mission was originally his.[49] Banks was born to an affluent bourgeois family in 1743 in Westminster,[50] and he attended Harrow from 1752 before transferring to Eton in 1756, but a bout of the pox ended his schooling early. He enrolled at Oxford University in late 1760 to study botany, and he inherited a handsome sum upon the death of his father in the following year. His financial independence allowed him to leave university without obtaining a degree and to devote himself to botany. For example, he sailed on the 1766 voyage to Newfoundland and Labrador on the HMS *Niger*, where he collected numerous animal and plant specimens yet unknown in Europe and priming his career as a botanist. Furthermore, he might have met James Cook in St. John's, Newfoundland, whom he was later to accompany on his first voyage to the South Sea.[51] In addition to his longstanding contacts to the London political scene, this contact allowed Banks to join Cook's first circumnavigation of the globe as a botanist (and bring seven more people with him). The flora and fauna he brought back from this voyage with his friend Daniel Solander secured his status as a botanist specializing on the South Sea and the Australian continent. On the one hand, his graphic descriptions of his romantic escapades in the South Sea contributed to colouring the image of the South Sea with an erotic tinge. On the other, he also wrote detailed descriptions of the flora on Tahiti and elsewhere, emphasizing the breadfruit's important socio-economic role. In a report in his travelogue entitled *Manners and Customs of South Sea Islands* he notes that the islanders must hardly toil for their living thanks to the breadfruit:

> Scarcely can it be said that they earn their bread with the sweat of their brow when their cheifest sustenance Bread fruit is procurd with no more trouble than that of climbing a tree and pulling it down.[52]

Even though one would have to initially plant the ten trees required for sustenance, the task would last hardly an hour, after which one's nourishment would be secured for life. These assumed characteristics of the breadfruit captivated his attention for years and well after his return to England. Banks shared the results of his research on the breadfruit tree with John Ellis, a close acquaintance of his. Ellis had been campaigning for the transfer of various crops, especially to the American colonies, and he proceeded to include the breadfruit tree in his long list of plants to be transplanted. He published the aforementioned text on the subject in 1775.[53] Other influential figures in the British colonies in the Caribbean were also in direct contact with Banks on this subject in the 1770s and 1780s, such as Valentine Morris, governor of St. Vincent, whom Banks had known at Eton, and Hinton East, the receiver general of Jamaica.

On returning to England after his voyage with Cook, Banks ascended to an unofficial position of government adviser in all botanical matters, on which he advised King George III. He also became the unofficial director of Kew Gardens and, owing to his excellent contacts in politics and business, he was consulted on virtually every question relating to the economic uses of plants in the colonies. This latter role led him to prepare the transfer of breadfruit from the South Sea to the Caribbean, which Banks saw as part of a larger British imperial plan. To secure easier access for Britain to high-quality cotton, it was slated for transplant to the Caribbean. Banks anticipated that, should the plan succeed and lead to cotton plantations in the Caribbean, even more slaves would be required to work them, and they in turn would increase the demand for cheap staples. However, food imports posed a significant challenge due to American independence and the curtailed grain imports that resulted from it. Banks sought to pre-empt shortages by prospectively transferring breadfruit, which then appears as just one move in a larger strategy of transplanting useful crops.[54]

His original plan was to use the voyage of the so-called First Fleet, which was to colonize Australia, to transfer breadfruit, but he decided against this approach in the course of 1787 in order not to tax the resources of the nascent Australian colony.[55] Instead, he presented the government and the Admiralty with a new plan to purchase and convert the *Bethia*, which would begin its new mission rechristened as the *Bounty*. Banks masterminded this mission, and it was he who proposed William Bligh as commander. Indeed, Banks became an important patron for Bligh and continued to support him after the mutiny by, for example, seeing to it that Bligh would also command the second breadfruit mission on the HMS *Providence*.

As it happens, Joseph Banks was a man of many interests and talents. Botany was just one of his scholarly pursuits, as his membership in the Royal Society testifies. He soon came into considerable wealth, and he was very well connected in London society. He was adventurous, travelled the world and was able to develop his own first-hand ideas about other societies and cultures. Importantly, Banks truly believed in the colonial vision and put his botanical and other expertise in the service of British colonial rule, especially when it came to making economic use of the colonial territories. Banks's many facets and interests as a historical actor cannot be credibly isolated from each other in order to evaluate the historical efficiency of each one. However, in the aggregate they do show the pivotal function that such actors play from the perspective of global history. Spaces and contexts of vastly different reaches came together in Banks's person, thoughts and actions, and his actorhood was inseparably and simultaneously embedded in them. His cognitive and opportunity structures allowed him to connect botanical science, the economics of Caribbean plantations, contemporary perceptions of the South Sea and the *Bounty*'s mission, to name just a few elements. His action was not located in any of these single contexts; rather, it brought them all into contact with each other.

Although Banks was not present for the mutiny, his actions beforehand contributed considerably to the convoluted circumstances on the breadfruit mission. By contrast, William Bligh (Figure 14), as commander of the *Bounty*, was one of the unwilling protagonists of the mutiny on the ship and the island of Tahiti: an actor on the scene who immediately shaped the course of events. While his action is typically viewed in the very local space of the ship, which

FIGURE 14 *William Bligh, as he liked to see himself in his books. William Bligh,* A Voyage to the South Sea, Undertaken by Command of His Majesty, for the Purpose of Conveying the Bread-Fruit Tree to the West-Indies, in His Majesty's Ship the *Bounty*, Commanded by Lieutenant William Bligh. *London 1792. Courtesy of Project Gutenberg, Australia.*

leads to his condemnation as cruel tyrant or lionization as heroic navigator, his thoughts and deeds were also embedded in frames of reference with very different ranges, though still differing from those of Joseph Banks.

Little is known about William Bligh's childhood.[56] He was born in 1754, probably in Plymouth, and he might have gone to sea already at the age of seven but no later than at fifteen. He served in the Royal Navy in various capacities until 1782. From 1776 to 1780 he was the master on the *Resolution* under James Cook, whose death he witnessed on Hawaii. This was a formative experience for Bligh, and it tainted his perception of native societies ever after. In 1781 he married Elizabeth Betham, the daughter of a Manx customs official. This marriage gave Bligh access to the better social circles on the Isle of Man, allowing him to leave the navy in 1783 in order to become a private captain in the West Indies trade. His employer was Duncan Campbell, a merchant-entrepreneur and Elizabeth's uncle. Campbell was, along with Banks, one of Bligh's most important patrons, and he went on to become deeply involved in the First Fleet. Due to his voyage with Cook, his knowledge of the West Indies and his connections on the Isle of Man, Bligh was entrusted with command of the *Bounty*. In this capacity he took Fletcher Christian and Peter Heywood on board, both of whom were from the upper ranks of Manx society. Bligh had commanded Christian before and had even promoted him. Heywood joined the *Bounty*'s crew on the recommendation of Bligh's father-in-law, who was well acquainted with the Heywoods. The two Manxmen spent considerable time together during the voyage, with Christian teaching the younger Heywood Latin, Greek and navigation.[57] Despite their friendship, their roles in the mutiny were very different. While Christian became a key figure, Heywood saw himself as uninvolved and completely blameless. Upon his arrest, Heywood was astounded to learn that Bligh and many others saw the matter very differently. Heywood was a decisive element in the conspiracy for Bligh, who fingered the Manxmen as its originators. This view is already apparent in the letter Bligh wrote to his wife from Coupang:

> It is incredible! these very young Men I placed every confidence in, yet these great Villains joined with the most able Men in the Ship got possession of the Arms and took the Bounty from me, with huzza's for Otaheite. I have now reason to curse the day I ever knew a Christian or a Heywood or indeed a Manks man.[58]

Bligh's structure of action and opportunity then were also the result of several overlapping contexts. He held a certain view of the South Sea, had had certain experiences with natives and brought a certain expertise about breadfruit. At the same time, he had also through Campbell become part of the Caribbean plantation complex, with which he was also quite familiar. He had served in the Royal Navy in various roles since his childhood, so he was also deeply socialized in its structures. A further piece of the puzzle was the immediate surroundings on the *Bounty* with its cramped spatial and social conditions. These several frameworks of interpretation and action structured Bligh's thought and action during and after the breadfruit mission. For all their differences and regional disparities, they directly intersect and interact in his person.

Conclusion: Actors in global history

Joseph Banks and William Bligh are particularly vivid examples of how very different frames of global meanings converge and interact in the persons of historical actors. It is the historical actors themselves – and not only prominent figures like Banks and Bligh – who lend historical efficiency to global connections by grounding their thoughts and actions simultaneously in diverse contexts. This pivot function is clearly manifest in the case of the mutiny on the *Bounty*, as the immediate connections between seemingly separate frames become dramatically apparent. These actors in global history are bound up in a multiplicity of contexts that vary greatly in their extension, and these are key to understanding subjects' actions. Accordingly, the genesis and meaning of the mutiny on the *Bounty* can only be sufficiently grasped if viewed in light of such global entanglements. Only this kind of gaze opens the vista of events and opportunity structures that the actors themselves faced, allowing their own view to be roughly approximated. As an inverse correlate it is also clear that examining a relatively isolated historical event, like the mutiny on the *Bounty*, from an actor-centric perspective can itself serve as an analytical prism through which the full spectrum of global connection patterns becomes visible. Such a perspective also sensitizes observers to the events' many overlapping layers of meaning and associated contexts. In short, focusing on the actors involved and how they are bound up in connections of global historical significance allows us to recognize entangled transregional lines of causality and to disentangle the strands of their meanings.

The mutiny is an apt case both because it is so well known and because of the wealth of sources available, which allow us to reconstruct the diverse entanglements in exceptional detail. However, the principle that actors perform a coalescent role is analytically useful in any scenario of global historical significance. The point is not merely to reveal the existence of global connections and processes of exchange in some context or other; rather, an actor-centric perspective allows the concrete causal relationships and modes of operation induced by such connections to be investigated. Indeed, this was already apparent in the Great Moon Hoax, the first case study discussed in this book. Richard Adams Locke, among others, cunningly used global connections and non-connections to orchestrate the hoax. Their strands converged in his person, and focusing on him makes those strands visible to us today. Historical actors' pivotal role was perhaps even more obvious in the section on space in global history, in which the oscillation between communicative proximity and geographical isolation showed how the protagonists in that chapter were bound up in different spaces and brought these into contact with each other. The shifts in the relations between the spaces were also manifested in and through the actors. The same applies to the telegraph users in the section on time, to the various actors seeking to build the Mont Cenis Tunnel in the following chapter and to Dr Crippen, who, in the final case study, tried to flee across the Atlantic. Each of them actuates processes of exchange between various frames of meaning through their thoughts and actions, and they lend historical efficiency to global connections along the way. At the same time, they are themselves subject to the effects of those same connections. These are but a few examples in global history of how focusing on actors allows us to detect the genesis of global connections, to investigate their historical efficiency in detail and to better understand their mechanisms.

Notes

1   See, for example, the praxeological approach in Pierre Bourdieu, *Entwurf einer Theorie der Praxis*. Frankfurt am Main, 1979.

2   See, for example, Giddens's model of structuration in: Giddens, *The Constitution of Society*.

3   There are now a vast number of textbooks for definitions of and introductions to historical anthropology. See, for example, Gert Dressel, *Historische Anthropologie. Eine Einführung*. Wien/Köln/Weimar, 1996; Richard van Dülmen, *Historische Anthropologie. Entwicklung, Probleme, Aufgaben*. 2. Aufl. Köln, 2001; Jakob Tanner, *Historische Anthropologie zur Einführung*. Hamburg, 2004.

4   With its focus on human agency, historical anthropology overlaps considerably with the neighbouring subfields of micro-history and the history of the everyday, though these engage with the subject matter with somewhat different interests and goals. See, for example, Alf Lüdtke, 'Alltagsgeschichte, Mikro-Historie, historische Anthropologie', in: Hans-Jürgen Goertz (Hrsg.), *Geschichte. Ein Grundkurs*. Reinbek, 1998, 565–7; Hans Medick, 'Mikro-Historie', in: Winfried Schulze (Hrsg.), *Sozialgeschichte, Alltagsgeschichte, Mikro-Historie. Eine Diskussion*. Göttingen, 1994, 40–53.

5   Michael Maurer, 'Historische Anthropologie', in: ders. (Hrsg.), *Aufriss der Historischen Wissenschaften. Bd. 7: Neue Themen und Methoden der Geschichtswissenschaft*. Stuttgart, 2003, 294–387, 379.

6   See Dressel, *Historische Anthropologie*, 162.

7   An excellent recent example is to be found in: Johannes Paulmann, 'Regionen und Welten. Arenen und Akteure regionaler Weltbeziehungen seit dem 19. Jahrhundert', in: *HZ* 296/3 (2013): 660–99.

8   Unless otherwise indicated, this reconstruction of the mutiny and its preludes is based on: Greg Dening, *Mr Bligh's Bad Language: Passion, Power and Theatre on the Bounty*. Cambridge/New York, 1992; Caroline Alexander, *The Bounty: The True Story of the Mutiny on the Bounty*. New York, 2004; Anne Salmond, *Bligh: William Bligh in the South Seas*. Berkeley, 2011.

9   For an overview, see Donald A. Maxton, *The Mutiny on HMS Bounty: A Guide to Non-Fiction, Fiction, Poetry, Film, Articles and Music*. Jefferson/London, 2008.

10 William Bligh, *Brief an Elizabeth Bligh*. Kupang, 1789. Mitchell Library of New South Wales, ZML Safe 1/45, 17–24.

11 Ibid.

12 Dening, *Bligh's Bad Language*, 9.

13 William Bligh, *Brief an Joseph Banks*. Anhang, Batavia, 13. Oktober 1789, Papers of Sir Joseph Banks. State Library of New South Wales, Series 46.27.

14 O.A., O.T., in: *Times* vom 26. März 1790, 3.

15 William Bligh, *A Narrative of the Mutiny, on Board His Majesty's Ship Bounty; and the Subsequent Voyage of Part of the Crew, in the Ship's Boat*

from Tofoa, One of the Friendly Islands, to Timor, a Dutch Settlement in the East Indies. London, 1790.

16   William Bligh, 'Extracts from Captain Bligh's Narrative', in: *Times* vom 7. September 1790, 3.

17   Bligh, *A Narrative of the Mutiny*, Eintrag vom April 1789.

18   Edward Christian and Stephen Barney, *Minutes of the Proceedings of the Court-Martial Held at Portsmouth, August 12, 1792. On Ten Persons Charged with Mutiny on Board His Majesty's Ship the Bounty. With an Appendix, Containing a Full Account of the Real Causes and Circumstances of that Unhappy Transaction, the Most Material of Which Have Hitherto Been Withheld from the Public.* London, 1794.

19   William Bligh, *An Answer to Certain Assertions Contained in the Appendix to a Pamphlet, Entitled Minutes of the Proceedings on the Court-Martial Held at Portsmouth, August 12th, 1792, on Ten Persons Charged with Mutiny on Board His Majesty's Ship the Bounty.* London, 1794.

20   Edward Christian, *A Short Reply to Capt. William Bligh's Answer.* London, 1795.

21   See Johannes Paulmann, 'Macht-Raum. Die Geschichte(n) von der Meuterei auf der Bounty', in: ders. (Hrsg.), *Ritual – Macht – Natur. Europäische-ozeanische Beziehungswelten in der Neuzeit.* (TenDenZen Sonderband.) Bremen, 2005, 53–74, 61–6.

22   Dening, *Bligh's Bad Language*, 63.

23   See Markus Pohlmann, 'Die Meuterei auf der Bounty – Über Revolution und einige der Mythen, die sich um sie ranken', in: Ingrid Artus and Rainer Trinczek (Hrsg.), *Über Arbeit, Interessen und andere Dinge. Phänomene, Strukuren und Akteure im modernen Kapitalismus.* München/Miring, 2004, 77–97.

24   Using the navy in this fashion as a transformative institution to mould the world was not unusual at the time. See Julia Angster, *Erdbeeren und Piraten. Die Royal Navy und die Ordnung der Welt 1770–1880.* Göttingen, 2012.

25   Dening, *Bligh's Bad Language*, 28.

26   The title of Greg Dening's book *Mr Bligh's Bad Language* alludes to this, especially to Bligh's often insecure, ambiguous use of lang the insecurespielt auf diesen Umstand, v.a. den unsicheren, zweideutigen und oft widersprüchlichen Einsatz von Sprache an.

27   Dening, *Bligh's Bad Language*, 22–3.

28   Ibid., 58, 86–7.

29   Bligh, *Brief an Joseph Banks.*

30   William Bligh, 'Chapter IX', in: ders., *A Voyage to the South Sea, Undertaken by Command of His Majesty, for the Purpose of Conveying the Bread-Fruit Tree to the West-Indies, in His Majesty's Ship the Bounty, Commanded by Lieutenant William Bligh.* London, 1792, 105–22. In many of his attempts to justify himself, Bligh mentions his suspicion that the mutineers knew an attempt to desert while at anchor in Tahiti would be fruitless because the natives would simply return them. According to him, this is why

they decided simply to take control of the ship instead: 'Desertions have happened, more or less, from many of the ships that have been at the Society Islands; but it ever has been in the commanders power to make the chiefs return their people: the knowledge, therefore, that it was unsafe to desert, perhaps, first led mine to consider with what ease so small a ship might be surprized, and that so favourable an opportunity would never offer to them again.' Bligh, *A Narrative of the Mutiny*, Entry of April 1789.

31 See Joachim Meißner, *Mythos Südsee. Das Bild von der Südsee im Europa des 18. Jahrhunderts*. Hildesheim, 2006.

32 Such exotic fantasies of the South Sea and Tahiti in particular are clearly reflected in the trailer of the 1962 film about *The Mutiny on the Bounty*, which boasts that the movie was shot in the original locations. The voiceover continues to exclaim: 'Tahiti! For generations the dream island of the Western world; a land of easy-going, fun-loving people; a land that has always represented escape from civilization; a land where there is no time, no tomorrow, only today.' Original Theatrical Trailer, in: Warner Brothers, *Mutiny on the Bounty (1962) Blu-Ray*. Los Angeles, 2011.

33 John Hawkesworth, *An Account of the Voyages Undertaken by the Order of His Present Majesty for Making Discoveries in the Southern Hemisphere, and Successively Performed by Commodore Byron Captain Wallis, Captain Carteret, and Captain Cook, in the Dolphin, the Swallow, and the Endeavour Drawn Up from the Journals Which Were Kept by the Several Commanders, and from the Papers of Joseph Banks*. Bd. 1/Part 2: *Captain Wallis's Voyage*. London, 1773, Kapitel VI, 280–301, 285–6.

34 Hawkesworth, *Captain Wallis's Voyage*, 290–1.

35 See Patty O'Brien, *The Pacific Muse: Exotic Femininity and the Colonial Pacific*. Seattle/London, 2006, 63–4.

36 Joseph Banks, 'Entry from 28 Mai 1769', *Endeavour Journal*. Bd. 1: 25 August 1768–14 August 1769, State Library of New South Wales, ML Safe 1/12; John Hawkesworth, *An Account of the Voyages Undertaken by the Order of His Present Majesty for Making Discoveries in the Southern Hemisphere, and Successively Performed by Commodore Byron Captain Wallis, Captain Carteret, and Captain Cook, in the Dolphin, the Swallow, and the Endeavour Drawn Up from the Journals Which Were Kept by the Several Commanders, and from the Papers of Joseph Banks*. Bd. 2/Part 1: *Lieutenant Cook's Voyage*. London, 1773, chapter XIII, 132–41, 132–3.

37 O'Brien, *The Pacific Muse*, 64.

38 Anthony Pagden, *The Enlightenment and Why It Still Matters*. Oxford, 2013, 186.

39 O.A., *An Epistle from Mr. Banks, Voyager, Monster-Hunter, and Amoroso, to Oberea, Queen of Otaheite*. London, 1773; O.A., *An Epistle from Oberea, Queen of Otaheite, to Joseph Banks Esq*. London, 1774.

40 O.A., *An Epistle from Mr. Banks to Oberea*, 13.

41 Translation from French original: ('Je le demande; comment retenir au travail, au milieu d'un spectacle pareil, quatre cents François, jeunes, marins, & qui depuis six mois n'avoient point vu de femmes?') Louis Antoine de

Bougainville, *Voyage autour du monde, par la frégate du Roi la Boudeuse, et la flûte l'étoile; en 1766, 1767, 1768 & 1769*. Paris, 1771, 190.

42 Ibid., 191.

43 Translation from French original: 'J'ai plusieurs fois été, moi second ou troisieme, me promener dans l'intérieur. Je me croyois transporté dans le jardin d'Eden; nous parcourions une plain de gazon, couverte de beaux arbres fruitiers & couplée de petites rivieres qui entretiennent une fraîcheur délicieuse, sans aucun des inconvéniens qu'entraîne l'humidité. Un peuple nombreux y jouit des trésors que la nature verse à pleine mains sur lui.' Ibid., 198.

44 Emma Spary and Paul White, 'Food of Paradise. Tahitian Breadfruit and the Autocritique of European Consumption', in: *Endeavour* 28/2 (2004): 75–80, 75–6.

45 Ibid.

46 John Ellis, *A Description of the Mangostan and the Bread-Fruit: The First, Esteemed One of the Most Delicious; the Other, the Most Useful of All the Fruits in the EAST INDIES*. London, 1775, 11.

47 See Norbert Ortmayr, 'Kulturpflanzen. Transfers und Ausarbeitungsprozesse im 18. Jahrhundert', in: Margarete Grandner and Andrea Komlosy (Hrsg.), *Vom Weltgeist beseelt. Globalgeschichte 1700–1815*. Wien, 2004, 73–102, 80; Richard B. Sheridan, 'Captain Bligh, the Breadfruit, and the Botanic Gardens of Jamaica', in: *Journal of Caribbean History* 23/1 (1989): 28–50, 28–30.

48 Spary and White, 'Food of Paradise', 79–80.

49 See David Mackay, 'Banks, Bligh and Breadfruit', in: *New Zealand Journal of History* 8/1 (1974): 61–77.

50 On Joseph Banks's biography, see, among others: John Gascoigne, 'Banks, Sir Joseph, Baronet', in: *Oxford Dictionary of National Biography 2004*. Version September 2013, in: URL= http://www.oxforddnb.com/view/artic le/1300?docPos=1 (accessed: 25 June 2016); Harold B. Carter, *Sir Joseph Banks, 1743–1820*. London, 1988; John Gascoigne, *Joseph Banks and the English Enlightenment: Useful Knowledge and Polite Culture*. Cambridge, 1994; Patrick O'Brian, *Joseph Banks: A Life*. Chicago, 1997.

51 Averil M. Lysaght, *Joseph Banks in Newfoundland and Labrador, 1766: His Diary, Manuscripts, and Collections*. Berkeley, 1971, 41. Other authors doubt whether the encounter took place. John C. Beaglehole, *The Life of Captain James Cook*. Stanford, 1974, 88; Richard Hough, *Captain James Cook: A Biography*. New York/London, 1997, 49.

52 Joseph Banks, 'Manners and Customs of the South Sea Islanders', in: ders., *Endeavour Journal*. Bd. 1: 25 August 1768–14 August 1769, State Library of New South Wales, ML Safe 1/12.

53 See Julia Bruce, 'Banks and Breadfruit', in: *RSA Journal* 141 (1993): 817–20, 818.

54 Ibid., 817; Alan Frost, *Sir Joseph Banks and the Transfer of Plants to and from the South Pacific, 1786–1798*. Melbourne, 1993.

55 Mackay, 'Banks, Bligh and Breadfruit', 86–70.

56 On William Bligh's biography, see Alan Frost, 'Bligh, William (1754–1817)', in: *Oxford Dictionary of National Biography 2004.* Version September 2013, in: URL= http://www.oxforddnb.com/view/article/2650?docPos=1 (accessed: 25 June 2016); Salmond, *Bligh.*

57 See Dening, *Bligh's Bad Language*, 258.

58 Bligh, *Brief an Elizabeth Bligh.*

6

Structures:

Breakthrough on Mont Cenis

Structures in global history

The concept of actorhood introduced in the previous chapter gains its analytical quality by appreciating actors' capacity for action, which is to say their agency. However, it simultaneously hints at the existence of conditions that constrain, guide or otherwise influence what actors can do. Thus, analytical use of the concept of actors always invokes the structure(s) that encompass and co-constitute their actions. Thomas Welskopp has identified the problem of the reciprocal relationship between action and structure and the question of 'whether conditions make subjects, or whether the converse proposition that subjects produce conditions is not more accurate' as one of the fundamental problems of social sciences and the humanities. Welskopp continues: 'Commitments to one of these two positions fundamentally affect the configuration of any social theory; obversely, they indelibly mark the physiognomy of every historical representation.'[1]

Different approaches to studying history often differ in precisely this regard. Researching history is a matter of reconstructing the thoughts and actions of historical actors as well as the contemporary circumstances in which they lived. History returns to the fundamental question of to what extent people make their own histories. How extensive is their freedom of action? What limits that freedom and how? How important are chance and contingency? When do structures determine historical trajectories? Where do such structures come from, and to what extent do they constrain the actions of particular subjects? These questions are unavoidable when trying to explain and understand remote thoughts and deeds in historical investigations. In the course of its development, different schools of thought in history have tried to answer these questions implicitly or explicitly and have made very different 'commitments' along the way.

Despite the increased popularity of terms like 'actor' and 'agency' in the historical discourse of recent decades, attention to humans as the makers of history is anything but new. Historical writing in the nineteenth century, which was coloured by historicism, focused principally on political history, that is, on the actions of statesmen, governments, diplomats and the military. Taken together, such events constituted history. The actors of interest to historical research of that time belonged to the social elite, and they accordingly had relatively broad freedom of action. This resonated in contemporary images of history, in which structural constraints were largely neglected, and the view is also reflected in Leopold von Ranke's famous phrase that 'every epoch is immediate to God, and its value does not rest on what eventuates from it, but on its own existence, on its own self',[2] and it is more broadly manifest in the historicists' contradiction of the visions of progress that were so popular among their contemporaries. Historicists discounted overarching, durable structures that channel social development along certain trajectories, as in the case of Enlightenment notions of progress.[3]

Various schools of historical thought began to clash in the twentieth century over the general avoidance of structure. The French *Annales* School and German social history (*Sozialgeschichte*) placed historical structures at the centre of their analyses, which increasingly became a feature of historical research in general after the Second World War. In 1973 Reinhart Koselleck summarized the change of orientation: 'With the recent ascendance of interest in social history, the words "structure" and, especially, "structural history" have taken root [...]. In terms of their temporality, structures are understood as contexts that do not arise strictly from the sequence of experienced events. In consequence, categories of relative duration, of medium and long terms, reintroduce – temporally speaking – the older "conditions" back into the investigation.'[4] Historians like Fernand Braudel, with his recognition of developments in the longue durée,[5] and Werner Conze,[6] one of the founders of German social history, exerted a lasting influence on historical research in (West) Germany well into the 1960s and 1980s. As in the research programme of the *Annales*, historical social science in that period prominently featured durable, often subliminal, structures in its outlook.

Returning to Welskopp's assessment, both historicism and post-war social history clearly made 'commitments' with regard to what space they allowed for the efficiency of human action, and both are located squarely in the tension between structure and agency. However, that does not mean that these two approaches neglected each other's insights. Indeed, Conze remarked in 1952, 'As passé as it might seem to continue the history of battles and royal dynasties, which was once as beloved as it was despised, it must be granted that history happens. This happening consists of more than mere development over time; it comprises decisions and deeds, destruction, creation and ordering in the domain of human opportunities that we perceive as freedom.'[7] Such words demonstrate the potential compatibility of the two positions, even if a synthesis that does justice to both perspectives and that gives due credit to subjects' capacity for action as well as to the guiding force of structures was not achieved overnight. However, proposals for just such a synthesis have since been developed, many of which originate in the writings of the British sociologist Anthony Giddens. In 1984 Giddens proposed a theory of structuration with which he attempted to analytically reconcile individual action with collective structures.[8] Briefly, Giddens postulated that the two aspects act on each other mutually, with structures making certain courses of action appear more reasonable than others and with the resulting actions (re) creating those guiding structures.[9]

In recent decades, such developments in sociology and other fields, like anthropology (see the chapter on actors), have inspired history in an attempt to adapt them to its own purposes, to better understand the relationship between structure and agency from a historical perspective. Historical research now generally assumes that subjects act autonomously, constituting their social worlds (and their history) in the process. At the same time, however, their actions collectively create structures that channel further activity and determine it to a certain degree. Although it is possible to deviate from the trodden path, doing so would also constitute action outside (or even against) the collective consensus.

Treating the relation between the one and the many in such a – for the most part – balanced fashion also allows one to deal with chance, contingency and the ubiquity of unintended consequences. This approach assumes that subjects' actions are always entangled with each other, and the resulting opportunity structures are so complex that the consequences of any particular action are unforeseeable, which gives structures a dynamic momentum of their own.[10] This is also why structures are not contained conceptually within subjects and their actions; rather, they demand attention in their own right, especially in global history. In investigating the role of transregional connections through history, global history seeks to understand how such connections manifest themselves in what people think and do as well as how these thoughts and deeds reproduce them. As transregional connections congeal, they evolve into connective structures that privilege certain practices and modes of global exchange. Processes of globalization and entanglement are unthinkable in the absence of their structures. Action over great distances, crossing cultural and other boundaries, is a very uncertain business, so it typically conforms tightly to existing structures. After all, the metaphor of 'entanglement' is itself structural in that it draws attention to durable connection patterns. There are countless examples of the importance of transregional structures. The intercontinental pattern of commerce known as transatlantic triangular trade, for instance, bears in its very name its basic structure. Connective infrastructures are also vital to global history in that they result from the material manifestation of structures, and they go on to make certain actions possible or practicable. Transregional connections make use of a wide variety of such infrastructures, ranging from streets and railways to telegraph cables. The materiality of such structures testifies to the vast effort invested in their erection and maintenance, and it typically adds another persistent feature.

The following section will survey a concrete case study to show how global infrastructures – representing structures more generally – become active in the deeds of particular actors, how they entwine developments from seemingly disparate areas, and how this leads actors in different regions to become implicated in each other's actions. The case study chosen to accomplish these tasks is the construction of a tunnel through Mont Cenis from 1857 to 1871.

Mont Cenis

In an article on the latest communicational developments around Mont Cenis, the *Times of London* succinctly but accurately summarized in 1865: 'Between France and Italy, as poets sing and conquerors discover, nature has interposed the Alps and snow.'[11] The Alps present a natural obstacle between Italy and the rest of Europe that travellers throughout the centuries have described in truly monumental terms. In 1768 Laurence Sterne sent his character Reverend Yorick on a *Sentimental Journey through France and Italy*, and when the latter's coach left Lyon and gradually entered more mountainous terrain, Yorick complained:

> Let the way-worn traveller vent his complaints upon the sudden turns and dangers of your roads – your rocks – your precipices – the difficulties of getting up – the horrors of getting down – mountains impracticable – and cataracts, which roll down great stones from their summits, and block up his road.[12]

In the novel, Yorick was about to traverse the pass over Mont Cenis, which was the second most important route to Italy over the Alps after the Simplon Pass in Valais.[13] The first part of the story ends abruptly in a shelter somewhere near Modane just after Yorick's lament, as Sterne died shortly after finishing it and could not continue the tale. Many readers were unsatisfied with the fact that

Yorick's journey found such an abrupt end at the threshold of Mont Cenis, but this only inadvertently reinforced the image of the mountain as an arduous obstacle on the road to Italy.[14]

The Mont Cenis massif stands between Savoy and Piedmont, building a natural border between today's France and Italy. It has always influenced trade and other kinds of exchange between the two sides by, on the one hand, impeding the regular traffic of people and goods and, on the other, providing a rich array of (often very clandestine and perilous) smuggling trails. Savoy and Piedmont have been connected by a traversable pass over Mont Cenis since at least the early Middle Ages, made famous by Henry IV in 1077 as the Road to Canossa. Still, the mountain has long presented a formidable obstacle to regional trade and communication.

Many aristocrats on the Grand Tour in the seventeenth and eighteenth centuries could testify to the difficulties involved in crossing the Alps over the Simplon Pass or Mont Cenis. For them, negotiating the Alpine passes was less a matter of experiencing natural grandeur and more a 'technical affair requiring coaches to be dismantled at the foot of the pass and transported across the mountains with mules'.[15] It was even common for horsemen to be carried across the pass in litters, but even then they usually saw the journey as arduous and risky.[16]

Between 1803 and 1810 Napoleon had the mule path upgraded into a paved road.[17] While this improvement theoretically facilitated the traversal and made it feasible to cross year-round, it still made a lasting impression on many travellers. The countless switchbacks up the mountain remained so steep that a rather large team of horses was required to ascend it. Once the climb was finally completed, one had to descend the other side, which often put the coaches' brakes as well as many a traveller's nerves to the test. Only a few local coachmen would regularly cross the pass with their teams, and though the road was treacherous in the summer, it was utterly hair-raising in the winter. Sleds replaced coaches as the preferred mode of transport. One traveller reported even in 1866 in the *Gartenlaube* magazine:

> We would shiver even in midsummer when climbing at night, not to mention the winter, when the masses of snow would accumulate in thirty-foot-high drifts. At such times it is very difficult to keep the road free of snow. Storms would howl down the ravines with untold rage and would threaten, with the terrible whirling snow that would enshroud the mountain, to hurl anything downward that was not as fast as the mountain's own rocks. On such days traffic would grind to a complete halt.[18]

The railway inspector Henry W. Tyler, who surveyed the route across Mont Cenis in the same year, came to a similar, but considerably more prosaic estimation. A direct rail line was available to St. Michel, where travellers had to transfer to the pass road: 'The service by horses and mules from St. Michel over the Mont Cenis to Susa can be performed, during the summer season, with as much regularity as any other part of the route, but it is uncertain during the winter.'[19] Tyler substantiated this description with precise measurements indicating that a mounted courier would need between seven and forty-eight hours to make the passage.[20] The route was especially difficult to gauge in the winter, which gravely irked Tyler. For him, Mont Cenis was more than just an obstacle to regional transportation; it hindered postal service on an intercontinental scale. Indeed, in 1866 Tyler was travelling through France and Italy at the behest of the British government in search of the best route for the so-called 'Eastern Mail' – the postal connection to the Asian colonies. Already on the first page of his report to the British postmaster general, Tyler wrote that efficiency practically dictated that the route lead from London to France, over Mont Cenis to Italy, then to Egypt and finally on to India. In the mid-nineteenth century, then, traversing Mont Cenis was one of the most important global communication routes of the age.

Building the tunnel through Mont Cenis

There were other routes to Asia. The British artist and war correspondent William Simpson described other possibilities in the introduction to his Chinese travelogue in 1872. He dismissed all overland routes as impractical or simply too dangerous, beyond contemplation for any ordinary travellers. He did, however, remark:

> The way round the Cape of Good Hope is not yet quite given up; but it has fallen into disuse since the opening of the Suez Canal. In 1859 I made the voyage to Calcutta round the Cape in a sailing-ship; and with the exception of a very distant view of Madeira, we saw no land all the way from Start Point to the sand-heads at the mouth of the Hooghly. We did the passage in ninety days, which was considered to be a quick voyage.[21]

The course around the Cape remained the favourite of sailing ships trading in the East Indies, but postal and passenger traffic had switched to other routes even before the Suez Canal was opened in 1869. Captain James Barber confirms as much in his popular 1850 travel guide:

> The sea route round the Cape of Good Hope still has its partisans, in spite of the tedium, extra risk and absence of all objects of interest, which

necessarily distinguish such a voyage.ᵗ […] Still in this – the comparative infancy of the steam route – nine-tenths of those whom fortune may carry to India will prefer the most expeditious manner of proceeding thither.[22]

In the mid-nineteenth century this most expeditious route led across the Mediterranean, through Egypt to the Red Sea, and then to Bombay via the Indian Ocean, which was possible largely due to steam power. Railways increasingly marked the European landscape from the 1830s, which, from a Britannic point of view, made reaching the Mediterranean considerably quicker and easier. At the same time, the rise of steamships made navigating the Red Sea much more feasible than was the case with large sailing ships, and there were a few variations on the Egyptian route by the mid-nineteenth century. Although it was possible to take a steamship from a British port all the way to Alexandria, travellers increasingly cut across the Continent, riding the railways to a Mediterranean port, usually Marseille, and caught a steamer to Alexandria from there. By mid-century a well-organized infrastructure had emerged in Egypt to convey globetrotters from Alexandria to Cairo and from there through the desert to Suez, where they would catch another steamer to Bombay.

It is clear from the introductory passages of Tyler's inspection report that, when speed was a factor, there was little alternative to the route across the Mediterranean and Egypt in the 1850s and 1860s. Writing about the postal service, Tyler related, 'Under the existing circumstances, the fast mails between Great Britain and the East must necessarily pass through Egypt, and it is only requisite to determine at present the best route through Europe towards Alexandria and Suez.'[23] However, the sustained efforts to improve transportation infrastructure on the Continent meant that the parameters of speed and difficulty were constantly changing mid-century. Tyler and his contemporaries reckoned that rail travel on land was more than twice as expeditious as a sea voyage:

> But inasmuch as it is practicable to travel more than twice as fast on land, where good railways are available, as by sea, and with less risk of delay from stress of weather, it becomes advantageous to decrease the sea passage as far as possible, when this can be done without too heavy a cost, in order to effect a saving of time.[24]

Accordingly, the construction of new rail lines would change the course of the then optimal route. Marseille was initially the preferred waypoint for transfer to steamers headed for Alexandria, but the railway in Savoy was extended to Modane at Mont Cenis in the 1850s, which allowed overland rail travel to continue from the south slope of the Alps to Bologna. The rail line was incrementally extended to Brindisi in the early 1860s,[25] which provided for a much shorter sea crossing to Alexandria than was the case from Marseille. Moreover, Brindisi Harbour was improved in the late 1860s, making it even more attractive as a transfer port. Through these continual improvements to the European transportation network, the route over Mont Cenis gained steadily in importance through the 1850s and 1860s. As a result, Mont Cenis graduated from a regional obstacle to a global bottleneck, and overcoming it inspired ever more exertion.

The idea of boring a tunnel through the Mont Cenis massif had been brewing since at least 1841,[26] but actual plans to do so remained fruitless due to either technical difficulties or political impediments. With the impending start of construction on the Suez Canal, however, the endeavour became more urgent. Once the Suez Canal was operational, obviating passage through the Egyptian desert, traversing Mont Cenis would remain as the final major obstacle on the route between Europe and Asia. As a result, the parliament of the Kingdom of Sardinia-Piedmont in Turin voted in June 1857 to build a tunnel between Modane in Savoy to Bardoneccia in Piedmont.[27] It was difficult to estimate the project's cost and duration. Due to technical innovations in tunnel construction the tunnel was eventually completed much sooner than what had originally been assumed. In the event, the tunnel was completed only fourteen years later in autumn 1871 (Figure 15). With the opening of the Suez Canal two years prior, this step concluded the route from Great Britain to the Indian colonies possible completely under steam power. Reporting on his 1872 journey, William Simpson wrote that 'any one wishing to reach Egypt by the quickest means will go by the Mont Cenis Tunnel'.[28]

Simpson reported that it only took 21 minutes to pass through the tunnel[29] and that doing so was not particularly unpleasant. 'And there was no smoke nor any of the disagreeables which French authorities had prophesied.'[30] As the Mont Cenis Tunnel reduced the time required to traverse the Alps by a remarkable seven to eight hours, if one heeds Tyler's survey, it represented a significant improvement in transportation.[31] However, that this acceleration of regional travel, even with the increased comfort for travellers, was enough to justify the costly construction of the tunnel is doubtful. Rather, improving the route has to be considered in a supra-regional or even global context. In his investigation, Tyler compared the Italian route over Mont Cenis with the one through Marseille in France, and the former beat the latter by 35 hours and 15 minutes even using the pass road.[32] The tunnel only served to increase this advantage. As Tyler mentioned at the end of his comparison, though, improving the predictability of the journey was even more important than shortening the duration of one stretch:

I have pointed out that, in laying down the periods of time on which the above calculations have been made, it was desirable to fix, not the shortest

FIGURE 15 *Portal of the railway tunnel through the Mont Cenis at Modane,* Illustrated London News, *1871.*

time in which the journey could be performed, but such rates of speed as would admit of punctuality. [...] I am of opinion, further, that the time may be kept with greater certainty *viâ* Brindisi than *viâ* Marseilles, because – (1) land transit generally may be performed more punctually than sea transit – (2) the sea passage would be less stormy and more certain, inasmuch as the worst part of it, across the Gulf of Lyons, would be avoided – (3) there would be a special railway service through Italy.[33]

This passage makes clear that, for the British, coordinating the various legs of the journey, reducing the number of transfers and synchronizing the connections had priority. As Tyler explains, minimizing the time at sea by taking the Italian route greatly aided such coordination, which amplified the difficulties induced by the highly variable duration of traversing over the pass. The habitual delays on the Mont Cenis transfers could start a chain reaction that would continue all the way to the port of Brindisi. Therefore, building the tunnel not only reduced the time required to traverse the Alps but also served to significantly reduce the total travel time well beyond the few hours saved at Mont Cenis. Furthermore, passenger service as well as postal delivery profited greatly from being able to anticipate the duration of the trip and plan accordingly. The colonial administration, merchants, investors and, to a certain degree, the general public needed to know the pace of communication between Europe and Asia, when their letters would arrive and when to expect replies.

In fact, securing predictability in communication and transport was one of the key innovative virtues of steam technology in that trains and steamers were much more resistant to environmental influences than were their predecessors. Currents, wind conditions and the availability of fresh draft animals were no longer concerns. This was especially noticeable at sea. Even though Tyler mentions that sea transit was less predictable than land transport in the previous passage, steamships provided some measure of regularity and predictability in maritime transport, and the improvement was greater on longer voyages. Contemporaries often valued predictability over even speed as the principle benefit of steamships. For instance, a report that appeared in the *Times of London* on 4 April 1857 exemplifies this clearly with its applause for the *Simla*, a steamer returning from Australia. The *Simla* was the first steamship to set out for Australia in 1856, and its return proved that regular steamer service to the antipodes was possible. As the *Times* wrote:

> [We] congratulate the public, and in especial the mercantile community. Nothing could have been more injurious to the operations of trade than the extreme uncertainty which has too long characterized our communications with our Australian Colonies. Had there simply been tediousness and delay, so long as the delay and the tediousness were of regular occurrence the inconvenience, deplorable enough in all cases, might have been borne; but, with dates, varying from three months and a half to two months, it was well-nigh impossible to use forecast for the future. [...] Our merchants must acquire the satisfactory conviction that they are not venturing their fortunes on a mere hazard when they engage in Australian operations, or else the trade will fall into the hands of mere speculators. Regularity, and then speed, are the necessary conditions of commercial intercourse.[34]

Thus, regularity and dependability of communications and transport trumped mere speed, especially on longer journeys. The *Times'* article principally focused on the long passage by steamship to Australia, which in this case still passed through Marseille. In contrast to the earlier route of sailing around the Cape under wind power, the *Simla* made the undertaking predictable, and the advantage is also directly applicable to optimizing the European leg of the journey. These developments were followed closely in Australia, and many Australian newspapers reported on Henry W. Tyler's inspection and his final report.[35] Even while the Mont Cenis Tunnel was still under construction, the *Argus* in Melbourne published a recommendation that had arrived by post from England:

> It is quite worth the while of homeward-bound travellers to take this route [i.e. via Brindisi] into serious consideration. [...] Thus, in comparison with

the Marseilles route, there are the advantages of a shortened sea voyage, a saving of from twelve to thirty-six hours in the home journey, and the opportunity of seeing Italy.[36]

According to the author, completion of the tunnel would bring further time savings, so piercing Mont Cenis promised to improve predictability on a scale comparable with that achieved by the *Simla*. Shortening the connection to Europe improved the economic prospects of distant colonies like Australia, and the same applied to British India and other Asian regions that were closely tied administratively or economically to Europe. Consequently, construction of

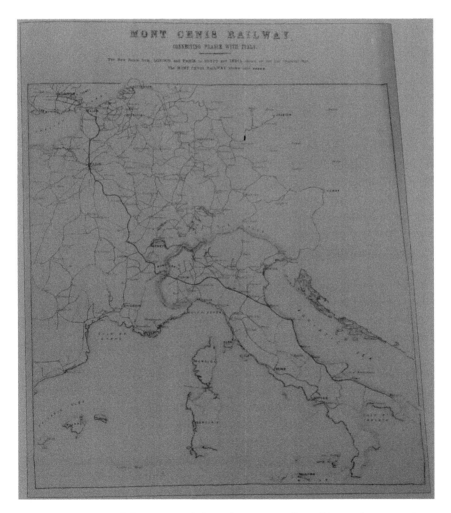

FIGURE 16 *Map of the course of the railway route through/over the Mont Cenis. Route Mont Cenis. Philip J. G. Ransom, The Mont Cenis Fell Railway. Truro, 1999, 15.*

the Mont Cenis Tunnel is best understood not as a regional or even European infrastructure project, but as one of global significance (Figure 16). In fact, the project of boring through an Alpine mountain was directly connected to the rise of steamships, the expansion of the European rail network, digging the Suez Canal and several other smaller infrastructure improvements, like expanding Brindisi Harbour. The reasons for building the tunnel and its seemingly inordinate importance are only intelligible in such a broad, integrated context. Every single development, construction plan and infrastructure project is connected to the others; they mutually conditioned each other, sometimes over great distances. The structural effects are unmistakable: the decision to dig a canal in Egypt bore concrete and definite consequences in the Alps. The construction of the Mont Cenis Tunnel aptly exemplifies the efficacy of emerging global structures (infrastructures, in this case) and their operative logics.

The Mont Cenis Pass Railway

The attempt to overcome Mont Cenis as an obstacle to global traffic reveals another particularity in that, parallel to the costly and technically demanding project of boring through the massif, there was another endeavour using very different equipment to achieve something similar. In reporting on his journey to China, in the course of which he passed through the tunnel already in 1872, William Simpson reflected on an earlier expedition that had taken him to Mont Cenis, but by other means. He writes:

> I had spent Christmas Day of 1868 in St. Michel, and I remember it as a very pleasant time. There was then a small English colony composed of the gentlemen who managed the Fell Railway over Mont Cenis. [...] The French railway ended at that date at St. Michel, and the Fell line began.[37]

The railroad Simpson referred to was the namesake of the British engineer John Barraclough Fell, who had developed a new propulsion system for railways on steep inclines, which he had successfully tested on a steep stretch of the Cromford and High-Peak Railway in Derbyshire in 1864. Fell wanted to lay a track based on his system over Mont Cenis and submitted his plans to the appropriate Italian commission, which approved the project. The British engineer then secured financing from investors and, between 1866 and 1868, eighty kilometres of track were laid along the pass road over Mont Cenis (Figure 17).[38] British journalist and alpinist Edward Whymper, who had achieved fame by being the first to climb the Matterhorn in 1865, described the pass railway thoroughly in his 1871 *Scrambles amongst the Alps*.

> The Fell railway follows the great Cenis road very closely, and diverges from it only to avoid villages or houses, or, as at the summit of the pass on the Italian side, to ease the gradients. The line runs from St. Michel to Susa. [...] From St. Michel to the summit of the pass it rises 4460 feet, or 900 feet more than the highest point of Snowdon is above the level of the sea; and from the summit of the pass to Susa, a distance less than that from London to Kew, it descends no less than 5211 feet! The railway itself is a marvel.[39]

Even before construction began, the plans had already attracted considerable attention. Captain Tyler, who submitted his complete report on the postal route to India a year later, also treated the feasibility of such a pass railway and attested to the practicability of Fell's designs. In fact, public interest was so great that Tyler's technical report was reproduced in full in the *Times of London* in 1865.[40] The project was so promising and Tyler's assessment was so positive that the *Times* questioned a few pages later in the same issue whether it was necessary to build the tunnel at all:

> It is rather too late now to raise the question, at any rate in the case before us, but [Tyler's] Report will certainly suggest an inquiry whether the Mont Cenis Tunnel was required at all. No doubt, when finished, it will make the line far more complete and the journey more expeditious, but the cost will be immense.[41]

The principal use that overcoming Mont Cenis was intended to achieve is perceptible even in this critical question about the tunnel's utility. Even though the author looked forward to the tunnel's completion and the 'more expeditious' travel that would result, he was not convinced that it was worth the effort. The pass railway would already secure predictability and connectivity. Given the noticeable progress in the tunnel's construction, the question as to what impetus remained to drive a track over the pass, however promising it may have been. In his 1866 report, Henry Tyler estimated the approximate date of completion for both projects, and he noted how difficult it was to foresee the course of construction in both cases. Nevertheless, he ventured some rough estimates, and he wrote in relation to the pass railway:

> The printed prospectus of the company refers to the 1st May 1867 as the date on which this railway is to be opened throughout from St. Michel to Susa for public traffic, and the calculations of the directors have been based upon that supposition; but to this end the line and works from Lanslebourg

to Molaret, 27 kilometres over the mountain, must be completed before the mountain is covered with snow in the autumn of this year[.][42]

This passage makes clear that Tyler did not rule out a delay of about a year, and the railway did in fact open in 1868. His estimate in regard to the tunnel proved similarly accurate in the event. Considering all the technical factors with a professional eye, Tyler expected the tunnel to open no earlier than late 1871,[43] which was only a few months too late. Tyler's appraisals are interesting in that they show that, even in the mid-1860s, it was possible to predict the tunnel's completion as well as the opening of the pass railway with respectable accuracy. Therefore, everyone – engineers, investors, those granting the concession – must have known that the pass railway would not operate for much more than five years in the best case. As soon as the tunnel was serviceable, no one would opt for the longer, more expensive and more arduous route over the mountain. In fact, the railway over Mont Cenis only operated for three years from 1868 until 1871.

For those responsible, however, the temporary nature of the endeavour did not disqualify it, as they were utterly desperate for a quick solution. As mentioned earlier, Tyler, the railway inspector, was in no doubt about the practicability of the pass railway. Eugène Flachat, a French engineer who had been occupied with overcoming Mont Cenis for years, wrote in the course of the tunnel's construction:

FIGURE 17 *Course of the Mont Cenis Pass Railway. O.A., 'Through and over the Mont Cenis' in:* The Gazebo 1866, 17, 269.

In our estimation passages across the Alps need not be abandoned due to delays in execution or the eventualities of projects already underway, because an immediate solution is required, even if provisional, so we must not hesitate to traverse the peaks under the open sky.[44]

Hence, Flachat thought it important not to restrict means of traversing the Alps to the long and dangerous construction of a tunnel and to find an immediate, if only provisional, solution to the problem. The correspondent for the *Times of London*, reporting directly from Lanslebourg, shared his opinion. His report, written on 2 July and not published in the *Times* until four weeks later on 29 July 1865, saw the pass railway as but one part of a larger transportation ensemble:

> As far then, as my opportunities and capacity permitted, I have examined, and with intense interest, the works of the tunnel and the railway on Mont Cenis, and have come to this conclusion, that so far from being rivals, they are necessary coadjutors, the one to the other. Such is the feeling which animates all concerned with the railway. The gigantic enterprise of piercing the mountain, and the means employed to effect the object, embody the highest poetry of genius. But when will this triumph of engineering be completed? Fresh obstacles may arise, and years may pass before that event takes place, and in this age, when infants go at a gallop, other lines of transit will be found, and the commerce which should have enriched the countries on either side Mont Cenis will be diverted into other channels. It cannot be long before the railway from Nice to Genoa is completed, and then, when a comparatively easy and rapid communication is opened from Marseilles to the north of Italy, what will become of the tunnel? It will remain a useless marvel.[45]

Thus, the correspondent saw the pass railway principally as a temporary measure to accomplish two basic objectives: first, to secure a regular connection across Mont Cenis until the tunnel was complete and, second, to sustain the attractiveness of the route in general in the interval so that the tunnel project would not lose value. His assessment reflects the spirit of a time when unforeseen and especially rapid technical progress – 'when infants go at a gallop' – and constant change were the rule. It may now seem doubtful whether, in light of the ease in travel and transportation gained through the tunnel, a pass railway was really necessary to keep interest in the overall route 'at a simmer' for the sake of the tunnel.

In terms of traversing the Alps efficiently and regularly until the tunnel opened, the Fell railway performed admirably. As Edward Whymper and others remarked, rail travel over the pass was not only a stunning feat of engineering, but also a thrill for the passengers. The steep inclines and many sharp bends made quite an impression:

> One looks down some three or four thousand feet of precipice and steep mountain-side. The next moment the engine turns suddenly to the left, and driver and stoker have to grip firmly to avoid being left behind; the next it turns as suddenly to the right; the next, there is an accession or diminution of speed from a change in the gradient. An ordinary engine, moving at fifty miles an hour, with a train behind it, is not usually very steady, but its motion is a trifle compared with that of a Fell engine when running down hill.[46]

The railway staff were also careful not to underestimate the risks of the route. Whymper recalled a conversation with a train engineer who had told him:

> Yes, mister, they told us as how the line was very steep, but they didn't say that the engine would be on one curve, when the fourgon was on another, and the carriages was on a third. Them gradients, too, mister [...] they didn't say as how we was to come down them in that snakewise fashion. It's worse than the [Great Indian Peninsular Railway], mister: there a fellow could jump off, but here, in them covered ways, there ain't no place to jump to.[47]

In spite of the route's demanding character, the pass railway was quite reliable, and there were very few accidents. With no small amount of pride, Fell reported on the railway's achievements at the annual meeting of the British Association for the Advancement of Science in 1870.[48] In two years and three months the trains had conveyed more than 100,000 passengers over the Alps, and the mail to and from Asia that the Mont Cenis Railway had been transporting since September 1869 was being delivered reliably and without major delays.

> Since the month of September last it has carried the accelerated Indian mail, and by the service thus established the delivery of the Indian mail in London viâ Marseilles has been anticipated by the Brindisi and Mont-Cenis route by about thirty hours. The ordinary mails between France and Italy have been carried by the Mont-Cenis Railway since its opening, and one night of travelling has been cut of the journey between Paris and Turin.[49]

The railway was able to operate profitably for most of its active life despite difficulties caused, for example, by heavy snow and floods.[50] Regardless, the pass railway ceased operation when the tunnel opened in September 1871. Although the *Illustrated London News* had mused that many travellers might prefer the route over Mont Cenis even after the tunnel had opened,[51] demand for pass railway trailed off into insufficiency by the end of 1871, although some travellers might have found the exciting trip over the Alps more attractive than the comparatively dull route through the tunnel. The Eastern Mail also switched to using the tunnel. The railway's operators reportedly inquired whether the local authorities might be interested in taking it over, but they refused.[52] In the end, the railway was dismantled, and the serviceable parts were sold to other concerns. The most obvious remnants of the short-lived venture are avalanche shields that were erected along the pass road.

Actors and structures

Everyone involved was aware that the pass railway was a temporary affair, and even the official concession to build and operate the track was only valid until the tunnel opened.[53] Investors, however optimistic they may have been, were certainly under no illusion about the serious financial risks involved in the project, which would hardly be able to recoup its construction costs despite annual profits. Instead, the railway's financing and construction is best understood in the context of supra-regional structures. Mont Cenis did not just separate Savoy and Piedmont or, later, France and Italy; rather, it was one of several formidable natural barriers between Europe and Asia from the perspective of transportation in the British Empire. In the English view, which sought the quickest possible route, the English Channel, the European landmass (including the Alps), the Mediterranean Sea, the isthmus in Egypt, the Red Sea and, finally, the Arabian Sea interposed themselves between the motherland and its most important colony in India. Most of these obstacles to communication and transportation were overcome in one way or another in the course of the nineteenth century. Railways transected the Continent regularly, without relying on draft animals, and steamships made punctual departures and arrivals possible in long-distance maritime travel regardless of wind, weather and sea currents. The Suez Canal promised to enable one to cross the Egyptian desert without having to transfer from one mode of transportation to another. Thanks to steam power, train and ship schedules could be regularized and coordinated with each other. Consequently, integrated chains of transportation and communication developed in the course of the nineteenth century along the routes to India and elsewhere. From about mid-century it was clear that the Alps would soon be the last remaining major obstacle on the India route. Unpredictability in crossing the Alps (especially in winter) affected the logistical synchronization of the entire chain, making Mont Cenis the weakest link in need of reinforcement.

Distant developments in the Egyptian desert and in the port of Brindisi, places that normally had little truck with snow-covered Alpine peaks, had reciprocating structural effects and brought actors in very different regions and circumstances into direct relations with each other. Such structural entanglements are especially pronounced in the provisional character of the pass railway, but the same applies to the tunnel – a European project of unprecedented scale. Decisions leading to the tunnel, too, are best understood in light of their position in a larger structural context. The plans and actions of very different actors were at once mostly independent of each other while still mutually implicating each other. The first to suggest building a tunnel through Mont Cenis was Joseph Médail, a developer. In the Kingdom of Sardinia-Piedmont, divided by the Alps, the king and other influential politicians, including Camillo Benso di Cavour, eagerly greeted the plan. The project started to gain momentum especially through the Belgian rail engineer, Jean-Marie Henri Maus, and plans for a railway from Genoa to Turin.[54] Rendering the vision of a twelve-kilometre tunnel feasible necessitated the expertise of many inventors and engineers, not least that of Paulin Talabot, a French railway pioneer who had played a key role in constructing the Suez Canal.[55] Even these few examples demonstrate that the decisions and actions preceding the tunnel's construction had been tightly intertwined with other locations and deeds from the very beginning, and the same applies to the pass railway. In the latter case, British rail engineers who had been busy building new railways throughout Europe, including in Savoy and northern Italy, provided the impetus. Thomas Brassey, John Barraclough Fell and other engineers who had earned their experience in the field proposed the idea of building a track over Mont Cenis[56] More keenly than most, they felt the sting caused by the gap between the cisalpine and transalpine rail networks, but their plans would never have been realized without the cooperation of the Italian government, coordination with those working on the tunnel and the support provided by Henry Tyler's reports.

The plans and actions of these and other actors were bound to each other by a larger structure, often without the conscious knowledge of those involved. Nonetheless, their decisions, investments, edifices and mutual adjustments created a structure and fed it with a mass of potential energy, which the structure then rearranged and allocated. In that sense, the structure itself, which in this case refers to the route to India and all of its many segments, gained a sort of agency. But on closer inspection, this is nothing more than the combined and rearranged agencies of the actors involved, which they could have hardly perceived at the moment. The structure developed a life of its own and directed human action.

Conclusion: Structures in global history

The example of overcoming Mont Cenis sheds new light on global history and the questions that drive it. It shows that transregional connections and the structures they induce affect the thoughts and deeds of local actors while simultaneously being products of these. This is not to say that regional and national considerations were irrelevant to the construction of the tunnel or the pass railway, which was not only to connect Savoy and Piedmont but also to improve the economic and political status of the newly founded Italy in Europe. Without considering the transnational knowledge and supra-regional interests of the actors involved, fully understanding their actions will remain impossible. The first element to consider are the British rail engineers who were on the lookout for new projects on the Continent in response to the increasing saturation of the domestic rail network, and who eventually found themselves working on improving the communication and transportation route between England and India. Enmeshed in a context of global structures, the actors involved made decisions whose consequences soon manifested themselves in several small Alpine villages. Beyond the obvious material traces that the tunnel and the pass railway left on the landscape, like the tracks, train stations, avalanche shields and a hole in the mountain, the construction projects triggered rapid social change. Hundreds of itinerant labourers would stay in the villages at the north and south tunnel entrances for years at a time, and they interacted with the local populations. Once the tunnel was complete, this region lay on a major European transportation corridor that brought considerable traffic as well as many foreign visitors to the area.

In the example presented here, regions at great remove from each other and the challenges they face are connected by subjects' actions, which themselves follow a certain, infinitely reproducible pattern. The repetition of individual acts congeals into structures, like travellers' choices of route and mode of transport, and the resulting structures then channel subsequent activity. Later travellers follow the same routes as earlier ones, and other actors offer services to assist them in the form of conveyances, shelter and other trappings. These many individual actions concatenate to benefit historical actors if they act according to a certain pattern, and they can even compel certain choices in particular situations. The types of benefit and compulsion can vary to include, for example, social, cultural or economic considerations. In the case of the decision to construct the Mont Cenis Tunnel, economic incentives dominated. The prime motivation in this example was the inclination to find the quickest and most efficient route for travel and postal transportation between Europe and Asia. This drive to optimize is what inspired the improvements along the route such that they complemented each other. No project could reach its full potential without certain other projects, yielding structural economic pressure to pursue certain courses of action. The resulting economic pressure bound various locations and actors together. Structures make an important contribution to the mechanics of global networking.

The worldwide telegraph network of the nineteenth and twentieth centuries discussed in the chapters on space and time provides another good example. Telegraphic communication also relies on a certain infrastructure that consists not only of certain practices but also of a stable material substratum, which in this case includes landlines, submarine cables and the attendant apparatus and stations. As already described, telegraphy was a new mode of communication that was based on dematerializing flows of information, which benefitted its users in certain ways. Most of these advantages were economic in nature, like rapid access to commercially relevant information and the means to more deftly control modes of transport, such as trains and steamships, but the telegraph was also valuable for military and administrative purposes. In order to realize these benefits in communication, users also had to come to terms with many disadvantages, and actions outside the predominant structure carried economic costs. The structure that resulted from the collective use of a new technology soon took on a life of its own.

Effective structures of very different kinds are, however, apparent at many points in this volume beyond those treating infrastructure. The case study on the voyage of the *Bounty* and the entanglements between the Caribbean and the colonial metropole are grounded in congealed administrative structures. The moon hoax relied on a structural flow of knowledge between Europe and the United States, and the hunt for Dr Crippen described in the next chapter took place in a broader context of colonial administrative structures. In each case it is necessary to understand structures in order to understand what opportunities historical actors faced in entangled global networks, how much freedom they really enjoyed in their decisions and what structural compulsions they encountered. Global entanglements constitute a kind of structure, and not in a merely metaphorical sense. The relation between these entanglements and global actors is one of the central questions of global history, and analysing it amounts to inquiring into the relation between structures and actors.

Notes

1   Translation from German original: 'ob eher die Verhältnisse den Menschen machen [...] oder ob nicht vielmehr umgekehrt der Mensch die Verhältnisse produziert [...] Eine Vorentscheidung für eine der beiden Positionen prägt die Bauprinzipien jeder Gesellschaftstheorie tiefgreifend; umgekehrt hinterläßt sie tiefe Spuren in der Physiognomie jeder historischen Darstellung.'

Thomas Welskopp, *Geschichte zwischen Kultur und Gesellschaft. Beiträge zur Theoriedebatte*. München, 1997, 39.

2 Translation from German original: 'Jede Epoche ist unmittelbar zu Gott, und ihr Wert beruht gar nicht auf dem, was aus ihr hervorgeht, sondern in ihrer Existenz selbst, in ihrem Eigenen selbst.' Theodor Schieder and Helmut Berding (Hrsg.), *Leopold von Ranke. Über die Epochen der neueren Geschichte. Historisch-kritische Ausgabe*. (Aus Werk und Nachlass, Bd. 2.) München, 1971, 60.

3 For an introduction, see Friedrich Jäger and Jörn Rüsen, *Geschichte des Historismus. Eine Einführung*. München, 1992.

4 Translation from German original: 'Nun hat sich unter dem Vorgebot sozialgeschichtlicher Fragestellungen in der jüngsten Historie das Wort ‚Struktur', speziell der ‚Strukturgeschichte' eingebürgert […]. Unter Strukturen werden im Hinblick auf ihre Zeitlichkeit solche Zusammenhänge erfaßt, die nicht in der strikten Abfolge von erfahrenen Ereignissen aufgehen. Damit werden – temporal gesprochen – die Kategorien der relativen Dauer, der Mittel- oder Langfristigkeit, werden die alten ‚Zustände' wieder in die Untersuchung einbezogen.' Reinhart Koselleck, 'Ereignis und Struktur', in: Reinhart Koselleck and Wolf-Dieter Stempel (Hrsg.), *Geschichte, Ereignis und Erzählung*. München, 1973, 560–70, 561–2.

5 Fernand Braudel, 'Histoire et Sciences Sociales. La Longue Durée', in: *Annales. Économies, Sociétés, Civilisations* 4/13 (1958): 725–53.

6 A prime example of Conze's brand of structural history is to be found in: Werner Conze, *Die Strukturgeschichte des technisch-industriellen Zeitalters als Aufgabe für Forschung und Unterricht*. (Arbeitsgemeinschaft für Forschung des Landes Nordrhein-Westfalen. Geisteswissenschaften, Bd. 66.) Köln/Opladen, 1957.

7 Translation from German original: 'So unzeitgemäß auch heute eine Fortführung der einst so beliebten wie verlästerten Geschichte der Bataillen und fürstlichen Häuser erscheint, so bleibt doch bestehen, daß Geschichte geschieht. Dies Geschehen aber ist mehr als bloße Entwicklung in der Zeit, es ist Entscheidung und Tat, Zerstören, Gestalten und Ordnen im Bezirk der uns als Freiheit erscheinenden menschlichen Möglichkeiten.' Werner Conze, 'Die Stellung der Sozialgeschichte in Forschung und Unterricht', in: *GWU* 3 (1952): 648–57, 652.

8 Giddens, *The Constitution of Society*.

9 For a nuanced and very helpful introduction to the relationship between structure and agency, see Thomas Welskopp: Thomas Welskopp, 'Der Mensch und die Verhältnisse. "Handeln" und "Struktur" bei Max Weber und Anthony Giddens', in: ders. and Thomas Mergel (Hrsg.), *Geschichte zwischen Kultur und Gesellschaft. Beiträge zur Theoriedebatte*. München, 1997, 39–70 und Ders., 'Die Dualität von Struktur und Handeln. Anthony Giddens' Strukturierungstheorie als "praxeologischer" Ansatz in der Geschichtswissenschaft', in: Andreas Suter and Manfred Hettling (Hrsg.), *Struktur und Ereignis*. (Geschichte und Gesellschaft, Sonderheft, Bd. 19.) Göttingen, 2001, 99–119.

10 Especially vivid examples of this are to be found in science and technology studies, where views on the relation between technology and human subjects have recently expanded to include actor-centric, structuring approaches, like actor-network theory. These are critically discussed in: Wenzlhuemer, *Connecting*, 50–6.

11 O.A., *The Times of London* vom 29. Juni 1865, 11.

12 Laurence Sterne, *A Sentimental Journey through France and Italy*. Basil, 1792, 149.

13 See Jean-Francois Bergier, *Pour une Histoire des Alpes, Moyen Age et Temps Modernes*. (Collected Studies Series, Bd. 587.) Aldershot, 1998, VII/39–49.

14 Cara Murray, *Victorian Narrative Technologies in the Middle East*. New York/Abingdon, 2008, 138.

15 Jan Pieper, 'Die Grand Tour in Moderne und Nachmoderne – Zur Einführung', in: ders. and Joseph Imorde (Hrsg.), *Die Grand Tour in Moderne und Nachmoderne*. Tübingen, 2008, 3–8, 4.

16 Edward Chaney, *The Evolution of the Grand Tour: Anglo-Italian Cultural Relations since the Renaissance*. London/Abingdon/New York, 1998, 330.

17 Tom F. Peters, *Building the Nineteenth Century*. Cambridge, 1996, 133.

18 Translation from German original: 'Auch im hohen Sommer fröstelt es uns, wenn wir Nachts hinaufsteigen, von dem Winter nicht zu reden, in welchem die Massen des Schnees sich oft zu dreißig Fuß hohen Mauern aufthürmen. In dieser Zeit hält es oft sehr schwer, die Straße frei zu halten. Der Sturm heult dann oft mit unerhörter Wuth durch diese Schluchten und droht in dem furchtbaren Schneewirbel, mit dem er den Berg umhüllt, Alles, was nicht fest ist wie seine Felsen, in die Abgründe hinabzuschleudern. An solchen Tagen stockt der Verkehr gänzlich.' Anonymous, 'Durch und über den Mont Cenis', *Die Gartenlaube* 17 (1866): 267–70, 267.

19 House of Commons. Parliamentary Paper 466, Tyler, Eastern Mails. Copy of Report from Captain Tyler, R. E., to Her Majesty's Postmaster General, of His Recent Inspection of the Railways and Ports of Italy, with Reference to the Use of the Italian Route for the Conveyance of the Eastern Mails, 1866, 6.

20 Ibid.

21 William Simpson, *Meeting the Sun: A Journey all round the World through Egypt, China, Japan and California, Including an Account of the Marriage Ceremonies of the Emperor of China*. London, 1874, 5.

22 James Barber, *The Overland Guide-Book: A Complete Vade-Mecum for the Overland Traveller*. London, 1845, 1–2.

23 Tyler, Eastern Mails, 1.

24 Ibid.

25 Ibid., 9.

26 Peters, *Building*, 133.

27 Ibid., 143.

28 Simpson, *Meeting the Sun*, 6.

29 Ibid., 13–14.

30 Ibid., 14. Construction of the Mont Cenis Tunnel attracted plenty of criticism in France due to fear about the Marseille route becoming insignificant.

31 Tyler, Eastern Mails, 12.

32 Ibid.

33 Ibid.

34 O.A., *The Times of London* vom 4. April 1857, 9.

35 Z.B. O.A., *South Australian Register* vom 1. Dezember 1866, 2; O.A., *Sydney Morning Herald* vom 19. Oktober 1869, 5.

36 O.A., *The Argus* vom 4. Juli 1867, 5.

37 Simpson, *Meeting the Sun*, 10–11.

38 Philip J. G. Ransom, *The Mont Cenis Fell Railway*. Truro, 1999, 33.

39 Edward Whymper, *Scrambles amongst the Alps in the Years 1860–69*. London/Murray, 1871, 49–50.

40 O.A., *The Times of London* vom 29. Juni 1865, 6.

41 Ibid., 11.

42 Tyler, Eastern Mails, 7.

43 Ibid., 8–9.

44 Translation from French original: 'D'accord avec nous que les passages des Alpes ne doivent être abandonées aux lenteurs d'exécutions et aux éventualités des projets en voie d'exécution, qu'il faut une solution immédiate, fût-elle provisoire, et qu'en conséquence il ne faut pas hésiter à passer les cols à ciel ouvert.' *Flachat Memoire,* zitiert nach Peters, *Building*, 155, Fußnote 173.

45 O.A., *The Times of London* vom 29. Juli 1865, 10.

46 Whymper, *Scrambles*, 52–3.

47 Ibid., 54–5.

48 O.A., *Report of the British Association of the Advancement of Science*. London, 1871, 216–18.

49 Ibid., 217.

50 Ransom, *Fell Railway*, 57; Peters, *Building*, 157.

51 O.A., *Illustrated London News* vom 10. Februar 1866, 146.

52 Ransom, *Fell Railway*, 62.

53 O.A., *British Association*, 216.

54 Peters, *Building*, 134–6.

55 Ibid., 143.

56 Ransom, *Fell Railway*, 12–22.

7

Transit:

Dr Crippen's getaway

Transit in global history

The basic units of observation in global history are global connections. The term suffers, however, from indiscriminate use, and it is generally confined to descriptive purposes, which sacrifices its conceptual potential. In the first case study on the Great Moon Hoax presented earlier, I discussed how to deal with the plurality of connections and how examining their interactions and tensions can lead to new insights about processes of globalization. Moreover, an analytically useful concept of connections has to allow for their role as historical phenomena in their own right with their own spatial and temporal facets. However, connections are generally conceptualized from their ending points, which is to say that most research focuses on actors, locations and objects that are already connected and maintain exchange relations with each other. These entities change and mutually influence each other by means of the transregional connections they maintain. Such approaches reduce connections to little more than intermediaries, in the sense of actor-network theory. There is contact at the termini, but otherwise they operate as practically inert transmission media. While connections can thus help to reconfigure relations between the connected entities and alter the meanings of those entities, the connections themselves are assumed to be incapable of creating new meanings.[1]

Research in global history, with its interest in the effectiveness of connections, must not settle for this view of connections as practically inert intermediaries but instead view them as mediators, to stay in the terminology of actor-network theory. Bruno Latour summarizes the function of mediators as follows: 'Mediators transform, translate, distort, and modify the meaning or the elements they are supposed to carry.'[2] That is, mediators meaningfully shape the relations between the connected entities. From the perspective of global history, this applies to all kinds of global and transregional connection. Such connections do not bring their termini into direct, unadulterated contact; rather, they interpose themselves as mediators, significantly affecting the mode of contact and, finally, the connected entities as well. Viewing connections – global and transregional connections in the case of global history – as mediators entails recalibrating the analytical focus of inquiries in global history. Connections have to be considered simultaneously with the connected entities and the reciprocal relations between them.[3]

Beyond their connective role, connections are also arenas of historical processes. They are possessed of duration, a temporal dimension, as well as a space of their own. Thus, connections display more or less conspicuous transit phases that should not be conflated with the connected entities and that operate according to their own rules. The term 'transit' evokes such things as transit depots and transit roads: certain places that witness high traffic volumes of people and goods, which characterize them to some degree. Some Alpine areas and the Suez Canal serve as intuitive examples, which is clear from the chapter on structures in that the focus is primarily on the transit zone, the latent entity, and how the traffic of subjects and goods affect it with their passage. In terms of global history, there is value in expanding this focus to include transit itself, which refers to the phase of motion from the perspective of the movers.

Transit denotes interstitial time and space. It is a historical setting in its own right where historical actors think, feel and act, where they experience decisive transitions and where meanings change. In short, life goes on in transit but under very different circumstances from those at the termini of a connection. It should be noted, though, that transit does not equate with transition. It is not a metamorphosis in the strict sense, not an incremental change that advances in proportion to the distance covered between the points of departure and arrival. Instead, transit is a stage of its own in which actors and objects passing through experience a peculiar combination of connection and disconnection and whose effects can be felt and remain active long after the transit period. The conditions of transit are also particular in that they feedback into the connections and affect their mediating qualities. As a result, how a given connection functions as a mediator depends primarily on the conditions of the associated transit. Every connection has a transit stage – whether global or local, long or short, slow or rapid. The principle applies just as well to immaterial, seemingly immediate forms of connection, like telegraphy. Only certain kinds of information are suitable for telegraphic transmission, and others are excluded. Telegraphy often omits context, messages can be forged, altered or lost in transit. Therefore, transit retains its mediating function even in cases of seemingly instantaneous exchange.

The role of transit is especially pronounced and discernible in connections over great distances and even more so in those involving the material transport of people and things. Such connections feature prominent spatial and temporal dimensions, which disclose new opportunities for observation. For example, trade goods can rot in transit, or their socio-cultural meaning can fundamentally change, as was the case in the chapter on actors, where the meaning of breadfruit changed dramatically between the South Sea and the Caribbean. Travellers, too, spend plenty of time in transit on board trains or ships, for example. They live in confined spaces with only limited opportunities to act and are confronted with extraordinary social situations.[4] For such historical actors, transit is a distinctive stage of their lives that operates according to its own rules and that alters the relation between the points of departure and arrival, changing the connection between the termini.

Maritime passages

To explore how transit affects its actors and its points of departure and arrival, I will consider an extraordinarily rich case study. The protagonists found themselves in transit on a steamer between two continents, situating the case in the broader field of maritime history. With its strong focus on maritime trade and communication, this field is an important point of reference in global history. Regional and transregional connections, such as crossings by ship, are some of the prime objects that maritime history investigates, but here as well the analysis too often concentrates on a journey's termini, privileging the connected at the cost of the connection itself. The field's preoccupation with port cities[5] as archetypical zones of contacts and melting pots is a good example. Ports are important gateways for transregional trade, mobility and intellectual exchange, making them excellent laboratories to observe what happens when different cultures come into contact. However, maritime history's gaze has not remained fixed on ports. Indeed, the concept of the seascape,[6] which basically refers to the region connected by a common sea, has expanded analytical horizons and integrated port cities into a broader regional context. Although Fernand Braudel's notion of a Mediterranean world connected by a shared sea inspired the idea,[7] it has since been applied, for example, to the Atlantic coasts[8] and the littoral of the Indian Ocean.[9] Port cities and the seascapes to which they belong are embedded in a dense net of transregional connections that begin and end there. In spite of some overtures by maritime history in this direction,[10] the field has long focused on the coasts

– the contact zones generated by such transoceanic connections. Maritime crossings tend to be viewed merely as conduits facilitating contact between A and B but not as historical settings in their own right. However important global connections might be for maritime history, what captures its attention are the points of departure and arrival, the connection's termini. Only recently have there been serious attempts to recalibrate the perspective. In many contexts, especially in relation to the maritime slave trade, ships and the crossings they make have started to attract more attention with new appreciation of the lives of historical actors on ships, like sailors, pirates and slaves.[11] Many of these studies view the ship as a historical setting of independent value and the crossing as a seminal period in the lives of those involved.

Maritime crossings have a pronounced spatiality and temporality determined by the layout of the ship and the duration of the crossing, which reinforces the claim that the connection must not be reduced to or conflated with its termini. Despite a host of technical innovations in the late nineteenth century that dramatically reduced the duration of intercontinental crossings, such voyages were lengthy affairs even in the golden age of steamships. For example, a voyage from Europe to India would commit passengers and crew to three or four weeks on board together. Even a crossing on the heavily trafficked route between Europe and North America over the North Atlantic would last about ten days. This time on board was not, however, 'downtime'; the passengers were not stuck in limbo.[12] On the contrary, life went on with passengers and crew sharing the (de)limited space on board for extended periods. Contact and exchange were virtually inevitable, and those on board were often presented with new, often unpleasant corporeal experiences regardless of personal background and social status.[13] Ships would foster new social networks[14] that might remain active well after the voyage. Cut off from the land, ships would become new normative spaces with their own rules, transgressions and conformity.[15] Hence, ship crossings are especially vivid examples of connections functioning as mediators.

As with all connections, maritime crossings converge with or diverge from other kinds of global connection, as I explained earlier with reference to the plurality of connections in the case of the Great Moon Hoax. Telegraph cables were often laid along important shipping routes, railways connected port cities with the interior, and radio signals 'whispered'[16] over the oceans, as in the current case. Ship crossings were embedded in a range of different connections, and the particular quality of transits results from their interplay. This becomes especially noticeable when considering the paradoxical relations between those on board ships and the rest of the world. On the one hand, transporting people, goods, animals and ideas around the world meant that ships were engaged in creating global connections. Their crossings are thus some of the basic constituents of globality and globalization. On the other hand, a ship in passage was in many senses an isolated space whose connection to the rest of the world was tenuous and fragile. Until radio technology became available on the big steamers at the beginning of the twentieth century, the only contact between a ship on the high seas and the rest of the world would consist of brief exchanges with other passing ships. Even with a radio-telegraph on board, a ship's connection to the world was often afflicted with limited capacity and frequent disruptions of various kinds, as will be seen later. Thus, while the passengers and crew were conjuring global connections in crossing from one continent to another, their own contact with the outside world simultaneously depended on a fragile, highly variable combination of connection and disconnection.

Crossings by ship are, therefore, appropriate cases with which to trace the socio-cultural meaning of transit. They lend themselves to investigation due to their clear spatial and temporal dimensions, and it will become clear how the conditions of any particular transit result from how it is embedded in various other connections. The following case deals with a notorious case of murder perpetrated in London at the beginning of the twentieth century. How the crime was perceived evolved as the steamship moved from the British capital to the mid-Atlantic, showing the particular character of transit in this instance. The spatiality and temporality involved in transit become tangible, as does the mercurial, malleable connection between the ship and the world.

The Crippen case

In the summer of 1910 an extraordinary murder case enthralled London.[17] Cora Crippen, an ambitious but largely unsuccessful singer who performed in music halls under the stage name *Belle Elmore*, had been missing since the beginning of the year. Her body was eventually found in the coal cellar of her house in North London. Cora was the second wife of Hawley Harvey Crippen, a homeopathic doctor from New York. After having to close his practice in New York, Dr Crippen took a position at Munyon's, a company that produced homeopathic pharmaceuticals. Munyon's sent him to London in 1897 to set up a new branch, and Cora accompanied her husband to Europe, where she hoped her singing career would take off. The doctor did what he could to support his wife, neglecting his own professional duties in the process, which caused to him leave Munyon's in 1899. Two years later he started a new position at the dubious Drouet's Institute for the Deaf, which sold questionable miracle cures to the deaf. There, Crippen met Ethel Le Neve, a stenographer, with whom he fell in love and started a relationship.

The Crippens' marriage had been dysfunctional for some time by the time he began his affair. The two were in many ways a poor match, and even the *Oxford Dictionary of National Biography* minces no words in describing Cora Crippen as a 'tipsy, plump, and unfaithful shrew with inordinate vanity and a miserly streak [whose] docile and submissive husband chafed at her dominion'.[18] As cutting as this assessment may be, Cora did indeed rage when she learnt of her husband's affair with Ethel Le Neve, which had been ongoing surreptitiously for years by that time, and she threatened to make it public. Then, in January 1910, Cora Crippen disappeared without a trace after a dinner party with friends at her house. When her friends started to ask after her, her husband explained that she had returned to America for health reasons. He later added that she had died there, but her friends became increasingly suspicious and eventually contacted Scotland Yard.

On 8 July 1910, more than five months after Cora's disappearance, Chief Inspector Walter Dew called on Crippen at his home in 39 Hilldrop Crescent in North London. Dew questioned Crippen as to Cora's whereabouts, but he failed to keep his story straight and eventually had to admit that he had in fact invented the whole story. Crippen then explained that his wife had left him, which had embarrassed him so badly that he fabricated another explanation. Although the inspector was initially satisfied with this new account, the interrogation perturbed Crippen, who then fled London with Ethel Le Neve. Upon hearing that he had absconded, the police searched the Crippen residence and eventually found a mutilated body in the coal cellar. Only a characteristic scar allowed the corpse to be identified as Cora's. She had been poisoned with hyoscine, a tranquilizer that is deadly at high doses and that Dr Crippen had been procuring in large quantities shortly before Cora's disappearance, as was later learnt.

Scotland Yard ordered an international manhunt for Crippen and Le Neve. Wanted posters appeared in newspapers throughout Europe, at first to no avail. The doctor and his mistress, who was apparently unaware of the suspicions against her lover, had fled across the channel to Antwerp, where they booked passage in Montreal on the steamer *Montrose*. The *Montrose* had been built in 1897 for Elder Dempster and Company; it was 136 metres long with a gross tonnage of 5440 tonnes. She had one chimney, four masts and was driven by a single propeller. Upon completion, the ship served as a passenger liner between Great Britain and her Canadian Dominion. After a stint as a troop transport during the Boer War, the *Montrose* was refitted for greater capacity. She was sold to the Canadian Pacific Steamship Company in 1903 and was able to carry 70 passengers in second class and 1,800 in third class. In the following years, the *Montrose* plied various routes across the North Atlantic, but principally between Great Britain, Belgium and Canada.[19]

On 20 July 1910 the *Montrose* left Antwerp harbour behind en route to Montreal. The passenger manifest included one Mr John Robinson and son, who had booked their second-class passage less than three hours before departure.[20] Crippen and Le Neve had thus boarded the ship in disguise, the doctor having shaven his beard and with Le Neve in short hair and an ill-fitting suit. The strange couple attracted the attention of Captain Henry Kendall only hours after casting off because of their odd behaviour. Kendall's suspicion grew, as Cora Crippen's murder had been a big story in the news. The captain perused the latest newspaper editions that had been brought aboard in Antwerp, searching for a picture of the suspects. Allegedly, he blotted out Dr Crippen's moustache in the picture using white chalk and compared the image with his passenger.[21] Once he had confirmed his suspicion, Kendall decided to inform the Canadian Pacific Steamship Company in Liverpool via radio-telegraph.

At the time, radio-telegraphy was still a relatively novel technology. The waning nineteenth century had witnessed countless experiments to transmit radio signals. The Italian Guglielmo Marconi was one of the many inventors and engineers working to advance the technology and file a patent on it,[22] but his real strength was as a businessman. In 1901 he began cooperating with Lloyd's, one of the most important shipping insurers of the time, which started restricting their policies to ships equipped with a Marconi radio-telegraph. This partnership provided Marconi's firm with a considerable competitive advantage, and radio-telegraph devices spread rapidly in the field of shipping.[23] In the opening years of the twentieth century, Marconi's devices were the most popular, counting the *Montrose* among the many ships equipped with one. Using that machine, Captain Kendall informed his employers in Liverpool of his discovery:

3 PM GMT Friday 130 miles west Lizard have strong suspicion that Crippen London Cellar Murderer and accomplice are among saloon passengers. Mustache taken off growing beard. Accomplice dressed as boy. Voice manner and build undoubtedly a girl. Both traveling as Mr. and Master Robinson. Kendall.[24]

The shipping line promptly passed the information about Crippen's location on to Scotland Yard, which itself had become the object of considerable criticism once news of Crippen's flight from London had become public. The failure of the police had even been the subject of parliamentary debate,[25] and Scotland Yard now mobilized immediately to atone for the blunder. Chief Inspector Dew embarked on the *Laurentic*, a brand-new steamer that would be able to overtake the slower *Montrose* before its arrival in Canada. While Dew took up the pursuit on the ocean, Scotland Yard was liaising with the Canadian Dominion Police to arrange for Crippen's immediate arrest, which occurred even before the murder suspect set foot on Canadian soil. As the *Montrose* was yet approaching the mouth of the Saint Lawrence River, Dew boarded the ship disguised as a pilot and apprehended Crippen.

The police, however, were not the only ones on Crippen's heels. In the early years of radio-telegraphy, its range was quite limited, and Kendall had sent his first message to Liverpool just before the coast fell out of the *Montrose*'s transmission radius. Every subsequent message between the ship and the British Isles had to be relayed by other ships, as was conventional practice at the time. With so many able to eavesdrop in the chain of relays, it is no wonder that the press soon learnt of Crippen's whereabouts. Newspaper editors around the world were able to follow the developments and embellished the fugitives' journey and the manhunt with melodramatic flourishes in their reports. One of many examples appeared in the 25 July edition of the *Daily Mail*:

> Friday afternoon must have been a dramatic time on board the ship. Ireland was a hundred and fifty miles astern, and Canada lay in front. The captain [...] sent a message – reaching Scotland Yard on Friday night – that he believed he had Dr. Crippen and Miss Le Neve on board. From the time that message was despatched a ceaseless, unobtrusive scrutiny must have been directed towards the couple, for a few hours later another message arrived from the captain to the effect that it was now known with certainty that 'Master Robinson' was in reality a woman.[26]

A host of news reports like this one detailed the voyage of the *Montrose*, informing a germinating global public about the dramatic events surrounding the doctor and his mistress. The fugitives, meanwhile, were oblivious, despite the 'ceaseless, unobtrusive scrutiny' until their arrest on 31 July. This extraordinary situation makes the role of the transit phase obvious. On the ship, Crippen and Le Neve were embedded in a unique cocoon of connections and non-connections, each of which shaped the contact between the ship and the world and helped to weave a unique transit situation.

Global interest

Thus, the flight of Hawley Harvey Crippen and Ethel Le Neve unravelled in a peculiar state of tension between global connection and isolation that in many ways recalls the examples presented in the chapter on space. Radio-telegraphy supplied the information that allowed the police and the public to keep tabs on the couple's location, and newspapers around the world took up reporting on the London murder case with renewed interest.[27] Not only did they trace the voyage of the *Montrose* and the pursuit of the *Laurentic* in detail (Figures 18 and 19),[28] they proceeded to revisit the entire case. Journalists returned to speak with the Crippens' former neighbours, they unearthed new information about Le Neve, and they tried to shed new light on Cora Crippen's failed singing career. Still, the media's fascination was concentrated on the ship itself, where Crippen and Le Neve were oblivious to the global media frenzy, slowing drifting into the police's trap. It was an odd and unprecedented situation. Tantalized by the media, a global public became increasingly captivated with the case, its attention fixed on a little ship in the middle of the Atlantic, where the doctor floated gradually 'into [the] clutch of the law'.[29] The transatlantic manhunt became a matter of global interest,[30] or, as John B. Priestley wrote in *The Edwardians*, a book on the *zeitgeist* around the *fin-de-siècle*, 'It was hot news indeed, something was happening for the first time in world history.'[31] Increasing global connectivity conspired with the fugitives' maritime seclusion, yielding a rare opportunity for observation. The media themselves frequently commented on the peculiarity and absurdity of the situation. On 26 July, the *New York Times* was already priming its readers

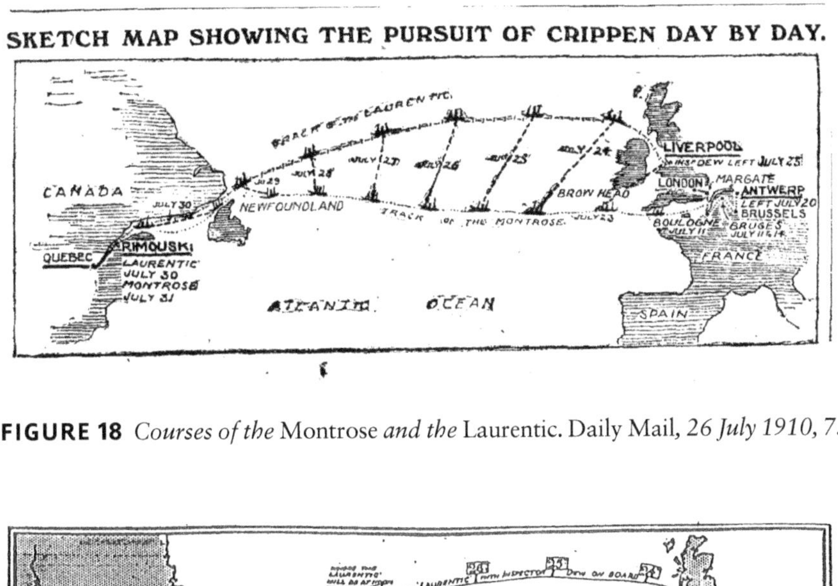

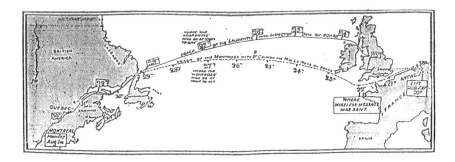

FIGURE 18 *Courses of the* Montrose *and the* Laurentic. Daily Mail, *26 July 1910, 7.*

FIGURE 19 *Courses of the* Montrose *and the* Laurentic. Daily Mirror, *27 July 1910, 3.*

for the inevitable and extraordinary conclusion of the case, '[Crippen and Le Neve are] steaming in almost pathetic helplessness towards the St. Lawrence and capture'.[32]

The *Daily Mirror* speculated on the following day on the other side of the Atlantic as to the 'sensations of the hunted Crippen and his companion caged in a floating trap'.[33] The paper even teased its captivated readers with a fictional monologue to represent their suppositions about Crippen's state on the ship:

> A harbour is the first place watched. One thirsts, one longs, when something is behind one, to get on to the sea. There's a sense of escape in the very wash of the environing waters! But the clever criminal resists the sea. Mysterious voices nowadays whisper across it; invisible hands stretch out upon it; viewless fingers draw near and clutch and hold there. Better a minor lodging in some big city. For I begin to see that the Captain has an odd look in his face.[34]

A few days later on 30 July, the *Daily Mail* quoted the Parisian *Liberté*: 'It is admirable and it is terrible. [...] [F]rom one side of the Atlantic to the other a criminal lives in a cage of glass [...] exposed to the eye of the public.'[35] On the same day, the *New York Times* ventured to explain why the media and the public seemed so obsessed with the case and the transatlantic manhunt. The author compared the situation to a play in that its setting and circumstances followed a standard dramaturgical rule:

> That rule is to let the audience or the spectators know exactly what is going to happen, while the people on the stage, or those of them upon whom interest is fastened, move forward to their predestined sorrow or joy in complete ignorance of coming events. The theory is that this gives to the observers a pleasant sense of superiority – of ability to see things hidden from others. That must be at least an approximation to the truth.[36]

Priestly, too, himself an author and playwright, saw a clear analogy to the fictional worlds of the theatre, writing:

> The people, who have a sure instinct in these matters, knew they had seats in a gallery five hundred miles long for a new, exciting, entirely original drama: *Trapped by Wireless!* There were Crippen and his mistress, arriving with a smile at the captain's table, holding hands on the boat deck, entirely unaware of the fact that Inspector Dew [...] was on his way to arrest them. While they were looking at the menu, several million readers were seeing their names again in the largest type.[37]

These comparisons to theatrical performances reveal a key aspect of the case in that the ability to observe the oblivious couple as flies on the wall equipped with contextual knowledge denied the fugitives was a fundamental component in the worldwide fascination. Both a smooth arrest and this specific mode of observation depended on secrecy. Any news about Crippen's identification or the pursuit reaching him on the *Montrose* would have broken the spell, as the *Daily Mail* related:

> Wireless messages are being flashed to and fro between the detective and the captain of the ship ahead. The tension in the Montrose must be extreme. How difficult it must be to keep the secret that a couple of passengers are suspect can only be realised by those who have made long voyages. If they are still at liberty life must be a tragic farce. In some mysterious way there may have crept among the passengers an indication that something is wrong.[38]

These excerpts of contemporary reports testify to the fact that public and media attention soon came to focus on the stage provided by ship's deck soon after Crippen's unmasking. However, the media had no access to the

FIGURE 20 *Photo series depicting how well-known costume designer Willy Clarkson turned a young woman into a boy. Jonathan Goodman,* The Crippen File. *London, 1985, 34.*

Montrose at the time. Rather, they occupied themselves and their readers with fictional internal monologues of the doctor's and speculation about the situation on board the ship. The *Illustrated London News* provided posterity with an especially vivid example of how outsiders tried to represent events on the ship by any means possible. The paper printed a photo series (Figure 20) intended to show how Willy Clarkson, a well-known contemporary costume designer, would disguise a young woman as a boy.[39] The jest was presented facetiously as advice to Ethel Le Neve, whose own disguise was apparently all too transparent. Soon, though, the media and the global public was freed from having to speculate about events on board the *Montrose*, when they obtained direct access to the confined space of the ship with the help of the radio-telegraph and the obliging Captain Kendall.

Caught in transit

On 28 November 1965, Henry George Kendall died at the age of ninety-two in a nursing home in London. He had led an eventful life, beginning his career at sea while still in his youth and suffering violence and abuse in the process.[40] In May 1914 he took command of the RMS *Empress of Ireland*, which collided with a Norwegian freighter in the same month and sank at the mouth of the Saint Lawrence River – very near where Crippen had been arrested four years prior. More than a thousand souls were lost in the disaster.[41] Kendall was catapulted from the deck and survived. Yet, his obituary in the *Times* made no mention of it.

> CAPTAIN HENRY GEORGE KENDALL, who in 1910 as master of the liner Montrose radioed to Scotland Yard that the murderer Crippen was on board, died in a London nursing home yesterday. He was 91.[42]

These brief words demonstrate to what extent Kendall was associated with the Crippen case throughout his life ever after. The demise of the *Empress of Ireland* paled by comparison. Kendall did indeed play a vital role in Dr Crippen's capture, which earned him the promised reward of 250 pounds sterling. Legend has it, though, that he never cashed the cheque and opted to have it framed instead,[43] which suggests that he also perceived the Crippen case as a landmark in his own biography.

Captain Kendall did all he could to keep the passengers on the *Montrose* in the dark about Crippen's identity and the ongoing pursuit. Thus, he greatly helped to construct and maintain the 'glass cage' in which the fugitives were trapped. Once he had seen through their disguises soon after putting out to sea, he started to control the flow of information between the ship and the outside world. He saw to it that no news regarding the Crippen case or the pursuit could reach the *Montrose* by radio-telegraph. Kendall gave the Marconi telegrapher a memo containing the following unequivocal instructions: 'All message re Dr. Crippen to any person or persons on board the above ship are to be filed, but not delivered, at the same time notifying me of their contents.'[44] He also made sure that the other passengers would not discover Crippen's identity in the manner he had, which would have ruined the operation. As Kendall explained later in a telegram:

> When my suspicions were aroused as to Crippen's identity I quietly collected all the English papers on the ship which mentioned anything of the murder, and I warned the chief officer to collect any he might see. This being done, I considered the road was clear.[45]

The captain informed but a handful of crewmembers, leaving everyone else on board the steamer – especially Crippen and Le Neve – clueless about the situation for the duration of the voyage. Kendall became the principal gatekeeper in control of all channels between the ship and the rest of the world. At first, he simply capped communication to and from the *Montrose*, which prevented any compromising information about Crippen from making its way on board and from escaping. After a few days, however, Kendall's interpretation of his role shifted as the media on land were running out of material to fuel the narrative. Detailing the transatlantic race between the *Montrose* and the *Laurentic* was no longer enough to keep the global public in rapture. For days they had been milking the story with every detail of the chase, recapitulating the murder case, explaining the miracle of radio-telegraphy to a fascinated public and providing a complete dossier on Captain Kendall. But they were in need of fresh material, and the most sensational angle about the events on board allowed only speculation.

Eventually, some reporters resorted to contacting Kendall directly via radio-telegram to the *Montrose* in order to press him for an update on the situation on board. Astonishingly, Kendall willingly obliged. The captain had been playing private detective from the beginning, ordering Crippen and Le Neve to be watched. He had also invited them to the captain's table under the pretence of a dinner to keep a closer eye on them.[46] After a while he even had them photographed clandestinely, and one of the resulting snapshots (Figure 21) is especially interesting in that it shows how perceptions of the murder case gradually changed over the course of the transit. Taken from behind the cover of a porthole, the picture shows Crippen and Le Neve from behind, the latter in her ill-fitting boy's suit, strolling along the deck. Neither their faces nor any other identifying features are visible. The image was irrelevant to the

FIGURE 21 *Crippen and Le Neve aboard the* Montrose, *secretly photographed through a porthole. Jonathan Goodman,* The Crippen File. *London, 1985, 38.*

impending arrest and had no value as evidence in the case. Nonetheless, the snapshot fascinated the media, so it reveals much more about Kendall's actual and perceived role in the affair than about the two subjects. Indeed, the photo's subjects increasingly became merely passive objects as Kendall and others became the authors of the story.

However, Kendall began to radically reinterpret his role as gatekeeper a few days before the planned arrest. Responding to the reporters' requests, he started to write his own telegraphic reports to the media in which he described how he had discovered the fugitives' identity, how he had confirmed his suspicions and how he was managing to keep the two in the dark. Kendall related his various observations in meticulous detail over many lines, and countless newspapers appreciatively reproduced his messages verbatim in part or whole. On 30 July the *Times* printed a telegram from Kendall that had originally been sent to the *Daily Mail*:

I am still confident Crippen and Le Neve on board. Crippen has shaved his moustache, and is growing a beard. He has no suspicion that he has been discovered. Passengers are also ignorant of the identity of the couple. Le Neve refrains from talking. They have no baggage. They are always together and very reticent with other passengers. Crippen has stated that he is a great traveller and has been many times in the United States. They spend most of their time reading books obtained from the ship's library. They are very sleepless at night. [...] They spend much time in their cabin. Both appear bright in presence of other passengers, but show signs of worry when alone together. [...] This is the first account that has been transmitted from this ship to any paper.[47]

In this telegram Kendall was mostly concerned with describing the fugitives' behaviour and routines in factual terms, with emotional and dramatic elements shining faintly through. For example, his mention of their insomnia could be intended as a sign of anxiety and perhaps of a guilty conscience, but this report was quite terse and factual overall. His next message, however, displayed a very different tone and intention. Indeed, the *Daily Mail* printed a telegram the very next day that was dripping voyeuristic detail:

I warned [my chief officer] that it must be kept absolutely quiet, as it was too good a thing to lose, so we made a lot of them, and kept them smiling. [...] Le Neve has the manner and appearance of a very refined, modest girl. [...] Her suit is anything but a good fit. Her trousers are very tight about the hips. [...] They have been under strict observation all the voyage, as if they smelt a rat, he might do something rash. I have not noticed a revolver in his hip pocket. [Crippen] continually shaves his upper lip, and his beard is growing nicely. I often see him stroking it and seeming pleased, looking more like a farmer every day. [...] He sits about on the deck reading, or pretending to read, and both seem to be thoroughly enjoying all their meals [...]. [Crippen] is now busy reading 'The Four Just Men', which is all about a murder in London and £1000 reward.[48]

Kendall had by this point abandoned any pretence of playing the dispassionate observer. He was intentionally feeding the suspense, noted his own role in the affair and the register of his expression is very colloquial. He intimated that Crippen might have been armed, despite the lack of any corroborating observation. Mentioning *The Four Just Men* as Crippen's choice of literature was the pinnacle in that Kendall was thereby alluding to Crippen's own situation. In a later telegram the captain remarked that he had covertly searched the fugitives' cabin, which led him to discover that Le Neve was washing her face in the morning with a piece of her underclothes.[49] These messages are evidence that Kendall had reinterpreted his role as captain and gatekeeper. Indeed, he did whatever he could to supply the outside world with any available information – no matter how trivial or salacious – and inching himself ever closer to centre stage in the drama.

The arrest

Kendall, along with a few crewmembers and radio-telegraphers, was not the only gatekeeper, and he was not the only one supplying the global public with information about Crippen and Le Neve. Once Crippen had fled London, Scotland Yard became the subject of plenty of mockery and derision for its imputed incompetence. However, the force was soon presented with the opportunity to redeem itself with the help of the very same media that had been ridiculing it. Fired by the tabloids, the public's anticipation for the day of the arrest reached a fever pitch. Days before the ship's arrival, lodgings around the mouth of the Saint Lawrence were already completely full of journalists and prying onlookers.[50] Scotland Yard painstakingly planned the crescendo and left nothing to chance – not only in terms of the apprehension but also of the media's reporting. It was important that their police work go over well. A steamboat was chartered for fifty journalists on the day of the arrest, but the *Eureka* was to wait out of sight of the *Montrose* until the arrest had been successfully completed. Then it was to approach the *Montrose* for the journalists to board and do their work.

The protagonist on the side of the law was Chief Inspector Walter Dew, the same officer who had investigated the disappearance of Cora Crippen in London.[51] Once Crippen had been discovered on board the *Montrose*, Dew boarded the *Laurentic* in Liverpool to intercept the fugitives before they could set foot on Canadian soil. Dew had been selected for this job because he was the only officer to have actually met the doctor and was thus able to positively identify him. Dew and Captain Kendall were in continuous contact by radio-telegraph during the Atlantic crossing and the *Montrose*'s anchorage in the mouth of the Saint Lawrence. Dew's role as officer-in-charge was no secret to the press and public:

> Captain Kendall, of the Montrose, kept Inspector Dew thoroughly informed of his disguised passengers' movements during Friday afternoon and Saturday, and the detective despatched instructions to guard against the possible use of poison or other means of suicide. This news and a hundred alarmist rumours intensified curiosity and induced the Press correspondents to sit up all Saturday night at Father Point with a special watchman placed over Inspector Dew![52]

As the *Montrose* approached the mouth of the Saint Lawrence, Dew and his Canadian counterparts mobilized. Disguised as pilots, they were rowed to the steamer and boarded. The *Times* revelled in the details of the arrest. Crippen and Le Neve were on deck with Dr Stuart, the ship's physician, and wondered about the conspicuously large number of pilots making their way towards the *Montrose*. Once on board they slowly and seemingly by chance approached Crippen and Le Neve; 'Then as Inspector Dew got a good, quick look at Crippen and the girl he gave the preconcerted signal, and the constables made the arrest.'[53] At this point the *Eureka* was ordered to pull up alongside to allow the press to embark, conduct interviews and take photographs.[54] The reporters proceeded to occupy the telegraph room of the *Montrose* for several hours in order to inform their various employers about the details of Crippen's arrest. Thanks to radio-telegraphy, the news spread so fast that even newspapers in Australia, which, after all, was half a day ahead of Montreal, were able to print the story in the 1 August editions.[55]

After the arrest, Crippen was detained in Quebec City while he awaited extradition to Great Britain under the *Fugitive Offenders Act of 1881*. In mid-August Crippen and Le Neve were placed on board the SS *Megantic* and returned to London, where they appeared in court in separate trials. After long and elaborate proceedings,[56] Hawley Harvey Crippen was found guilty of murdering his wife Cora and sentenced to death by hanging.[57] The sentence was executed on 23 November 1910 in London's HM Prison Pentonville. For

FIGURE 22 *Ethel Le Neve poses as Master Robinson for the studio camera.* Daily Mirror, *21 November 1910, 15.*

her part, Ethel Le Neve was acquitted and, on the day of Crippen's hanging, emigrated to North America.

However, a large-format picture of Ethel Le Neve had appeared a few days prior in the *Daily Mirror*[58] and in *Lloyd's Weekly News*[59] that depicted her in her poorly fitting suit (Figure 22). This picture was not one of Kendall's photos taken in secret on the *Montrose*, but a carefully staged dupe taken in a studio. The story goes that she appeared in the Bow Street police station after her acquittal and asked if she could borrow the suit she had worn during the voyage. She had apparently been offered a handsome sum to don her costume once again and pose as Master Robinson so that certain scenes on the *Montrose* could be re-enacted and photographed.[60] The printed photograph showed an androgynous Ethel Le Neve sitting on a chair, staring off into the distance. The *Daily Mirror* even ventured to detect a (pitifully strained) similarity between Le Neve and her lover: 'It will be noticed that she bears a strong likeness to Dr. Crippen.'[61]

Conclusion: Transit in global history

The photographic re-enactment of Le Neve's time on the *Montrose* clearly demonstrates the tension between connection and non-connection in cases of transit by sea. Radio technology and Captain Kendall's intervention allowed an emerging global public to follow events on the ship almost immediately, but such contact was fragile and feeble. The radio-telegraph had a limited range and transmission capacity, enabling the captain to act as gatekeeper and control connectivity to the outside world by this medium. As a result, the ship's integration in a globalized world was unbalanced and incomplete in that in was unidirectional. Crippen, Le Neve, the other passengers and even most of the crew were unaware of the media frenzy surrounding the voyage of the *Montrose*. Kendall fed the media with soupçons of information about the situation, whetting their insatiable appetites for sensational news and scandal – an appetite that Kendall's radio-telegraphic morsels and fuzzy images could not satisfy. Only in the retrospective re-enactment did the public finally gain full access to the transit area.

The story of Dr Crippen's flight and eventual arrest is an extraordinary historical episode, but it nonetheless can serve the purposes of history by revealing how ships represent influential, transformative transit settings. A ship on the high seas is not detached from the rest of the world, from time and space, as a thoroughly self-contained unit, as Michel Foucault's famous phrase calling the ship the 'heterotopia *par excellence*' would suggest.[62] On the contrary, the especially pronounced spatial and temporal dimensions of sea voyages disclose the connections that result from such voyages' mediation. This, in turn, allows us to chart what they mean(t) to the people and places involved. That one voyage on the *Montrose* was a long, distinct phase in the lives of those concerned, those whose thoughts and actions were confined to a restricted and restrictive physical and social space. In this sense, the passengers were simultaneously cut off from the rest of the world and embedded in a mesh of diverse global connections. In this case, too, the multiplicity of transregional connections, which was already discussed more thoroughly earlier, becomes visible, for it created a unique transit situation.

The Crippen case illustrates how and why history, especially global history, ought to view transregional connections as mediators. The scene of the actual crime was London. The prime suspect was American and sought to flee across the Atlantic back to North America. The passage by steamship would conventionally be viewed as a mere interlude bridging two more interesting locations. This case, however, makes eminently clear that a seminal chapter of the story unfolded in transit and how the particular configuration of the transit phase made this possible in the first place. Thanks to the story's high drama and the abundant documentary evidence it yielded, we can precisely reconstruct what the transit phase meant and how the connection came to life as a historical setting in its own right. As is the case with a few other recent contributions to the literature in this area,[63] analysing this case shows that sea voyages must be seen as historical places and times that exert decisive influences on the lives of the people on board. When one recalibrates one's analytical focus so that the ship and the world, the connection and the connected, are viewed simultaneously, the significance of transit is simply striking. As mentioned earlier, sea voyages are particularly apt objects for such an integrated perspective because they bring the spatial and temporal dimensions of transit into particularly stark relief. This feature was especially pronounced in the preceding section treating the mutiny on the *Bounty*, which focused on the role of historical actors. After all, Greg Dening had good reason to depict the mutiny as a performance and the *Bounty* as a stage.[64] Still, the insights about voyages at sea derived here are more broadly applicable, and they contribute to a more nuanced understanding of global connections in a more general sense.

Although not all connections display spatial and temporal dimensions as definitely as do intercontinental crossings, they all possess spatial and temporal characteristics that lend transit a particular form with a particular mediating role. Processes of contact and exchange exhibit their own spaces and times beyond the deck of a steamship. The space of a given connection permeates the way in which places and people are and can be connected, what can be communicated or not, and how stable that connection will prove to be. A connection's time profoundly affects matters of synchronicity and the interactions with other connections, as the case of telegraphic connections illustrates. While the spatial and temporal elements of transit are relatively easy to grasp when imagining the circumstances on board a hundred-metre ship during a voyage of several weeks, telegraphy complicates them. But telegraphic connections, too, are possessed of spatial and temporal features (which should not be confused with their relations to space and time, a topic discussed more thoroughly in the previous chapters). In the first place, a telegraphic connection extends in material terms beyond its mere wires and electricity to include paper telegrams and the telegraph office. Moreover, the electrons displaced in the process also have a space of their own – a very limited one indeed – in which certain kinds of information can be transmitted and others have no place, so to speak. The temporal dimension of telegraphic connections is just as unmistakable in relation, for example, to other kinds of connection and the virtual immediacy of telegraphy, as was discussed in the chapter on time. Thus, telegraphic connections also display a distinct transit phase that is responsible for their mediating character. The concept of transit can also be generalized beyond the context of sea voyages and other types of travel and transportation, which indicates that something important happens in connections: they are historical settings in their own right, and they are most usefully conceptualized in global history as mediators rather than as mere intermediaries.

Notes

1 See, for example, Bruno Latour, *Reassembling the Social: An Introduction to Actor-Network-Theory.* (Clarendon Lectures in Management Studies.) Oxford, 2005, 39.

2 Ibid.

3 Martin Dusinberre and Roland Wenzlhuemer, 'Editorial – Being in Transit: Ships and Global Incompatibilities', in: *Journal of Global History* 11/2 (2016): 155–62.

4 See Roland Wenzlhuemer and Michael Offermann, 'Ship Newspapers and Passenger Life aboard Transoceanic Steamships in the Late Nineteenth Century', in: *Transcultural Studies* 8/1 (2012): 79–80; Johanna de Schmidt, 'This Strange Little Floating World of Ours. Shipboard Periodicals and Community-Building in the "Global" Nineteenth Century', in: *Journal of Global History* 11/2 (2016): 229–50.

5 For example, see Dilip K. Basu (Hrsg.), *The Rise and Growth of the Colonial Port Cities in Asia.* (Monograph Series/Center for South and Southeast Asia Studies, Bd. 25.) Lanham, 1985; Frank Broeze (Hrsg.), *Brides of the Sea: Port Cities of Asia from the 16th–20th Centuries.* Honolulu, 1989; Ders. (Hrsg.), *Gateways of Asia: Port Cities of Asia in the 13th–20th Centuries.* London,

1997; Gordon Jackson, Lewis R. Fischer and Adrian Jarvis (Hrsg.), *Harbours and Havens: Essays in Port History in Honour of Gordon Jackson*. (Research in Maritime History, Bd. 16.) St. John's, 1999; Sandip Hazareesingh, 'Interconnected Synchronicities. The Production of Bombay and Glasgow as Modern Global Ports c. 1850–1880', in: *Journal of Global History* 1/4 (2009): 7–31.

6   Reinwald and Deutsch (Hrsg.), *Space on the Move*; Bentley, Bridenthal and Wigen (Hrsg.), *Seascapes*.

7   Fernand Braudel, *La Méditerranée et le Monde Méditerranéen à l'Époque de Philippe II*. Paris, 1949.

8   O'Rourke and Williamson, *Globalization and History*; Linebaugh and Rediker, *The Many-Headed Hydra*; Armitage and Braddick (Hrsg.), *The British Atlantic World, 1500–1800*; Gilroy, *The Black Atlantic*; Rediker, *Villains of all Nations*.

9   Kenneth McPherson, *The Indian Ocean: A History of People and the Sea*. Oxford, 1993; Michael Pearson, *The Indian Ocean*. London, 2003; Sugata Bose, *A Hundred Horizons: The Indian Ocean in the Age of Global Empire*. Cambridge, 2006; Himanshu Ray and Edward Alpers (Hrsg.), *Cross Currents and Community Networks: The History of the Indian Ocean World*. Oxford, 2007; Markus Vink, 'Indian Ocean Studies and the New "Thalassology"', in: *Journal of Global History* 2/1 (2007): 41–62; Pier Larson, *Ocean of Letters: Language and Creolization in an Indian Ocean Diaspora*. Cambridge, 2009.

10 For a recent example, see Michael B. Miller, *Europe and the Maritime World: A Twentieth Century History*. Cambridge, 2012.

11 Most of these studies focus on the crew's professional life, on pirates and on the significance of the 'Middle Passage' in the transatlantic slave trade. See, for example, Linebaugh and Rediker, *Many-Headed Hydra*; Jonathan Hyslop, *Steamship Empire: Asian, African and British Sailors in the Merchant Marine c. 1880–1945*, in: *Journal of Asian and African Studies* 44/1 (2009): 49–67; Frances Steel, *Oceania under Steam: Sea Transport and the Cultures of Colonialism, c. 1870–1914*. Manchester 2011; Marcus Rediker, *Between the Devil and the Deep Blue Sea: Merchant Seamen, Pirates and the Anglo-American Maritime World, 1700–1750*. Cambridge 1993; Ders., *Villains of all Nations*; Michael Kempe, *Fluch der Weltmeere. Piraterie, Völkerrecht und Internationale Beziehungen, 1500–1900*. Frankfurt am Main 2010; Ders., '"Even in the Remotest Corners of the World". Globalized Piracy and International Law, 1500–1900', in: *Journal of Global History* 5/3 (2010): 353–72; Emma Christopher, Cassandra Pybus and Marcus Rediker (Hrsg.), *Many Middle Passages: Forced Migration and the Making of the Modern World*. Berkeley 2007; Maria Diedrich, Henry L. Gates and Carl Pedersen (Hrsg.), *Black Imagination and the Middle Passage*. Oxford 1999; Marcus Rediker, *The Slave Ship: A Human History*. London 2007; Stephanie E. Smallwood, *Saltwater Slavery: A Middle Passage from Africa to American Diaspora*. Cambridge 2007; Paul Ashmore, 'Slowing Down Mobilities: Passengering on an Inter-War Ocean Liner', in: *Mobilities* 8/4 (2013): 595–611.

12 Wenzlhuemer and Offermann, *Ship Newspapers and Passenger Life*.

13 Tamson Pietsch, 'Bodies at Sea: Travelling to Australia in the Age of Sail', in: *Journal of Global History* 11/2 (2016): 209–28.

14 Leonard Woolf, *Growing: An Autobiography of the Years 1904 to 1911*. London, 1961, 12.

15 See, for example, de Schmidt, 'This Strange Little Floating World of Ours'.

16 O.A., *Daily Mirror* vom 27. Juli 1910, 7.

17 Unless otherwise indicated, the reconstructions of Crippen's biography and the murder case are based on: Filson Young, *The Trial of Hawley Harvey Crippen*. Edinburgh, 1950; Julie English Early, 'Technology, Modernity and "The Little Man". Crippen's Capture by Wireless', in: *Victorian Studies* 39/3 (1996): 309–37; Jonathan Goodman, *The Crippen File*. London, 1985; Nicolas Connell, *Walter Dew: The Man Who Caught Crippen*. Stroud, 2005; Ders., *Dr. Crippen: The Infamous London Cellar Murder of 1910*. Stroud, 2013; Martin Fido, 'Crippen, Hawley Harvey (1862–1910)', in: *Oxford Dictionary of National Biography 2004*. Version January 2011, in: URL = http://www .oxforddnb.com/view/article/39420 (accessed: 21 June 2016); Tom Cullen, *Crippen: The Mild Murderer*. London, 1977; Erik Larson, *Thunderstruck*. New York, 2007; O.A., 'Trial of Crippen, Hawley Harvey. October 1910', in: *Old Bailey Proceedings Online*. Version 7.2, in: URL = http://www.oldbailey online.org/browse.jsp?id=def1-74-19101011&div=t19101011-74 (accessed: 21 June 2016).

18 Fido, *Crippen*.

19 O.A., 'Ship Descriptions – M', in: *The Ships List*. Version 25. September 2008, in: URL = http://www.theshipslist.com/ships/descriptions/ShipsMM. shtml (accessed: 21 June 2016).

20 O.A., *Daily Telegraph* vom 25. Juli 1910; Goodman, *Crippen File*, 28.

21 Although this is the most popular account of how Crippen was unmasked, there are other variants. The *Berliner Tageblatt*, for example, reported that a ship's steward who had lived in Crippen's neighbourhood in London recognized him. O.A., *Berliner Tageblatt* vom 30. Juli 1910, 5.

22 For a short depiction of radio-telegraphy from the perspective of the history of technology, see Huurdeman, *The Worldwide History of Telecommunications*, 199–216.

23 Hugill, *Global Communications since 1844*, 93–4.

24 Goodman, *Crippen File*, 28.

25 *Hansard*, HC Deb, Bd. 19, CC1240-1 vom 20. Juli 1910.

26 O.A., *Daily Mail* vom 25. Juli 1910, 7.

27 This section generally relies on excerpts and quotations from British and American newspapers, which displayed the most intense interest and had the most immediate access to the events. These sources include especially the *Daily Mail, Daily Mirror, Times of London*, and *New York Times*. However, newspapers around the world followed the Crippen case, including *Le Matin, Die Neue Zeitung* and the *Berliner Tagblatt* in Europe; the *Los Angeles Times* on the American west coast; the *Times of India* in Asia; and the *Sydney Morning Herald* in Australia, to name a few.

28 Many newspapers printed maps following the courses of the *Montrose* and the *Laurentic*. See, for example O.A., *Daily Mirror* vom 27. Juli 1910, 3; Dies. vom 26. Juli 1910, 7.

29 O.A., *Los Angeles Times* vom 29. Juli 1910, 1.

30 O.A., *Daily Mail* vom 30. Juli 1910, 6.

31 John B. Priestley, *The Edwardians*. New York, 1970, 197.

32 O.A., *New York Times* vom 26. Juli 1910, 6; Goodman, *Crippen File*, 33.

33 O.A., *Daily Mirror* vom 27. Juli 1910, 7.

34 Ibid.

35 O.A., *Daily Mail* vom 30. Juli 1910, 6.

36 O.A., *New York Times* vom 30. Juli 1910, 6; Goodman, *Crippen File*, 37.

37 Priestley, *Edwardians*, 200.

38 O.A., *Daily Mail* vom 25. Juli 1910, 7; Goodman, *Crippen File*, 29.

39 Goodman, *Crippen File*, 34.

40 Larson, *Thunderstruck*, 1–2.

41 O.A., *Times of London* vom 1. Juni 1914, 8.

42 O.A., *Times of London* vom 29. November 1965, 12.

43 Larson, *Thunderstruck*, 376.

44 Goodman, *Crippen File*, 30.

45 O.A., *Daily Mail Sonderausgabe* vom 31. Juli 1910 und O.A., *Daily Mail* vom 1. August 1910, 5.

46 Ibid.

47 O.A., *Times of London* vom 30. Juli 1910, 6.

48 O.A., *Daily Mail* vom 1. August 1910, 5.

49 Cullen, *Mild Murderer*, 126.

50 O.A., *Daily Mail* vom 27. Juli 1910, 7; Goodman, *Crippen File*, 35.

51 For more background information on Dew's life and career, see Connell, *Walter Dew*.

52 O.A., *Times of London* vom 1. August 1910, 7.

53 Ibid.

54 O.A., *Lloyd's Weekly News* vom 31. Juli 1910, 1.

55 Z.B. O.A., *Sydney Morning Herald* vom 1. August 1910, 9.

56 Young, *Trial of Crippen*.

57 *Old Bailey Proceedings*, Trial of Crippen, Hawley Harvey.

58 O.A., *Daily Mirror* vom 21. November 1910, 15.

59 O.A., *Lloyd's Weekly News* vom 20. November 1910; Goodman, *Crippen File*, 74.

60 Goodman, *Crippen File*, 74.

61 O.A., *Daily Mirror* vom 21. November 1910, 15.

62 Michel Foucault and Jay Miskowiec, 'Of Other Spaces', in: *Diacritics* 16/1 (1986): 22–7, 27.

63 For example, see the contributions to a special issue of the *Journal of Global History* 11/2 (2016); Tamson Pietsch, 'A British Sea: Making Sense of

Global Space in the Late Nineteenth Century', in: *Journal of Global History*
5/3 (2010): 423–46; Michael Pesek, 'Von Europa nach Afrika. Deutsche
Passagiere auf der Dampferpassage in die Kolonie Deutsch-Ostafrika', in:
Werkstatt Geschichte 53 (2009): 68–88; James R. Ryan, '"Our Home on
the Ocean": Lady Brassey and the Voyages of the Sunbeam, 1874–1887',
in: *Journal of Historical Geography* 32 (2006): 579–604; Wenzlhuemer and
Offermann, *Ship Newspapers and Passenger Life.*

64 Dening, *Bligh's Bad Language.*

8

Doing global history

Consolidating the field

The preceding six chapters have covered the concepts of connection, space, time, actor, structure and transit and have attempted to show, with concrete examples, how these six concepts can be applied to help answer the key questions driving research in global history. Global connections are the key units of observation in the study of global history. As I argued in the opening pages of this book, they have not received too much attention in investigations of global history, but far too little. A firm conceptual grasp of global connections is a fundamental precondition for any productive research in global history. Focusing on space and time helps, on the one hand, to frame the setting in which any global historical episode takes place as well as, on the other hand, to elucidate how the events that unfold in that frame relate to global connections. Thus, the two chapters on space and time were especially concerned with how global connections affect the shape of their own historical contexts. One inference of particular interest is that how temporal and spatial strata change as a whole is perhaps less important than how specific spaces and times change relative to each other. Examining actorhood led to the conclusion that connections – be they local or global – emerge through human thoughts and actions, which they also influence reciprocally. Global history seeks to understand and interpret precisely this interaction, and applying the concept of actorhood to global history is most helpful in this regard. Conversely, elaborating the concept of structure in global history allows us to observe how connections emerge, stabilize and potentially disintegrate again. It directs attention to the conditions that stabilize connections more or less durably, conditions that emerge from, and feed into, actors' thoughts and actions. The point is to understand how structures and actors interact from the perspective of global history. Finally, transit is nothing more than reappraising the concept of connection from the perspective of the connection itself rather than from the connected objects. The concept emphasizes connections' substance, their spatial and temporal dimensions, and especially their experiential autonomy thanks to their mediating character. Taken together, these concepts provide relatively unmediated analytical purchase on the questions that drive research in global history.

Hopefully, this has become clear in the individual case studies. As mentioned in the introduction that opened this book, the case selection obeyed no compelling internal logic and drew instead on the empirical repertoire I have acquired. The fact that all cases occurred in the so-called 'long nineteenth century', that they all revolved somehow around Europe and European colonialism, especially the British Empire, is merely an artefact of my own research interests and approaches. This particular composition does not reflect an overarching epistemological or didactic purpose. Indeed, the analytical concepts and the case studies could be combined otherwise. Each history could illustrate several conceptual approaches, just as each term could be fruitfully applied to very different histories. However, the approach to global history presented in this book should not be read as groundless or arbitrary. Rather, its broad applicability is the product of its more fundamental analytical precision.

While the six terms introduced here constitute neither a compulsory nor an exhaustive instrumentarium, I am still confident that they are of central importance to global history, and that they yield great potential to formulate and operationalize that which makes the field so interesting. Of course, the list of terms could easily be extended to include other relevant aspects of global history. The relation of global connections and cultural transfer, for example, comes to mind as a means of analysing how the ascription of meanings changes. Another fruitful topic would be how the media and other technologies affect processes of globalization, although this question has been treated indirectly in several places in this book. Information and knowledge are also challenging and promising concepts among the many others that would enrich our insights about global history. In short, manifold pathways of enquiry lie open before us. A lot of different conceptual approaches promise interesting results. Many of them are already being tried and tested; others will be developed in the future. I find it difficult to make any reliable prognosis about which concepts and approaches will prove most fruitful and interesting in the years to come. I am much more confident about the key challenge of the field of global history that hovers over the question of how to conceptually approach a history of global connections. Global history is currently entering into a phase of consolidation. This entails finding its place in the broader ensemble of historiography. This is quite a substantial issue and a lot is at stake here. So far, global history has mostly defined itself in opposition to the so-called mainstream of historical research, in opposition to historians who, for instance, privileged the nation state over other frameworks of enquiry or indulged in an often unquestioned Eurocentrism. However, this definition *ex negativo* is becoming less and less satisfying as global history has started to establish itself firmly in the broader field of historical enquiry. The outsider's role does not work well anymore.

Consolidation means re-evaluation. The most important questions in this context revolve around the issue of what global history can contribute to historiography. It seems less important what global history is. The question is what it can and must do for the profession as such. In this regard, it is key to think about the bridges, the synergies but also about the borders global history maintains with other fields of historical enquiry. In the next years, therefore, practitioners in the field will have to think about two principal questions: in order to best contribute to historical research and interpretation, which stories shall we tell and how shall we tell them? Or: what do we have to say about human history and how can we say it in a way that is meaningful, understandable and maybe even entertaining?

First, which stories to tell? This issue revolves around a number of different but related questions that the field will have to think and discuss intensely in the years to come. Does global history have its own object of study or is it 'only' a perspective? Do we want to produce bird's eye syntheses or rather analytical close-ups? Or both? What should be our main analytical angle? I have touched upon all these issues in the course of this book. As pointed out already, my answer to these and other open issues – in this book and beyond – rests in an analytical emphasis on global connections. Therefore, I believe that global historians will have to develop this approach much further in the coming years. We will have to learn to think of global connections not in the singular but rather as bundles of connections. We will have to develop a sensorium for the tensions that result from the shifts and interactions between the connections in a bundle. We will have to learn to adequately acknowledge the role of disconnections and non-connections in global history. In short, we will have to sharpen our analytical tools, which will then give shape to the stories we can and must tell.

But how to tell these stories? I strongly believe that the historian should always be a storyteller in the actual sense of the word. Good historians have a deep interest in the stories of their actors and should be able to weave all those stories together into a grasping narrative that is both scientifically insightful and entertaining to read. This is, one could say, a question of the last mile. How can we convince other people to dedicate some of their precious time to thinking about the results of our research that has occupied us for so long? An intriguing while, of course, accurate story will help. Weaving the insights of global historical research into a compelling narrative often poses a formidable challenge. Global history has a certain tendency to produce placeless stories. When in this book I suggest to analytically focus on global connections and to pay more attention to the in-between, to the connection instead of the connected, what does this mean for the setting of the resulting narrative, for the pace of the story, for the dramatis personae? How can we tell a story without a centre, a story whose very point it is to transgress established frames of analysis and, hence, of narration? This is the second big issue that will necessitate intense discussion and experimentation in the following years.

This book can also be seen as my own small contribution to this discussion. Throughout the book, I emphasize the importance of developing and employing analytical concepts in history and particularly in global history. It is the main idea to bring these concepts into direct correspondence with their case studies, with the stories that need telling. Here, I have taken inspiration from micro-historical approaches. This is not to imply that from the perspective of classical micro-history, which was so formative in the 1970s and 1980s,[1] my cases would count as 'real' micro-history in that sense. The histories here most likely do not plumb the minutiae deeply enough or describe the specific socio-cultural circumstances in sufficient detail. Moreover, micro-history was often conceived in terms of the history of the everyday or of the 'common people'.[2] To the extent that such considerations inform the examples chosen here, they do so in muted form, if at all. Their narrative scope, however, fits comfortably in a micro-historical approach. And so does the fact that most of the cases presented here revel in the unusual or display some peculiar socio-cultural configuration. These cases are generally memorable episodes whose peculiarity makes them particularly vivid. Consequently, one might doubt to what extent they are representative or to what degree the insights they yield can be generalized, which is also a perennial sticking point for micro-historical studies. In what sense, then, can these intricate, extraordinary stories teach us anything worthwhile about history?

Indeed, many historians have recently wrestled with the question[3] as to how well micro-historical approaches are suited to the 'age of global history', as Francesca Trivellato put it.[4] The crux of the dilemma is the apparent irreconcilability of the detail that micro-history demands and to which it owes its name and the macro-perspective of global history. In almost every case, the scholars who venture to solve this dilemma come to the conclusion that the micro- and macro-perspectives are not as incompatible as they might seem at first. Compelling arguments that are meant to illustrate their compatibility tend to follow. Perhaps the most compelling is Trivellato's enlightening essay, in which she proposes the following preliminary, but certainly apt, solution:

> Italian microhistory aimed to be 'big history' not because it sought to embrace 13 billion years of human life on earth, but because it wished

to say something big about history. At a minimum, it aimed to raise big questions about how social and cultural systems emerge and evolve, as well as the methods humanists and social scientists adopt to interpret them.[5]

This cogent and succinct statement also applies to the case studies in this book: they are small, but meticulously researched histories, which enable more profound conclusions in combination with the attendant concepts. In terms of the interpretative scope of the individual case studies, then, I share precisely that micro-historical goal. The stories I have told here are often intricate, if not convoluted. They are stories of a hoax with great aspirations but little effect, of telegraphers on tiny islands, of short cons on horse races. When it comes to the more renowned stories, like the mutiny on the *Bounty* or the tunnel through Mont Cenis, I touch only cursorily on their historical significance, preferring to examine the intricate mechanisms that underlie them. This style is perhaps most pronounced in the case of Dr Crippen's transit. Although they focus on the little things, on the kinds of details more familiar to micro-history, each of the cases presented contributes to global history, to understanding the emergence and historical efficiency of global connections. Moreover, the oft-lamented conflict between micro-history and global history dissolves entirely on closer inspection. From the perspective of global history understood as the history of connections – as it is here – there is no necessary conflict, since global history does not simply imply macro-history. As mentioned above in the chapter on space, the global is an opportunity, not a predetermined lens through which global history must be observed. An approach that focuses on the emergence of global connections and what they mean for subjects' thoughts and actions is not by definition macro-historical. Indeed, the proximity to historical actors described above often implies the opposite. Therefore, the relationship between micro-history and global history is not contradictory or tense or complicated in any other sense.

Carlo Ginzburg has recently been contemplating the relationship of the two fields, and he opened his recent article on the topic in *Cambridge World History* with the observation that micro-history is an 'indispensable tool' for global history.[6] As true as his characterization rings for my own habits, I must still qualify that, for the sake of the systematicity to which this book strives, 'indispensable' perhaps goes too far, because micro-history is a valuable, but not strictly necessary, tool for global history. In the final analysis, micro-history is a boutique method, an instrument that can help to answer significant questions in global history, but it is only one method among many, and it can be applied to many contexts beyond global history.[7] This is not to understate the value of scalability[8] but just to emphasize that questions of scale apply to global history just as they do to any other historiographical approaches.

But what can one say about the episodic nature of the cases chosen here, and, perhaps more importantly, what deeper insights can they yield in light of their seeming peculiarity? The Crippen manhunt is a good example of a socio-cultural constellation that seems to verge on the absurd. It seems to fortuitously combine countless factors – an emerging global public, newly invented radio technology, transoceanic crossings by steamer – whose coexistence was restricted to a very short window of historical opportunity. This is anything but the rule. The pass railway over Mont Cenis was a similarly extraordinary undertaking that required a very particular motivation. The Great Moon Hoax was a similarly exceptional episode, and even contemporary observers considered the mutiny on the *Bounty* to be an event without precedent. One advantage that results from the cases' peculiarity is that readers are likely to remember them and perhaps even to delight in the combination of their oddity with serious historical analysis, or so an author would hope. In fact, these episodes might serve a valuable didactic purpose by making the business of history somewhat more agreeable, if not enjoyable.[9]

Although it is certainly not a defect, this pleasant side effect did not guide the selection of such unusual cases, which, in many cases, was more heavily influenced by the availability of sources and what our ancestors elected to preserve for posterity. Studying global phenomena often entails delving into archives and other source collections in diverse national and regional contexts, making it difficult in practice to tell a seamless story from start to finish through its various way stations. One is often left with fragments – a common affliction in history. It does, however, make assessing the generalizability of terms and concepts difficult beyond anecdotal contexts, but trails of evidence that can be followed through diverse archives and sources help considerably. Unusual, eye-catching cases are more likely to have been well recorded, because even contemporaries were often equally interested, inspiring them to preserve the requisite sources.

Classical micro-history is no stranger to such obstacles. In fact, a work like Carlo Ginzburg's *The Cheese and the Worms: The Cosmos of a Sixteenth Century Miller* is propelled by the peculiarity of the story and its protagonist.[10] Had Menocchio and his point of view not struck his contemporaries as odd and worthy of investigation, we would not have the sources necessary to reconstruct his story in micro-historical detail. In such instances, micro-history invokes the epistemological value of 'extraordinary normality', referring to the possibility of reaching generalizable conclusions from extraordinary documents (or circumstances) using the right kind of interpretation.[11] I would gladly subscribe to this line of argument. In many of the cases discussed here, it is precisely the exceptional circumstances and constellations that reveal a mechanism, a relation, a cause in uncommon clarity. The extraordinary then becomes an amplifier, helping us to read and interpret a situation. While the stories might be unusual, the forces and relations that surface in their explanations are not – nor are the insights derived from them. Indeed, this is the point of analysing global history with the greatest possible conceptual precision: to distil those elements that contribute to our knowledge of global history and that can be integrated into broader historical horizons from extraordinary stories (or ordinary ones, if available). Combining a conceptual abstraction with a suitable case can achieve exactly that. The peculiarity of the episodes fades into the background, making room for conclusions that can be extrapolated to other contexts and that perhaps, due to the unusual stories that spawned them, remain memorable, unmistakable and perhaps even entertaining

Conclusion: The grasp of global history

Global history tends to be underestimated. As the interest in the broader field for research in global history has grown, so too has the diversity of its interests, approaches and methodologies. As a result, its contours can become blurred, which makes it even more difficult for global historians, and especially for colleagues from other fields, to remain cognizant of the contribution global history can and should make to the discipline of history as a whole. Therefore, I have tried, despite my appreciation of a broad and internally diverse research programme, to identify some key questions and epistemological directions for global history as well as a few ways to approach and answer them. I believe that concentrating on global connections is the most fruitful way to engage with global history, which is a matter of determining how they emerge and how they affect the thoughts and actions of historical actors. To do so, global history needs a clear analytical picture of what global connections are in the first place – a question asked far too seldom – and what distinguishes them from other kinds of connection.

Properly handled, global history can complement other approaches, such as those that privilege the nation state. It can expand and enrich such approaches, but it should not be seen as a replacement for them. Metaphorically speaking, global history should be viewed as a carefully calibrated counterweight that helps to achieve a better balance – not as an attempt to create new imbalances with yet another master narrative. In the end, global history will have achieved its goal when it makes itself obsolete. That is, it should not aim to *over*write other modes of historical research, but rather to *in*scribe itself within them such that any attempt to interpret history automatically includes the role of global connections in the analysis. This does not mean to give global connections top priority; it is simply a matter of giving them their due consideration.

In many contexts, considering global connections might indeed lead to the conclusion that they play no significant role. In reading this book it should have become clear that I, as a practising global historian, accord the field an important, but not supreme, status in the wider ensemble of modern historical research. Supremacy always implies elevating oneself over others, and such an attitude would only hinder dialogue and productive cross-fertilization with other modes of inquiry. For me, global history can enrich history in general with its complementarity, and complementarity logically precludes exclusivity. The concepts and analytical tools presented in this book reflect my conviction that openness is indeed the highest value.

Finally, there remains the question about the purpose of all these thoughts, qualifications and elaborations, given that the goal of global history is to integrate itself into the broader discipline and to eventually render itself obsolete. The answer is as important as it is mundane: as with all the social sciences and humanities generally – and history in particular – the point of global history is to sharpen our critical judgement. In our case, the object of our curiosity is just a deeply entangled world. And it is to that end that I have tried to make a small contribution with the ideas contained in this book.

Notes

1 Some of the most renowned examples would include Carlo Ginzburg, *The Cheese and the Worms: The Cosmos of a Sixteenth Century Miller.* Baltimore, 1980; Emmanuel Le Roy Ladurie, *Montaillou. Cathars and Catholics in a French Village, 1294–1324.* London, 1978; Natalie Zemon Davis, *The Return of Martin Guerre.* Cambridge/London, 1983; Giovanni Levi, *Inheriting Power: The Story of an Exorcist.* Chicago, 1988.

2 See Angelika Epple, 'Globale Mikrogeschichte. Auf dem Weg zu einer Geschichte der Relationen', in: Ernst Langthaler and Ewald Hiebl (Hrsg.), *Im Kleinen das Große suchen. Mikrogeschichte in Theorie und Praxis.* Hanns Haas zum 70. Geburtstag. (Jahrbuch für Geschichte des ländlichen Raumes 2012.) Innsbruck, 2012, 37–47, 38–9.

3 Rebekka Habermas, 'Der Kolonialskandal Atakpame – eine Mikrogeschichte des Globalen', in: *Historische Anthropologie* 17/3 (2009): 295–319; Tonio Andrade, 'A Chinese Farmer, Two African Boys, and a Warlord: Toward a Global Microhistory', in: *Journal of World History* 21/4 (2010): 573–91; Matti Peltonen, 'Clues, Margins, and Monads: The Micro-Macro Link in Historical Research', in: *History and Theory* 40/3 (2001): 347–59; Epple, 'Globale Mikrogeschichte'.

4 Francesca Trivellato, 'Is There a Future for Italian Microhistory in the Age of Global History?' in: *California Italian Studies* 2/1 (2011), unter: eScholarship. University of California, in: URL= http://escholarship.org/uc/item/0z94n9hq (accessed: 23 June 2016).

5 Trivellato, 'Italian Microhistory', Kap. IX.

6 Carlo Ginzburg, 'Microhistory and World History', in: Jerry H. Bentley et al. (Hrsg.), *The Cambridge World History*. (Bd. 6.) Cambridge, 2015, 446–73, 446.

7 This is a feature that micro-history shares with the comparative method, which studies in global history often rely on more or less explicitly.

8 See Bernhard Struck, Kate Ferris and Jacques Revel, 'Introduction: Space and Scale in Transnational History', in: *International History Review* 33/4 (2011): 573–84; insbesondere aber Martin Dusinberres Gedanken zu 'Incompatibilities' in Martin Dusinberre and Roland Wenzlhuemer, 'Editorial – Being in Transit', 161.

9 On this point, see the introductory thoughts in the chapter 'Narrating World History', in: Manning, *Navigating World History*, 107.

10 Ginzburg, *The Cheese and the Worms*.

11 Trivellato, 'Italian Microhistory', Kap. II.

Further reading

Andrade, Tonio, 'A Chinese Farmer, Two African Boys, and a Warlord: Toward a Global Microhistory', *Journal of World History* 21/4 (2010): 573–91.

Drayton, Richard and Motadel, David, 'Discussion: The Futures of Global History', *JGH* 13/1 (2018): 1–21.

Dusinberre, Martin, 'Japan, Global History, and the Great Silence', *History Workshop Journal* 83/1 (2017): 130–50.

Ginzburg, Carlo, *The Cheese and the Worms: The Cosmos of a Sixteenth Century Miller*. Baltimore, 1980.

Magnússon, Sigurður Gylfi, 'Far-reaching Microhistory: The Use of microhistorical Perspective in a Globalized World', *Rethinking History* 21/3 (2017): 312–41.

Sand, Jordan, 'Gentlemen's Agreement, 1908: Fragments for a Pacific History', *Representations* 107/1 (2009): 91–127.

Trivellato, Francesca, 'Is There a Future for Italian Microhistory in the Age of Global History?' *California Italian Studies* 2/1 (2011), unter: eScholarship. University of California, URL= http://escholarship.org/uc/item/0z94n9hq (accessed: 23 June 2016).

Bibliography

Sources

Banks, Joseph, Eintrag vom 28. Mai 1769, in: ders., *Endeavour Journal*. Bd. 1: 25. August 1768–14. August 1769, State Library of New South Wales, ML Safe 1/12.

Banks, Joseph, Manners and Customs of the South Sea Islanders, in: ders., *Endeavour Journal*. Bd. 1: 25. August 1768–14. August 1769, State Library of New South Wales, ML Safe 1/12.

Barber, James, *The Overland Guide-Book: A Complete Vade-Mecum for the Overland Traveller*. London, 1845.

Bennett, James Gordon, The Astronomical Hoax Explained, in: *New York Herald* vom 31. August 1835, 1.

Berliner Tageblatt.

Bligh, William, *A Narrative of the Mutiny, on Board His Majesty's Ship Bounty; and the Subsequent Voyage of Part of the Crew, in the Ship's Boat from Tofoa, one of the Friendly Islands, to Timor, a Dutch Settlement in the East Indies*. London, 1790.

Bligh, William, *An Answer to Certain Assertions Contained in the Appendix to a Pamphlet, Entitled Minutes of the Proceedings on the Court-Martial Held at Portsmouth, August 12th, 1792, on Ten Persons Charged with Mutiny on Board His Majesty's Ship the Bounty*. London, 1794.

Bligh, William, *Brief an Elizabeth Bligh*. Kupang, 1789. Mitchell Library of New South Wales, *ZML Safe* 1/45, 17–24.

Bligh, William, *Brief an Joseph Banks*. Anhang, Batavia, 13. Oktober 1789, Papers of Sir Joseph Banks. State Library of New South Wales, Series 46.27.

Bligh, William, Chapter IX, in: ders., *A Voyage to the South Sea, Undertaken by Command of His Majesty, for the Purpose of Conveying the Bread-Fruit Tree to the West-Indies, in His Majesty's Ship the Bounty, Commanded by Lieutenant William Bligh*. London, 1792, 105–22.

Bligh, William, Extracts from Captain Bligh's Narrative, in: *Times* vom 7. September 1790, 3.

Bougainville, Louis Antoine de, *Voyage autour du monde, par la frégate du Roi la Boudeuse, et la flûte l'étoile; en 1766, 1767, 1768 & 1769*. Paris, 1771.

British Library. General Reference Collection, Shelfmark 8761.b.62. 'Souvenir of the Inaugural Fête [Held at the house of Mr. John Pender], in Commemoration of the Opening of Direct Submarine Telegraph with India', 23 June 1870.

British Library. Oriental Collections IOR/V/24/4284. Administration Report of the Indian Telegraph Department for 1862–1863, 1863.

Cable and Wireless Archive. British-Indian Submarine Telegraph Co Ltd DOC/
    BISTC/6/2. Souvenir of the Inaugural Fete to Celebrate the Opening of Direct
    Submarine Telegraphic Communication to India, 2. Juni 1870.
Christian, Edward, *A Short Reply to Capt. William Bligh's Answer*. London, 1795.
Christian, Edward and Barney, Stephen, *Minutes of the Proceedings of the Court-
    Martial Held at Portsmouth, August 12, 1792. On Ten Persons Charged with
    Mutiny on Board His Majesty's Ship the Bounty. With an Appendix, Containing
    A Full Account of the Real Causes and Circumstances of that Unhappy
    Transaction, the Most Material of Which Have hitherto Been Withheld from
    the Public*. London, 1794.
Cincinnati Mirror & Western Gazette of Literature and Science.
Clauson-Thue, William, *The ABC Universal Commercial Electric Telegraphic Code
    Specially Adapted for the Use of Financiers, Merchants, Shipowners, Brokers,
    Agents*. 4. Aufl. London, 1881.
Daily Mail.
Daily Mirror.
Daily News.
Daily Telegraph.
Die Gartenlaube.
Dilke, Charles Wentworth, Extraordinary Discoveries by Sir John Herschel, in:
    Athenaeum 440 vom 2. April 1836, 244.
Ellis, John, *A Description of the Mangostan and the Bread-Fruit: The First,
    Esteemed One of the Most Delicious; The Other, the Most Useful of All the
    Fruits in the East Indies*. London, 1775.
Emory, Kenneth P., Occasional Papers of Bernice P. Bishop Museum 15/17,
    Additional Notes on the Archaeology of Fanning Island, 1939, 179–89.
Greene, Asa, *A Glance at New York. The City Government, Theatres, Hotels,
    Churches, Mobs, Monopolies, Learned Professions, Newspapers, Rogues,
    Dandies, Fires and Firemen, Water and Other Liquids &C. &C*. New York, 1837.
Hansard, HC Deb, Bd. 19, CC1240-1 vom 20. Juli 1910.
Hawkesworth, John, *An Account of the Voyages Undertaken by the Order of
    His Present Majesty for Making Discoveries in the Southern Hemisphere,
    and Successively Performed by Commodore Byron Captain Wallis, Captain
    Carteret, and Captain Cook, in the Dolphin, the Swallow, and the Endeavour
    Drawn Up from the Journals Which Were Kept by the Several Commanders,
    and from the Papers of Joseph Banks* (3 Bd.). London, 1773.
Herschel, Sir John, Extracts of a Letter from Sir J. Herschel to M. Arago, in:
    Athenaeum 478, 24. Dezember 1836, 908.
House of Commons. Parliamentary Paper 466, Tyler, Eastern Mails. Copy of
    Report from Captain Tyler, R. E., to Her Majesty's Postmaster General, of His
    Recent Inspection of the Railways and Ports of Italy, with Reference to the
    Use of the Italian Route for the Conveyance of the Eastern Mails, 1866.
House of Commons. Parliamentary Papers C. 304. Telegraphs. Report by Mr.
    Scudamore on the Re-Organization of the Telegraph System of the United
    Kingdom. Presented to the House of Commons by Command of Her Majesty.
    London, 1871.
Illustrated London News.
Jones, Thomas P. (Hrsg.), *Journal of the Franklin Institute of the State of
    Pennsylvania and American Repertory of Mechanical and Physical Science*,

Civil Engineering, the Arts and Manufactures and of American and Other Patented Inventions. Philadelphia, 1845, 203.

Kenyon, Eustace Alban, Brief an Tizie, Cambridge 1891, in: *Cambridge South Asian Archive*, Centre of South Asian Studies, University of Cambridge.

Library of Congress. Prints & Photographs Division, Reproduktion (LC-USZ62-61482) von Charles Dana Gibson, Mr. A. Merger Hogg is Taking a Much Needed Rest at His Country Home, Zeichnung, in: *Life* 41 vom 4. Juni 1903, 518–19.

Literatur- und Intelligenzblatt für Neu-Vorpommern und Rügen. Beilage zur Sundine.

Lloyd's Weekly London Newspaper.

Locke, Richard Adams, Celestial Discoveries, in: *The Sun* vom 21. August 1835, 2.

Locke, Richard Adams, Great Astronomical Discoveries. Lately Made By Sir John Herschel, L. L. D. F. R. S. &c. At the Cape of Good Hope [From Supplement to the Edinburgh Journal of Science.], in: *The Sun* vom 25. August 1835, 1.

Locke, Richard Adams, Great Astronomical Discoveries. Lately Made By Sir John Herschel, L. L. D. F. R. S. &c. At the Cape of Good Hope [From Supplement to the Edinburgh Journal of Science.] [continued from yesterday's Sun], in: *The Sun* vom 26. August 1835, 1.

Locke, Richard Adams, Great Astronomical Discoveries. Lately Made By Sir John Herschel, L. L. D. F. R. S. &c. At the Cape of Good Hope [From Supplement to the Edinburgh Journal of Science.] [continued from yesterday's Sun], in: *The Sun* vom 27. August 1835, 1.

Locke, Richard Adams, Great Astronomical Discoveries. Lately Made By Sir John Herschel, L. L. D. F. R. S. &c. At the Cape of Good Hope [From Supplement to the Edinburgh Journal of Science.] [continued from yesterday's Sun], in: *The Sun* vom 28. August 1835, 1.

Locke, Richard Adams, Great Astronomical Discoveries. Lately Made By Sir John Herschel, L. L. D. F. R. S. &c. At the Cape of Good Hope [From Supplement to the Edinburgh Journal of Science.] [continued from yesterday's Sun], in: *The Sun* vom 29. August 1835, 1.

Locke, Richard Adams, Great Astronomical Discoveries. Lately Made By Sir John Herschel, L. L. D. F. R. S. &c. At the Cape of Good Hope [From Supplement to the Edinburgh Journal of Science.] [concluded.], in: *The Sun* vom 31. August 1835, 1.

Locke, Richard Adams, To the Editor of the Evening Star, in: *New York Herald* vom 1. September 1835, 1.

Locke, Richard Adams and Nicollet, Joseph Nicolas, *The Moon Hoax; Or, a Discovery that the Moon Has a Vast Population of Human Beings.* New York, 1859.

Los Angeles Times.

Martineau, Harriet, *Retrospect of Western Travel*, Bd. 3. London, 1838.

Mücke, Hellmuth von, *The 'Ayesha': Being the Adventures of the Landing Squad of the 'Emden'.* Boston, 1917.

New Anecdote Library (Hrsg.), *The London Anecdotes. For All Readers. Part 1: Anecdotes of the Electric Telegraph.* London, 1848.

New York Times.

New Zealand Spectator and Cook's Strait Guardian.

New Zealander.

O.A., *An Epistle from Mr. Banks, Voyager, Monster-Hunter, and Amoroso, to Oberea, Queen of Otaheite*. London, 1773.

O.A., *An Epistle from Oberea, Queen of Otaheite, to Joseph Banks Esq*. London, 1774.

O.A., *Report of the British Association of the Advancement of Science*. London, 1871.

O.A., The Emden's Fatal Visit to Cocos, in: *The Zodiac* 8, 1915, 62–8.

O'Brien, Frank, The Story of the Sun. Part 2, in: *Munsey's Magazine*, Juni 1917, 99–115.

Original Theatrical Trailer, in: *Warner Brothers*, Mutiny on the Bounty (1962) Blu-Ray. Los Angeles, 2011.

Paula Gruithuisen, Franz von, Olbers, Wilhelm and Gauss, Carl Friedrich, The Moon and Its Inhabitants, in: *Edinburgh New Philosophical Journal* 1 (1826): 389–90.

Poe, Edgar Allan, Richard Adams Locke, in: ders., *The Literati of New York City. Some Honest Opinions at Random Respecting Their Autorial Merits, With Occasional Words of Personality*, Bd. 6. O.O. 1846, 159–61.

Porthcurno Telegraph Museum, DOC//5/107/1-3, Letters from the Fanning Islands.

Ross, Nelson E., How to Write *Telegrams Properly*. (Little Blue Book Bd. 459.) Girard, 1928.

Siemens, Werner von, Brief an Carl von Siemens vom 12. April 1870, zitiert nach: Hans Pieper/Kilian Kuenzi, in: Museum für Kommunikation (Hrsg.), *In 28 Minuten von London nach Kalkutta. Aufsätze zur Telegrafiegeschichte aus der Sammlung Dr. Hans Pieper im Museum für Kommunikation, Bern.* (Schriftenreihe des Museums für Kommunikation, Bern.) Zürich, 2000, 209.

Simpson, William, *Meeting the Sun. A Journey all Round the World through Egypt, China, Japan and California, Including an Account of the Marriage Ceremonies of the Emperor of China*. London, 1874.

South Australian Register.

Sterne, Laurence, *A Sentimental Journey through France and Italy*. Basil, 1792.

Sydney Morning Herald.

The Argus.

Times.

Times of London.

Whymper, Edward, *Scrambles amongst the Alps in the Years 1860-69*. London/Murray, 1871.

Scholarly literature

Adelman, Jeremy, What Is Global History Now? in: *Aeon*, 2 March 2017, https://aeon.co/essays/is-global-history-still-possible-or-has-it-had-its-moment (accessed 1 June 2018).

Alexander, Caroline, *The Bounty. The True Story of the Mutiny on the Bounty*. New York, 2004.

Andrade, Tonio, A Chinese Farmer, Two African Boys, and a Warlord. Toward a Global Microhistory, in: *Journal of World History* 21/4 (2010): 573–91.

Angster, Julia, *Erdbeeren und Piraten. Die Royal Navy und die Ordnung der Welt 1770-1880*. Göttingen, 2012.

Antunes, Cátia and Fatah-Black, Karwan (Hrsg.), *Explorations in History and Globalization*. London, 2016.

Armitage, David and Braddick, Michael (Hrsg.), *The British Atlantic World, 1500–1800*. Basingstoke/New York, 2002.

Ashmore, Paul, Slowing Down Mobilities. Passengering on an Inter-War Ocean Liner, in: *Mobilities* 8/4 (2013): 595–611.

Assmann, Aleida, *Ist die Zeit aus den Fugen? Aufstieg und Fall des Zeitregimes der Moderne*. München, 2013.

Austin, Gareth, Global History in (Western) Europe: Explorations and Debates, in: Sven Beckert and Dominic Sachsenmaier (Eds.), *Global History, Globally: Research and Practice around the World*. London/New York, 2018, 21–44.

Barth, Boris, Gänger, Stefanie and Petersson, Niels P. (Hrsg.), *Globalgeschichten. Bestandsaufnahme und Perspektiven*. (Reihe 'Globalgeschichte', Bd. 17.) Frankfurt am Main, 2014.

Barton, Roger N., Brief Lives. Three British Telegraph Companies 1850-56, in: *The International Journal for the History of Engineering and Technology* 80/2 (2012): 183–98.

Basu, Dilip K. (Hrsg.), *The Rise and Growth of the Colonial Port Cities in Asia*. (Monograph Series/Center for South and Southeast Asia Studies, Bd. 25.) Lanham, 1985.

Bayly, Christopher A., 'Archaic' and 'Modern' Globalization in the Eurasian and African Arena, *c*. 1750-1850, in: Anthony G. Hopkins (Hrsg.), *Globalization in World History*. New York, 2002, 47–73.

Bayly, Christopher A., *The Birth of the Modern World, 1780–1914. Global Connections and Comparisons*. Oxford, 2004.

Beaglehole, John C., *The Life of Captain James Cook*. Stanford, 1974.

Beck, Ulrich, *Macht und Gegenmacht im globalen Zeitalter. Neue weltpolitische Ökonomie*. (Edition Zweite Moderne.) Frankfurt am Main, 2002.

Beckert, Sven and Sachsenmaier, Dominic (Eds.), *Global History, Globally: Research and Practice around the World*. London/New York, 2018.

Belich, James, Darwin, John, Frenz, Margret and Wickham, Chris, *The Prospect of Global History*. Oxford, 2016.

Bentley, Jeremy H., Bridenthal, Renate and Wigen, Kären (Hrsg.), *Seascapes. Maritime Histories, Littoral Cultures, and Transoceanic Exchanges*. (Perspectives on the Global Past.) Honolulu, 2007.

Bergier, Jean-Francois, *Pour une Histoire des Alpes, Moyen Age et Temps Modernes*. (Collected Studies Series, Bd. 587.) Aldershot, 1998, VII/39–49.

Bose, Sugata, *A Hundred Horizons. The Indian Ocean in the Age of Global Empire*. Cambridge, 2006.

Bourdieu, Pierre, *Entwurf einer Theorie der Praxis*. Frankfurt am Main, 1979.

Braudel, Fernand, Histoire et Sciences Sociales. La Longue Durée, in: *Annales. Économies, Sociétés, Civilisations* 4/13 (1958): 725–53.

Braudel, Fernand, *La Méditerranée et le Monde Méditerranéen à l'Époque de Philippe II*. Paris, 1949.

Broeze, Frank (Hrsg.), *Brides of the Sea. Port Cities of Asia from the 16th-20th Centuries*. Honolulu, 1989.

Broeze, Frank (Hrsg.), *Gateways of Asia. Port Cities of Asia in the 13th-20th Centuries*. London, 1997.

Bruce, Julia, Banks and Breadfruit, in: *RSA Journal* 141 (1993): 817–20.

Burke, Peter, Reflections on the Cultural History of Time, in: *Viator. Medieval and Renaissance Studies* 35 (2004): 617–26.

Carey, James, Technology and Ideology. The Case of the Telegraph, in: ders., *Communication as a Culture. Essays on Media and Society*. Boston, 1989, 201–30.

Carter, Harold B., *Sir Joseph Banks, 1743–1820*. London, 1988.

Castagnaro, Mario, Lunar Fancies and Earthly Truths. The Moon Hoax of 1835 and the Penny Press, in: *Nineteenth-Century Contexts. An Interdisciplinary Journal* 34/3 (2012): 253–68.

Castells, Manuel, Informationalism, Networks, and the Network Society: A Theoretical Blueprint, in: ders. (Hrsg.), *The Network Society. A Cross-Cultural Perspective*. Cheltenham, Northampton, 2004, 3–45.

Chaney, Edward, *The Evolution of the Grand Tour. Anglo-Italian Cultural Relations since the Renaissance*. London, 1998.

Choudhury, Deep Kanta Lahiri, India's First Virtual Community and the Telegraph General Strike of 1908, in: Aad Blok and Greg Downey (Hrsg.), *Uncovering Labour in Information Revolutions, 1750–2000*. (IRSH. Supplements, Bd. 11.) Cambridge/New York/Melbourne, 2003, 45–71.

Choudhury, Deep Kanta Lahiri, Treasons of the Clerks. Sedition and Representation in the Telegraph General Strike of 1908, in: Crispin Bates (Hrsg.), *Beyond Representation. Colonial and Postcolonial Constructions of Indian Identity*. Oxford, 2006, 300–321.

Christopher, Emma, Pybus, Cassandra and Rediker, Marcus (Hrsg.), *Many Middle Passages. Forced Migration and the Making of the Modern World*. Berkeley, 2007.

Connell, Nicolas, *Dr. Crippen: The Infamous London Cellar Murder of 1910*. Stroud, 2013.

Connell, Nicolas, *Walter Dew: The Man Who Caught Crippen*. Stroud, 2005.

Conrad, Sebastian, *Globalgeschichte. Eine Einführung*. (Beck'sche Reihe, Bd. 6079.) München, 2013.

Conrad, Sebastian, *What Is Global History?* Princeton/Oxford, 2016.

Conrad, Sebastian and Eckert, Andreas, Globalgeschichte, Globalisierung, Multiple Modernen. Zur Geschichtsschreibung der modernen Welt, in: Dies., Ulrike Freitag (Hrsg.), *Globalgeschichte*. Theorien, Ansätze, Themen. Frankfurt am Main, 2007, 7–49.

Conrad, Sebastian, Eckert, Andreas and Freitag, Ulrike (Hrsg.), *Globalgeschichte. Theorien, Ansätze, Themen*. Frankfurt am Main, 2007.

Conze, Werner, Die Stellung der Sozialgeschichte in Forschung und Unterricht, in: *GWU* 3 (1952): 648–57.

Conze, Werner, *Die Strukturgeschichte des technisch-industriellen Zeitalters als Aufgabe für Forschung und Unterricht*. (Arbeitsgemeinschaft für Forschung des Landes Nordrhein-Westfalen. Geisteswissenschaften, Bd. 66.) Köln, 1957.

Cooper, Frederick, *Colonialism in Question Theory, Knowledge, History*. Berkeley/ Los Angeles, 2005.

Cooper, Frederick, What Is the Concept of Globalization Good For? An African Historian's Perspective, in: *African Affairs* 100/399 (2001): 189–213.

Crossley, Pamela Kyle, *What Is Global History?* Cambridge, 2008.

Crowe, Michael J., A History of the Extraterrestrial Life Debate, in: *Zygon* 32/2 (1997): 147–62.

Crowe, Michael J., *The Extraterrestrial Life Debate 1750–1900. The Idea of a Plurality of Worlds from Kant to Lowell.* Cambridge, 1986.

Cullen, Tom F., *Crippen. The Mild Murderer.* London, 1977.

Dening, Greg, *Mr Bligh's Bad Language. Passion, Power and Theatre on the Bounty.* Cambridge/New York, 1992.

Diedrich, Maria, Gates, Henry L. and Pedersen, Carl (Hrsg.), *Black Imagination and the Middle Passage.* Oxford, 1999.

Döring, Jörg and Thielmann, Tristan (Hrsg.), *Spatial Turn. Das Raumparadigma in den Kultur- und Sozialwissenschaften.* 2. Aufl. Bielefeld, 2009.

Drayton, Richard and Motadel, David, Discussion: The Futures of Global History, in: *Journal of Global History* 13/1 (2018): 1–21.

Dressel, Gert, *Historische Anthropologie. Eine Einführung.* Wien/Köln/Weimar, 1996.

Dülmen, Richard van, *Historische Anthropologie. Entwicklung, Probleme, Aufgaben.* 2. Aufl. Köln, 2001.

Dusinberre, Martin, Japan, Global History, and the Great Silence, in: *History Workshop Journal* 83/1 (2017): 130–50.

Dusinberre, Martin and Wenzlhuemer, Roland, Editorial – Being in Transit. Ships and Global Incompatibilities, in: *Journal of Global History* 11/2 (2016): 155–62.

Early, Julie English, Technology, Modernity and 'The Little Man'. Crippen's Capture by Wireless, in: *Victorian Studies* 39/3 (1996): 309–37.

Eckert, Andreas, Globalgeschichte und Zeitgeschichte, in: *APuZ* 62/1–3 (2012): 28–32.

Edgerton, David, *The Shock of the Old. Technology and Global History since 1900.* Oxford, 2007.

Epple, Angelika, Globale Mikrogeschichte. Auf dem Weg zu einer Geschichte der Relationen, in: Ernst Langthaler and Ewald Hiebl (Hrsg.), *Im Kleinen das Große suchen. Mikrogeschichte in Theorie und Praxis. Hanns Haas zum 70. Geburtstag.* (Jahrbuch für Geschichte des ländlichen Raumes 2012.) Innsbruck, 2012, 37–47.

Epple, Angelika, Kaltmeier, Olaf and Lindner, Ulrike (Hrsg.), *Entangled Histories. Reflecting on Concepts of Coloniality and Postcoloniality.* (Comparativ, Bd. 21/1.) Leipzig, 2011.

Espagne, Michel and Werner, Michael (Hrsg.), *Transferts. Les relations interculturelles dans l'espace franco-allemand (xviiie–xixe siècles).* Paris, 1988.

Evans, David S., *Herschel at the Cape: Diaries and Correspondence of Sir John Herschel, 1834–1838.* Cape Town, 1969.

Fletcher, Paul, The Uses and Limitations of Telegrams in Official Correspondence between Ceylon's Governor General and the Secretary of State for the Colonies, circa 1870–1900, in: Roland Wenzlhuemer (Hrsg.), *Global Communication. Telecommunication and Global Flows of Information in the Late 19th and Early 20th Century.* (HSR 35/1. Special Issue: Global Communication.) Köln, 2010, 90–107.

Flynn, Dennis O. and Giráldez, Arturo, Born Again: Globalization's Sixteenth Century Origins (Asian/Global Versus European Dynamics), in: *Pacific Economic Review* 13/3 (2008): 359–87.

Flynn, Dennis O. and Giráldez, Arturo, Born with a 'Silver Spoon': The Origin of World Trade in 1571, in: *Journal of World History* 6/2 (1995): 201–21.

Foucault, Michel and Miskowiec, Jay, Of Other Spaces, in: *Diacritics* 16/1 (1986): 22–7.

Frost, Alan, *Sir Joseph Banks and the Transfer of Plants to and from the South Pacific, 1786–1798*. Melbourne, 1993.

Gagen, Wendy, Not Another Hero. The Eastern and Associated Telegraph Companies. Creation of the Heroic Company, in: Stephen McVeigh and Nicola Cooper (Hrsg.), *Men after War*. London, 2013, 92–110.

Gagen, Wendy, The Manly Telegrapher. The Fashioning of a Gendered Company Culture in the Eastern and Associated Telegraph Companies, in: Michaela Hampf and Simone Müller-Pohl (Hrsg.), *Global Communication Electric. Business, News and Politics in the World of Telegraphy*. New York, 2013, 170–96.

Gascoigne, John, *Joseph Banks and the English Enlightenment. Useful Knowledge and polite Culture*. Cambridge, 1994.

Giddens, Anthony, *A Contemporary Critique of Historical Materialism. Bd. 1: Power, Property and the State*. London, 1981.

Giddens, Anthony, *The Consequences of Modernity*. Stanford, 1990.

Giddens, Anthony, *The Constitution of Society. Outline of the Theory of Structuration*. Cambridge, 1984.

Gills, Barry K. and Thompson, William R., Globalizations, Global Histories and Historical Globalities, in: dies. (Hrsg.), *Globalization and Global History*. New York/Abingdon, 2006, 1–15.

Gilroy, Paul, *The Black Atlantic: Modernity and Double-Consciousness*. 3. Aufl. London, 2002.

Ginzburg, Carlo, Microhistory and World History, in: Jerry H. Bentley et al. (Hrsg.), *The Cambridge World History*. (Bd. 6). Cambridge: Cambridge University Press, 2015, 446–73.

Ginzburg, Carlo, *The Cheese and the Worms: The Cosmos of a Sixteenth Century Miller*. Baltimore, 1980.

Goodman, Jonathan, *The Crippen File*. London, 1985.

Goodman, Matthew, *The Sun and the Moon. The Remarkable True Account of Hoaxers, Showmen, Dueling Journalists, and Lunar Man-Bats in Nineteenth-Century New York*. New York, 2008.

Grandner, Margarete, Rothermund, Dietmar and Schwentker, Wolfgang (Hrsg.), *Globalisierung und Globalgeschichte*. (Globalgeschichte und Entwicklungspolitik, Bd. 1.) Wien, 2005.

Griggs, William, *The Celebrated "Moon Story", Its Origins and Incidents*. New York, 1852.

Habermas, Rebekka, Der Kolonialskandal Atakpame – eine Mikrogeschichte des Globalen, in: *Historische Anthropologie* 17/3 (2009): 295–319.

Harvey, David, Between Space and Time. Reflections on the Geographical Imagination, in: *Annals of the Association of American Geographers* 80/3 (1990): 418–34.

Harvey, David, *Social Justice and the City*. London, 1973.

Harvey, David, *The Condition of Postmodernity. An Enquiry into the Origins of Cultural Change*. Cambridge, 1990.

Hazareesingh, Sandip, Interconnected Synchronicities. The Production of Bombay and Glasgow as Modern Global Ports c. 1850–1880, in: *Journal of Global History* 1/4 (2009): 7–31.

Headrick, Daniel R., *The Invisible Weapon. Telecommunications and International Politics, 1851–1945*. New York/Oxford, 1991.

Hennessey, Roger, *Worlds without End*. Gloucestershire, 1997.

Herold, Heiko, *Reichsgewalt bedeutet Seegewalt. Die Kreuzergeschwader der Kaiserlichen Marine als Instrument der deutschen Kolonial- und Weltpolitik 1885 bis 1901*. (Beiträge zur Militärgeschichte, Bd. 74, zugleich Phil. Diss. Heinrich-Heine-Universität Düsseldorf 2010.) München, 2013.

Hochfelder, David, *The Telegraph in America, 1832–1920*. Baltimore, 2012.

Hochfelder, David, 'Where the Common People Could Speculate': The Ticker, Bucket Shops, and the Origins of Popular Participation in Financial Markets, 1880–1920, in: *The Journal of American History* 93/2 (2006): 335–58.

Holtorf, Christian, *Der erste Draht zur Neuen Welt. Die Verlegung des transatlantischen Telegrafenkabels*. Göttingen, 2013.

Hopkins, Anthony G., Introduction: Globalization – An Agenda for Historians, in: ders. (Hrsg.), *Globalization in World History*. New York, 2002, 1–10.

Hough, Richard, *Captain James Cook. A Biography*. New York/London, 1997.

Hugill, Peter J., *Global Communications since 1844. Geopolitics and Technology*. Baltimore, 1999.

Hunt, Lynn, Globalization and Time, in: Chris Lorenz and Berber Bevernage (Hrsg.), *Breaking up Time: Negotiating the Borders between Present, Past and Future*. (Schriftenreihe der FRIAS School of History, Bd. 7.) Göttingen, 2013, 199–215.

Huurdeman, Anton A., *The Worldwide History of Telecommunications*. Hoboken, 2003.

Hyslop, Jonathan, Steamship Empire. Asian, African and British Sailors in the Merchant Marine c. 1880–1945, in: *Journal of Asian and African Studies* 44/1 (2009): 49–67.

Jackson, Gordon, Fischer, Lewis R. and Jarvis, Adrian (Hrsg.), *Harbours and Havens. Essays in Port History in Honour of Gordon Jackson*. (Research in Maritime History, Bd. 16.) St. John's, 1999.

Jäger, Friedrich and Rüsen, Jörn, *Geschichte des Historismus. Eine Einführung*. München, 1992.

John, Richard, *Network Nation. Inventing American Telecommunications*. Cambridge, u.a. 2010.

Kempe, Michael, 'Even in the Remotest Corners of the World'. Globalized Piracy and International Law, 1500–1900, in: *Journal of Global History* 5/3 (2010): 353–72.

Kempe, Michael, *Fluch der Weltmeere. Piraterie, Völkerrecht und Internationale Beziehungen, 1500–1900*. Frankfurt am Main, 2010.

Keohane, Robert O. and Nye, Joseph S., Globalization: What's New? What's Not? (And So What?) in: *Foreign Policy* 118/1 (2000): 104–19.

Kern, Stephen, *The Culture of Time and Space, 1880–1918. With a New Preface*. 2. Aufl. Cambridge/London, 2003.

Kieve, Jeffrey, *The Electric Telegraph. A Social and Economic History*. New Abbot, 1973.

Komlosy, Andrea, *Globalgeschichte. Methoden und Theorien*. (UTB Geschichte, Bd. 3564.) Wien/Köln/Weimar, 2011.

Koselleck, Reinhart, Ereignis und Struktur, in: Reinhart Koselleck and Wolf-Dieter Stempel (Hrsg.), *Geschichte, Ereignis und Erzählung*. München, 1973, 560–70.

Koselleck, Reinhart, *Vergangene Zukunft. Zur Semantik geschichtlicher Zeiten*. (Suhrkamp Taschenbuch Wissenschaft, Bd. 757.) 8. Aufl. Frankfurt am Main, 2013.

Koselleck, Reinhart, *Zeitschichten. Studien zur Historik*. (Suhrkamp Taschenbuch Wissenschaft, Bd. 1656.) Frankfurt am Main, 2003.

Ladurie, Emmanuel Le Roy, *Montaillou: Cathars and Catholics in a French Village, 1294-1324*. London, 1978.

Landwehr, Achim, *Geburt der Gegenwart. Eine Geschichte der Zeit im 17. Jahrhundert*. (S. Fischer Geschichte.) Frankfurt am Main, 2014.

Larson, Erik, *Thunderstruck*. New York, 2007.

Larson, Pier, *Ocean of Letters. Language and Creolization in an Indian Ocean Diaspora*. Cambridge, 2009.

Latour, Bruno, *Reassembling the Social. An Introduction to Actor-Network-Theory*. (Clarendon Lectures in Management Studies.) Oxford, 2005.

Lefebvre, Henri, *La Production de l'Espace*. Paris, 1974.

Leipold, Andreas, *Die deutsche Seekriegsführung im Pazifik in den Jahren 1914 und 1915*. Wiesbaden, 2012.

Levi, Giovanni, *Inheriting Power. The Story of an Exorcist*. Chicago, 1988.

Linebaugh, Peter and Rediker, Marcus, *The Many-Headed Hydra. Sailors, Slaves, Commoners, and the Hidden History of the Revolutionary Atlantic*. Boston, 2000.

Löhr, Isabella and Wenzlhuemer, Roland, Introduction. The Nation State and Beyond. Governing Globalization Processes in the Nineteenth and early Twentieth Centuries, in: dies. (Hrsg.), *The Nation Sate and Beyond. Governing Globalization Processes in the Nineteenth and Early Twentieth Centuries*. Berlin/Heidelberg, 2013, 1–26.

Lorenz, Chris and Bevernage, Berber (Hrsg.), *Breaking up Time. Negotiating the Borders between Present, Past and Future*. (Schriftenreihe der FRIAS School of History, Bd. 7.) Göttingen, 2013.

Löw, Martina, *Raumsoziologie*. Frankfurt am Main, 2001.

Lüdtke, Alf, Alltagsgeschichte, Mikro-Historie, historische Anthropologie, in: Hans-Jürgen Goertz (Hrsg.), *Geschichte. Ein Grundkurs*. Reinbek, 1998, 565–7.

Lysaght, Averil M., *Joseph Banks in Newfoundland and Labrador, 1766. His Diary, Manuscripts, and Collections*. Berkeley, 1971.

Mackay, David, Banks, Bligh and Breadfruit, in: *New Zealand Journal of History* 8/1 (1974): 61–77.

Magnússon, Sigurður Gylfi, Far-Reaching Microhistory: The Use of Microhistorical Perspective in a Globalized World, in: *Rethinking History* 21/3 (2017): 312–41.

Maliszewski, Paul, Paper Moon, in: *Wilson Quarterly* 29/1 (2005): 26–34.

Manning, Patrick, *Navigating World History. Historians Create a Global Past*. New York, 2003.

Marx, Karl, *Ökonomische Manuskripte 1857/58* (Grundrisse der Kritik der politischen Ökonomie). (Marx-Engels-Gesamtausgabe [MEGA], Abt. 2/Bd. 1.) 2. Aufl. Berlin, 2006.

Massey, Doreen B., *For Space*. Los Angeles, 2005.

Massey, Doreen B., Politics and Space-Time, in: *New Left Review* 196 (1992): 65–84.

Massey, Doreen B., *Space, Place and Gender*. Cambridge, 1994.

Maurer, Michael, Historische Anthropologie, in: ders. (Hrsg.), *Aufriss der Historischen Wissenschaften. Bd. 7: Neue Themen und Methoden der Geschichtswissenschaft*. Stuttgart, 2003, 294–387.

Maxton, Donald A., *The Mutiny on HMS Bounty. A Guide to Non-Fiction, Fiction, Poetry, Film, Articles and Music*. Jefferson/London, 2008.

Mazlish, Bruce, *The New Global History*. New York/Abingdon, 2006.

Mazlish, Bruce and Iriye, Akira, Introduction, in: dies. (Hrsg.), *The Global History Reader*. New York/Abingdon, 2005, 1–15.

McPherson, Kenneth, *The Indian Ocean. A History of People and the Sea*. Oxford, 1993.

Medick, Hans, Mikro-Historie, in: Winfried Schulze (Hrsg.), *Sozialgeschichte, Alltagsgeschichte, Mikro-Historie. Eine Diskussion*. Göttingen, 1994, 40–53.

Meißner, Joachim, *Mythos Südsee. Das Bild von der Südsee im Europa des 18. Jahrhunderts*. Hildesheim, 2006.

Middell, Matthias and Naumann, Katja, Global History and the Spatial Turn. From the Impact of Area Studies to the Study of Critical Junctures of Globalization, in: *Journal of Global History* 5/1 (2010): 149–70.

Miller, Michael B., *Europe and the Maritime World. A Twentieth Century History*. Cambridge, 2012.

Morus, Iwan R., The Nervous System of Britain. Space, Time and the Electric Telegraph in the Victorian Age, in: *The British Journal for the History of Science* 33/4 (2000): 455–75.

Müller-Pohl, Simone, The Transatlantic Telegraphs and the Class of 1866. Transnational Networks in Telegraphic Space, 1858-1884/89, in: *Historical Social Research* 35/1 (2010): 237–59.

Munn, Nancy D., The Cultural Anthropology of Time. A Critical Essay, in: *Annual Review of Anthropology* 21 (1992): 93–123.

Murray, Cara, *Victorian Narrative Technologies in the Middle East*. New York/ Abingdon, 2008.

O'Brian, Patrick, *Joseph Banks: A Life*. Chicago, 1997.

O'Brien, Patrick, Historiographical Traditions and Modern Imperatives for the Restoration of Global History, in: *Journal of Global History* 1/1 (2006): 3–39.

O'Brien, Patty, *The Pacific Muse: Exotic Femininity and the Colonial Pacific*. London/Seattle, 2006.

O'Rourke, Kevin H. and Williamson, Jeffrey G., *Globalization and History: The Evolution of a Nineteenth Century Atlantic Economy*. Cambridge, 1999.

O'Rourke, Kevin H. and Williamson, Jeffrey G., Once More: When Did Globalisation Begin? in: *European Review of Economic History* 8/1 (2004): 109–17.

O'Rourke, Kevin H. and Williamson, Jeffrey G., When Did Globalisation Begin? in: *European Review of Economic History* 6/1 (2002): 23–50.

Ortmayr, Norbert, Kulturpflanzen. Transfers und Ausarbeitungsprozesse im 18. Jahrhundert, in: Margarete Grandner and Andrea Komlosy (Hrsg.), *Vom Weltgeist beseelt. Globalgeschichte 1700–1815*. Wien, 2004, 73–102.

Osterhammel, Jürgen and Petersson, Niels P., *Globalization. A Short History*. Princeton/Oxford, 2005.

Pagden, Anthony, *The Enlightenment and Why It Still Matters*. Oxford, 2013.

Paulmann, Johannes, Macht-Raum. Die Geschichte(n) von der Meuterei auf der Bounty, in: ders. (Hrsg.), *Ritual – Macht – Natur. Europäisch-ozeanische Beziehungswelten in der Neuzeit.* (TenDenZen Sonderband.) Bremen, 2005, 53–74.

Paulmann, Johannes, Regionen und Welten. Arenen und Akteure regionaler Weltbeziehungen seit dem 19. Jahrhundert, in: *Historische Zeitschrift* 296/3 (2013): 660–99.

Pearson, Michael, *The Indian Ocean*. London, 2003.

Peltonen, Matti, Clues, Margins, and Monads: The Micro-Macro Link in Historical Research, in: *History and Theory* 40/3 (2001): 347–59.

Perry, Charles, The Rise and Fall of Government Telegraphy in Britain, in: *Business and Economic History* 26/2 (1997): 416–25.

Pesek, Michael, Von Europa nach Afrika. Deutsche Passagiere auf der Dampferpassage in die Kolonie Deutsch-Ostafrika, in: *Werkstatt Geschichte* 53 (2009): 68–88.

Peters, Tom F., *Building the Nineteenth Century*. Cambridge, 1996.

Pieper, Jan, Die Grand Tour in Moderne und Nachmoderne – Zur Einführung, in: ders., Joseph Imorde (Hrsg.), *Die Grand Tour in Moderne und Nachmoderne*. Tübingen, 2008, 3–8.

Pietsch, Tamson, A British Sea. Making Sense of Global Space in the Late Nineteenth Century, in: *Journal of Global History* 5/3 (2010): 423–46.

Pietsch, Tamson, Bodies at Sea. Travelling to Australia in the Age of Sail, in: *Journal of Global History* 11/2 (2016): 209–28.

Pohlmann, Markus, Die Meuterei auf der Bounty – Über Revolution und einige der Mythen, die sich um sie ranken, in: Ingrid Artus and Rainer Trinczek (Hrsg.), *Über Arbeit, Interessen und andere Dinge. Phänomene, Strukuren und Akteure im modernen Kapitalismus*. München/Mering, 2004, 77–97.

Pratt, Mary Louise, *Imperial Eyes. Travel Writing and Transculturation*. London, 1992.

Priestley, John B., *The Edwardians*. New York, 1970.

Randeria, Shalini, Geteilte Geschichte und verwobene Moderne, in: Jörn Rüsen, Hanna Leitgeb and Norbert Jegelka (Hrsg.), *Zukunftsentwürfe. Ideen für eine Kultur der Veränderung*. Frankfurt am Main, 1999.

Randeria, Shalini and Conrad, Sebastian, Geteilte Geschichten. Europa in einer postkolonialen Welt, in: dies. (Hrsg.), *Jenseits des Eurozentrismus. Postkoloniale Perspektiven in den Geschichts- und Kulturwissenschaften*. Frankfurt am Main, 2002.

Ransom, Philip J. G., *The Mont Cenis Fell Railway*. Truro, 1999.

Ray, Himanshu and Alpers, Edward (Hrsg.), *Cross Currents and Community Networks. The History of the Indian Ocean World*. Oxford, 2007.

Rediker, Marcus, *Between the Devil and the Deep Blue Sea. Merchant Seamen, Pirates and the Anglo-American Maritime World, 1700-1750*. Cambridge, 1993.

Rediker, Marcus, *The Slave Ship. A Human History*. London, 2007.

Rediker, Marcus, *Villains of all Nations. Atlantic Pirates in the Golden Age*. Boston, 2004.

Reinwald, Brigitte and Deutsch, Jan-Georg (Hrsg.), *Space on the Move. Transformations of the Indian Ocean Seascape in the Nineteenth and Twentieth Centuries*. Berlin, 2002.

Rosa, Hartmut, *Beschleunigung. Die Veränderung der Zeitstrukturen in der Moderne.* (Suhrkamp-Taschenbuch Wissenschaft, Bd. 1760.) 9. Aufl. Frankfurt am Main, 2012.

Rothermund, Dietmar, Globalgeschichte und Geschichte der Globalisierung, in: ders., Margarete Grandner and Wolfgang Schwentker (Hrsg.), *Globalisierung und Globalgeschichte.* (Globalgeschichte und Entwicklungspolitik, Bd. 1.) Wien, 2005, 12–35.

Rüsen, Jörn, Einleitung. Zeit deuten – kulturwissenschaftliche Annäherungen an ein unerschöpfliches Thema, in: ders. (Hrsg.), *Zeit deuten. Perspektiven, Epochen, Paradigmen.* Bielefeld, 2003, 11–22.

Ruskin, Steven, A Newly-Discovered Letter of J.F.W. Herschel Concerning the 'Great Moon Hoax', in: *Journal for the History of Astronomy* 33/1 (2002): 71–4.

Ryan, James R., 'Our Home on the Ocean'. Lady Brassey and the Voyages of the Sunbeam, 1874–1887, in: *Journal of Historical Geography* 32 (2006): 579–604.

Sachsenmaier, Dominic, *Global Perspectives on Global History. Theories and Approaches in a Connected World.* Cambridge, 2011.

Salmond, Anne, *Bligh. William Bligh in the South Seas.* Berkeley, 2011.

Sand, Jordan, Gentlemen's Agreement, 1908: Fragments for a Pacific History, in: *Representations* 107/1 (2009): 91–127.

Schieder, Theodor and Berding, Helmut (Hrsg.), *Leopold von Ranke. Über die Epochen der neueren Geschichte. Historisch-kritische Ausgabe.* (Aus Werk und Nachlass, Bd. 2.) München, 1971.

Schlögel, Karl, *Im Raume lesen wir die Zeit. Über Zivilisationsgeschichte und Geopolitik.* 3. Aufl. Frankfurt am Main, 2009.

de Schmidt, Johanna, This Strange Little Floating World of Ours. Shipboard Periodicals and Community-Building in the 'Global' Nineteenth Century, in: *Journal of Global History* 11/2 (2016): 229–50.

Scholte, Jan Aart, *Globalization: A Critical Introduction.* 2. Aufl. New York, 2005.

Schwentker, Wolfgang, Globalisierung und Geschichtswissenschaft. Themen, Methoden und Kritik der Globalgeschichte, in: ders., Margarete Grandner and Dietmar Rothermund (Hrsg.), *Globalisierung und Globalgeschichte.* (Globalgeschichte und Entwicklungspolitik, Bd. 1.) Wien, 2005, 36–59.

Sheridan, Richard B., Captain Bligh, the Breadfruit, and the Botanic Gardens of Jamaica, in: *Journal of Caribbean History* 23/1 (1989): 28–50.

Smallwood, Stephanie E., *Saltwater Slavery: A Middle Passage from Africa to American Diaspora.* Cambridge, 2007.

Soja, Edward W., *Postmodern Geographies: The Reassertion of Space in Critical Social Theory.* London/New York, 1989.

Soja, Edward W., *Thirdspace. Journeys to Los Angeles and Other Real and Imagined Places.* 18. Aufl. Malden, 2014.

Spary, Emma and White, Paul, Food of Paradise. Tahitian Breadfruit and the Autocritique of European Consumption, in: *Endeavour* 28/2 (2004): 75–80.

Sprenger, Florian, Between the Ends of a Wire. Electricity, Instantaneity and the Globe of Telegraphy, in: Michaela Hampf and Simone Müller-Pohl (Hrsg.), *Global Communication Electric. Actors of a Globalizing World.* Frankfurt am Main, 2013, 355–81.

Standage, Tom, *The Victorian Internet. The Remarkable Story of the Telegraph and the Nineteenth Century's On-Line Pioneers.* 2. Aufl. New York, 2014.

Steel, Frances, *Oceania under Steam. Sea Transport and the Cultures of Colonialism, c. 1870–1914*. Manchester, 2011.

Stein, Jeremy, Annihilating Space and Time. The Modernization of Fire-Fighting in Late Nineteenth-Century Cornwall, Ontario, in: *Urban History Review* 24/2 (1996): 3–11.

Stein, Jeremy, Reflections on Time. Time-Space Compression and Technology in the Nineteenth Century, in: Jon May and Nigel Thrift (Hrsg.), *Timespace. Geographies of Temporality*. (Critical Geographies, Bd. 13.) London/New York, 2001, 106–19.

Struck, Bernhard, Ferris, Kate and Revel, Jacques, Introduction. Space and Scale in Transnational History, in: *International History Review* 33/4 (2011): 573–84.

Subrahmanyam, Sanjay, Connected Histories: Notes towards a Reconfiguration of Early Modern Eurasia, in: *Modern Asian Studies* 31/3 (1997): 735–62.

Tanner, Jakob, *Historische Anthropologie zur Einführung*. Hamburg, 2004.

Vink, Markus, Indian Ocean Studies and the 'New Thalassology', in: *Journal of Global History* 2/1 (2007) 41–62.

Walle, Heinrich, *Deutschlands Flottenpräsenz in Ostasien 1897–1914. Das Streben um einen 'Platz an der Sonne' vor dem Hintergrund wirtschaftlicher, machtpolitischer und kirchlicher Interessen*. (Jahrbuch für europäische Überseegeschichte 9.) Wiesbaden, 2009.

Welskopp, Thomas, Der Mensch und die Verhältnisse. 'Handeln' und 'Struktur' bei Max Weber und Anthony Giddens, in: ders., Thomas Mergel (Hrsg.), *Geschichte zwischen Kultur und Gesellschaft. Beiträge zur Theoriedebatte*. München, 1997, 39–70.

Welskopp, Thomas, Die Dualität von Struktur und Handeln. Anthony Giddens' Strukturierungstheorie als 'praxeologischer' Ansatz in der Geschichtswissenschaft, in: Andreas Suter and Manfred Hettling (Hrsg.), *Struktur und Ereignis*. (Geschichte und Gesellschaft, Sonderheft 19.) Göttingen, 2001, 99–119.

Welskopp, Thomas and Mergel, Thomas (Hrsg.), *Geschichte zwischen Kultur und Gesellschaft. Beiträge zur Theoriedebatte*. München, 1997.

Wenzlhuemer, Roland, *Connecting the Nineteenth-Century World. The Telegraph and Globalization*. Cambridge, 2013.

Wenzlhuemer, Roland, 'I had occasion to telegraph to Calcutta'. Die Telegrafie und ihre Rolle in der Globalisierung im 19. Jahrhundert, in: *Themenportal Europäische Geschichte*. Version von 2011, http://www.europa.clio-online. de/2011/Article=513 (accessed: 23 June 2016).

Wenzlhuemer, Roland, Globalization, Communication and the Concept of Space in Global History, in: ders. (Hrsg.), *Global Communication. Telecommunication and Global Flows of Information in the Late 19th and Early 20th Century*. (HSR 35/1. Special Issue: Global Communication.) Köln, 2010, 19–47.

Wenzlhuemer, Roland, Verbrechen, Verbrechensbekämpfung und Telegrafie. Kriminalhistorische Perspektiven auf die Entkoppelung von Transport und Kommunikation im langen 19. Jahrhundert, in: *Historische Zeitschrift* 301/2 (2015): 347–74.

Wenzlhuemer, Roland and Offermann, Michael, Ship Newspapers and Passenger Life aboard Transoceanic Steamships in the Late Nineteenth Century, in: *Transcultural Studies* 8/1 (2012): 77–121.

Werner, Michael and Zimmermann, Bénédicte, Beyond Comparison. Histoire Croisée and the Challenge of Reflexivity, in: *History and Theory* 45/1 (2006): 30–50.

Winseck, Dwayne R. and Pike, Robert M., *Communication and Empire. Media, Markets and Globalization, 1860–1930*. Durham/London, 2007.

Woolf, Leonard, *Growing: An Autobiography of the Years 1904 to 1911*. London, 1961.

Young, Filson, *The Trial of Hawley Harvey Crippen*. Edinburgh, 1950.

Zemon Davis, Natalie, Decentering History. Local Stories and Cultural Crossings in a Global World, in: *History and Theory* 50/2 (2011): 188–202.

Zemon Davis, Natalie, *The Return of Martin Guerre*. Cambridge/London, 1983.

INDEX

Index of Names